THE
APPLE FAMILY

Scenes from Life in the Country

OTHER BOOKS BY RICHARD NELSON
AVAILABLE FROM TCG

Frank's Home

Goodnight Children Everywhere and Other Plays
INCLUDES:
Franny's Way
New England
Some Americans Abroad
Two Shakespearean Actors

Rodney's Wife

IN A TRANSLATION SERIES
WITH RICHARD PEVEAR AND LARISSA VOLOKHONSKY:

The Inspector

The Cherry Orchard

A Month in the Country

THE
APPLE FAMILY

Scenes from Life in the Country

RICHARD NELSON

THEATRE COMMUNICATIONS GROUP
NEW YORK
2014

The Apple Family: Scenes from Life in the Country is published by Theatre Communications Group, Inc., 520 Eighth Avenue, 24th Floor, New York, NY 10018-4156

The publication of *The Apple Family: Scenes from Life in the Country*, by Richard Nelson, through TCG's Book Program, is made possible in part by the New York State Council on the Arts with the support of Governor Andrew Cuomo and the New York State Legislature.

Special thanks to Long Wharf Theatre for its generous support of this publication.

TCG books are exclusively distributed to the book trade by Consortium Book Sales and Distribution.

Due to space constraints of this copyright page, credit information for excerpted material may be found at the back of the book.

LIBRARY OF CONGRESS CATALOGING-IN-PUBLICATION DATA
Nelson, Richard, 1950–
The Apple family : scenes from life in the country / Richard Nelson.
pages cm
ISBN 978-1-55936-456-0 (paperback)
ISBN 978-1-55936-775-2 (ebook)
1. Rhinebeck (N.Y.)—Drama. 2. Domestic drama. I. Title.
PS3564.E4747A85   2014
812'.54—dc23   2014006961

Book design and composition by Lisa Govan
Cover design by Mark Melnick
Cover photograph: Arvind Garg / The Image Bank / Getty Images

First Edition, November 2014

CONTENTS

An American Saga
An Introduction
By Oskar Eustis   vii

THE APPLE FAMILY:
SCENES FROM LIFE IN THE COUNTRY

That Hopey Changey Thing
A Conversation in Rhinebeck
Election Night, November 2nd
2010   1

Sweet and Sad
A Conversation on September 11th
The Tenth Anniversary of 9/11
2011   87

SORRY
Conversations on Election Day
Election Day, November 6th
2012   183

REGULAR SINGING
Conversations on November 22nd
The Fiftieth Anniversary of the Assassination
of President John F. Kennedy
2013   273

Author's Notes   369

Acknowledgments   375

AN AMERICAN SAGA

By Oskar Eustis

The Apple Family: Scenes from Life in the Country began with
Richard Nelson not giving me what I wanted.

It was early in 2009. I had asked Richard out to breakfast
and proposed that he write a large-scale, research-based play,
set in Washington, about our war in Afghanistan. Early in my
tenure at The Public Theater, in the spring of 2006, we had
produced David Hare's remarkable play *Stuff Happens*, about
the origins of our war in Iraq. I loved everything about that
play, and its production, with one exception: the only play on
the subject we had was written by a Brit. A Brit we loved and
admired, but nonetheless a Brit. We had no Americans writing
that kind of large-scale, public-issue plays with the expertise
and craft that Hare brought to *Stuff Happens*. And no wonder,
as I said publicly at the time: for thirty years Hare had been
writing large-cast, big-issue plays, and every year the National
Theatre of Great Britain produced them. He could master the
challenges of the epic form, and write with tremendous speed
and grace, because he had been afforded a lifetime's worth of
production opportunities to hone his skills. It isn't that Ameri-

can writers can't do this work: it's that the American theaters hadn't given them the opportunity and demand to do so.

After deep discussions within our artistic staff, we determined that Richard was the writer we were close to who had all the brains, knowledge and artistry to pull off such a task. Our relationship was long-term and deep; we had just had a wonderful success with Richard's *Conversations in Tusculum*; we knew Richard could write both rapidly and with depth; and his long-term interest in politics and curiosity about the world made him, we reasoned, a perfect candidate for this job.

Richard is also unfailingly polite and, as I remember, he let me talk at great length about my proposal, making occasionally encouraging replies. I did notice that there was one aspect, in particular, that seemed to excite him about the project: the idea that we would work rapidly, setting an opening date as soon as we shook hands on the commission. We parted with him agreeing to come back to me with a proposal.

Within a week he did. His proposal was almost exactly what you now have in your hands, the only substantive difference being that originally there were only three *Apple Family* plays. The fourth was conceived after the success of the first.

Richard suggested a set of family plays, all set in the Apple Family household in Rhinebeck, New York, all opening on the day they were set, and therefore all being rewritten up to the last minute. Each of the opening days would be a date of national significance, and hence have a public aspect to them, and yet the plays would be very much intimate, conversational, family dramas. His proposal brilliantly fulfilled one of The Public's desires: to have plays that deal with great national events in a timely (how could they be more timely!) fashion, and completely ignored our desire to have an epic play about our war in Afghanistan.

From such selective responses great artists make their work.

We agreed, and set the opening dates for the first three *Apple Family* plays then and there: November 2, 2010 (the date of the midterm elections); September 11, 2011 (the tenth anniversary of 9/11); and November 6, 2012 (presidential election day). The fourth play, conceived later, was set on November 22, 2013, fifty years after JFK was shot in Dallas.

In order to fulfill that plan, we had to create a company of actors, and we were blessed to assemble an amazing group: Jay O. Sanders, Maryann Plunkett, Laila Robins and Jon deVries were with us for the whole journey; J. Smith Cameron for the first three, and Shuler Hensley for the first two. J. and Shuler were brilliantly replaced by Sally Murphy and Stephen Kunken. In this way, we achieved that rarest of American theatrical beasts, a long-term (albeit small) acting company.

These actors, and the extraordinary brilliance of their playing, demonstrated the powerful artistic rewards of long-term ensemble acting. This process also revealed what writers have known at least since Shakespeare's time, but which the current American theater rarely allows: playwrights benefit enormously when they are writing for specific actors who they know well. Characters can develop in amazing complexity and depth when they are the creation, not only of the writer who composes them, but of the actor who embodies them. The creation of this mini-company was a huge achievement in its own right, reminding us that one of the core original promises of the not-for-profit theater movement was to create better working (and living!) conditions for our actors.

The plays themselves turned out to be minor miracles, intimate conversations of a depth and thematic resonance we rarely experience in the theater. This is theater for grown-ups, theater that takes seriously its obligation to map and record our national psyche. Richard has made almost a second profession of his versions of Russian drama, both classic and contemporary, and one feels the gracing presence of Chekhov throughout these plays. Like Chekhov's characters, the Apples are decent, highly educated, caring people who love their country, understand that something has gone terribly wrong in its politics, and have no confidence in their own ability to change it. They are the worried citizens of a nation on the brink of great upheaval, and they register with seismographic sensitivity and precision the temblors to come.

Richard is allergic to the shouting that makes up much of contemporary American political discourse, and much of American drama, and these plays avoid any easy melodramatics or posturing. He is interested in the conversations which don't happen in public anymore, conversations based less on conflict than on self-exposure, where the interest of the characters is not in relentlessly pursuing their objectives but in attempting to share their deepest reflections, and thereby become less lonely. I know of no American plays which so effortlessly incorporate literature and American history; these characters are able to listen to Walt Whitman, and allow us to listen to Whitman, because they aren't busily and noisily pursuing their own desires. They want to connect with each other, and in so doing, allow us in the audience to connect with them, and with ourselves.

The Apple Family plays model not only a different kind of drama, but a different idea of humanity; one based not on conflict but on collegiality, not on achievement but on being; not on selfishness, but on listening, and love. The Apples struggle with fragility, with their own limitations, and with that greatest of human limitations, death. They struggle, but they struggle together. And as they talk, and eat, and take care of each other, they remember both their own history and their nation's.

Adorno said: "All reification is a forgetting"; these plays take memory as their great subject because Richard knows that it is only by remembering that we can blow life back into a frozen world; only by sharing our past that we can actually create a shared human future. Uncle Benjamin's loss of short-term memory is, in these terms, a subtly constructed Brechtian Verfremdungseffekt; by making memory contingent and problematic, Richard is drawing attention to how much we need memory to be fully human.

Richard has been a tireless champion of the rights of artists in the American theater; The Public's stance toward taking subsidiary rights from the plays they produce has changed entirely because of his activism. He has lived a life that embodies the values his plays talk about, and is that rare American artist who can actually serve as an exemplar of how to live an artistic life driven by moral as well as aesthetic values.

These plays reflect Richard's deep love of family, of actors, of writers, and of the theater. Like Chekhov's Konstantin before him, he despairs of the theater we have but has enormous faith in what the theater can become. Unlike Konstantin, but like Chekhov, Richard can actually create that theater. For those of us who were privileged to watch *The Apple Family* plays come into existence, year by year, the return to The Public every fall became a kind of secular religious ritual. I was not the only audience member whose eyes would tear up at the start of each play, watching those beloved characters walk back on stage and set the table to begin a new chapter in their, and our, saga. These plays, as radical in their quiet way as anything I have ever seen, are small masterpieces.

New York City
September 2014

THAT
HOPEY CHANGEY
THING

———

A Conversation in Rhinebeck
Election Night, November 2nd
2010

For Corin Redgrave

———

PRODUCTION HISTORY

That Hopey Changey Thing was commissioned by and first produced at The Public Theater (Oskar Eustis, Artistic Director; Andrew D. Hamingson, Executive Director) in New York on November 2, 2010. The director was Richard Nelson; the set and costume design were by Susan Hilferty, the lighting design was by Jennifer Tipton, the sound design was by Scott Lehrer; the assistant director was David F. Chapman, the production stage manager was Pamela Salling, the stage manager was Amber Wedin. The cast was:

RICHARD APPLE	Jay O. Sanders
BARBARA APPLE	Maryann Plunkett
MARIAN APPLE PLATT	Laila Robins
JANE APPLE HALLS	J. Smith-Cameron
BENJAMIN APPLE	Jon DeVries
TIM ANDREWS	Shuler Hensley

In December 2013, the complete series of *The Apple Family* was presented at The Public Theater in rotating repertory. *That Hopey Changey Thing* was revived with Sally Murphy playing Jane and Stephen Kunken as Tim.

CHARACTERS

The Apples:

RICHARD APPLE, a lawyer in the State Attorney General's office, lives in Manhattan.

BARBARA APPLE, his sister, a high school English teacher, lives in Rhinebeck.

MARIAN APPLE PLATT, his sister, a second grade teacher, lives in Rhinebeck.

JANE APPLE HALLS, his sister, a nonfiction writer and teacher, lives with Tim in Manhattan.

BENJAMIN APPLE, his uncle, a retired actor, lives with Barbara in Rhinebeck.

TIM ANDREWS, an actor, lives with Jane in Manhattan.

TIME

The play takes place between approximately seven P.M. and nine P.M. on the night of Tuesday, November 2, 2010—election night.

PLACE

Rhinebeck, New York: a small historic village one hundred miles north of New York City; once referred to in an article in the *New York Times* as "The Town That Time Forgot." A room in Barbara Apple's house on Center Street.

How's that hopey changey thing workin' for ya?

—*Sarah Palin*

In the dark. A wooden table and four wooden chairs. A few flowers, with most of their stems cut off, in a small glass vase on the table. Rugs.

Suddenly, a sick dog lets out an awful, painful scream, and then begins to whimper. Underneath the whimper, a distant church bell tolls seven.

Joanna Newsom's "Good Intentions Paving Company" begins. After a moment, Barbara enters with a chair. She is soon followed by Richard, Jane and Tim with another chair and a folded-up wooden card table. They unfold the card table and set the chairs around the room in a kind of circle. The women put tablecloths on the tables, set out glasses, etc. All this as the music continues to play.

They make a few trips back and forth, bringing out serving dishes—a chicken dish, green beans, boiled potatoes, salad; as well as glasses, a couple of bottles of wine and a pitcher of water—all for a buffet dinner. By now, Benjamin has joined them as well. Barbara has gone back to the kitchen when the music stops.

Election Day

Seven P.M. A room in Barbara Apple's home on Center Street, Rhine-beck. As the lights come up, Richard is in the middle of a story/joke:

RICHARD: "Fuck you Andrew Cuomo!"

(The others laugh or disagree or just react.)

"Fuck you Dark Prince!"
TIM: Who's the Dark—?
RICHARD: That's what they call him.
BENJAMIN: Who calls him that?
RICHARD: Everyone in the office, Uncle Benjamin. *(Continues)* "Fuck you Albany." "Fuck everyone in Albany!"

(Barbara enters with dishes of food.)

BARBARA: Do you have to keep using that word?
JANE: He's telling a joke.
BARBARA: I know that, Jane. *(Noticing)* We don't have any napkins.
RICHARD: "And fuck—"
JANE *(Interrupting; laughing, to Tim)*: This is funny. He told me this on the phone. "And fuck—"
BARBARA: How often do you and Richard talk on the phone?
JANE *(Continuing)*: "And fuck—" Fuck. What's her real name? I always want to call her Christine.
RICHARD *(Continuing with the joke)*: "And fuck Kirsten Gilli-brand—"
JANE: Kirsten! Not Christine.
RICHARD: "And the horse—"
JANE *(Excited, finishes Richard's joke)*: "And the horse she rode in on whose name is—Charles!"

RICHARD *(Correcting her)*: "Chuck." The horse's name is Chuck. Chuck—Schumer.

(A little laughter.)

It was very funny.

BARBARA *(To Jane)*: Does Richard call you or do you call him?

JANE: I don't know.

BARBARA *(To Richard)*: You never call me, Richard.

(And she is off to get the napkins.)

RICHARD: I call her . . .

JANE *(Not loud enough for Barbara to hear)*: Let me help . . . *(To Richard)* I guess she didn't hear me.

(Short pause. They are uncomfortable. Tim smiles at Richard, then:)

TIM *(To Richard and Jane)*: And then what happened?

RICHARD *(Mind on something else)*: With what?

TIM: In your office. The guy who quit.

RICHARD: Oh. He then picked up a couple of things—from his desk, I think a photo of his wife—and walked out.

(Barbara is returning.)

(To Barbara) Can we help? *(No response)* Barbara. We could have just eaten out. I suggested this.

JANE *(Explaining to Benjamin)*: Mr. Cuomo's Richard's boss—

RICHARD: He wasn't there. Of course. Cuomo.

JANE: He wasn't? You didn't tell me that.

RICHARD: And this guy, he didn't really quit. He was just— blowing off steam. Like lawyers do. It was funny. *(To himself, as he looks over the food)* "Fuck Andrew Cuomo." It's fun just to say . . .

BARBARA *(To Benjamin)*: Do you know who Cuomo is, Uncle Benjamin?

(No response.)

He's our next—

JANE *(Interrupting)*: In about— *(Looks at her watch)* two hours, he'll be our governor. I'm sure we all voted for him. But that's very funny. *(To herself)* "Fuck you Albany."

BARBARA: I wish you both wouldn't keep—

JANE: "Fuck Albany." Come on, you must want to say it. You're a public schoolteacher.

(Barbara ignores her.)

We're doing this as a buffet? *(To Richard)* It would have been better if Cuomo'd been there.

BARBARA: Is buffet all right with everyone? You want to sit around a table?

JANE: Whatever is easiest, Barbara. We don't want to put you out.

BARBARA: A buffet is not necessarily easier than—

TIM *(To Barbara)*: Thank you for doing all this.

BARBARA: You're welcome— *(Turns to Jane)*

JANE: "Tim."

BARBARA: Tim.

(They are at the tables, filling their plates.)

RICHARD: Actually, I don't really like Andrew. I liked working for Eliot more; he had his bad days, but mostly . . . With Eliot it wasn't *all* about politics. So—in my mind, Eliot was better. *(Looks at the others)* But then again—I didn't have to have sex with him.

(He smiles. Jane smiles.)

(Joke to Jane) We've heard how that could be a little rough . . .

BENJAMIN: Why would you have to have sex with him?

JANE *(After a glance at Richard)*: It's a long long story, Uncle. Richard was making another joke.

BARBARA: Since when did everything become a joke to you?

RICHARD *(Ignoring her)*: I'm glad we decided not to go to Gigi's. Last time we went there—it's like being in New York.

BARBARA: I don't go there. Only New Yorkers go there.

(Short pause, as they fill their plates.)

JANE: Like us.

(No response.)

RICHARD: Barbara, I brought you and Marian bagels. They're in the car. You too, Uncle Benjamin. I know how much you love your bagel.

BENJAMIN: Do I?

BARBARA: We have bagels in Rhinebeck. We have a whole "bagel shop" on West Market.

(Richard and Jane share a look.)

TIM: I'm sorry I missed the fall foliage. I hear that's spectacular up here.

BARBARA: It's very nice.

JANE: Tim and I walked around the village a little. We got here early.

BARBARA: You could have—

JANE: He'd never been to Rhinebeck.

TIM: What a beautiful village . . .

RICHARD: The Beekman Arms—

JANE: We went in. Where should we sit?

BARBARA: Anywhere . . .

(They hesitate.)

RICHARD: Washington, Lafayette stayed there. *(To Barbara)* Who else?

BARBARA: I don't know.

JANE: I showed him the sign. You could hardly read it. Don't they clean it anymore? I'll bet they cleaned it for Chelsea's wedding.

RICHARD *(To Tim)*: Did she point out the muskets on the ceiling?

JANE *(Before Tim can answer)*: He loved Stickle's. They don't have five-and-dimes like that anymore . . .

RICHARD: Barbara saved an article from the *New York Times* that called this "The Town That Time Forgot." *(To Barbara)* Is it still on your refrigerator?

BARBARA: Probably.

(No one has sat down.)

RICHARD: Maybe I should— Uncle Benjamin—why don't you sit at the table? That'll be easier.

(Directing them to seats.)

Jane and—Tim. And I'll sit . . . Barbara—I don't want to tell you where to sit in your own house . . .

(Barbara sits.)

And our sister, when she comes . . . *(Another chair)*

(Then:)

And we are sure she's not going to be angry that we started without her?

JANE: Do you care?

RICHARD: No.

BARBARA: It was getting cold.

(Short pause.)

(To say something) I didn't tell you—Mrs. Stickle's son-in-law—not the one who works in the store, the other one?
JANE: I don't live here. I've never even met Mrs. Stickle.
BARBARA *(To Richard)*: He wrote that vampire book about President Lincoln.
JANE: There's a vampire book about Lincoln? *(Smiles)*
RICHARD: I don't know it.
BARBARA: It's very—successful.

(They begin to eat.)

RICHARD: Good.

(They eat.)

JANE *(To Tim)*: What does Lincoln have to do with vampires?
TIM: I have no idea.

(They eat.)

BARBARA *(To Tim)*: Mrs. Stickle has been here forever. Longer even than Marian.
RICHARD: You are looking good, Uncle Benjamin. The country air is doing you wonders. *(To Barbara)* He does look better.
BARBARA: The bean salad is Marian's.
RICHARD *(Standing)*: Should I pour the wine? Who wants wine and who wants—water? Is that the choice?
BARBARA *(Starting to stand up)*: What else do you want?
JANE: Sit down. Barbara, sit down.

(Various responses: "Wine," "Water," etc.)

BARBARA *(To Richard)*: You know Marian worked for Gillibrand—so I wouldn't . . . She might not find your story funny.

JANE *(Eating)*: What did she do?

BARBARA: I think she made—phone calls? Her first campaign for the House. So—Marian thinks she was there in on the "beginning."

RICHARD: The "beginning" of what?

(He shrugs.)

They scared everyone else off. Is that what we now call an election?

BARBARA: Marian likes her. So . . . *(Looks at her watch)* I'm sure Adam's got Marian doing things. *(The explanation)* It's election day.

(They eat. The lights fade.)

Oliver

A short time later, in the same seats, eating.

JANE: We're just up for this week.

(Then:)

I was going to call . . . And we didn't have a car. Today we had to borrow a car . . . Anyway, what a treat to be together. And to see you looking so well, Uncle Benjamin.

(They eat.)

BARBARA: How's Billy? *(To Tim)* Billy's her son.

TIM: I know. We've met.

JANE: Billy's at Haverford. He doesn't know what he wants to do.

BARBARA: Nothing wrong with that. Don't make him feel bad.

JANE: I'm not doing that.

BARBARA: Don't push him. I see kids being pushed by their parents all the time.

JANE: I'm not pushing.

BARBARA *(With difficulty)*: And Alfred? Can I ask about him?

JANE *(After a look at Richard and then Tim)*: Why not?

BARBARA: He's written me twice. And I've written him back.

JANE: Then why ask me about him?

BARBARA: Jane, you have nothing to be ashamed of . . .

(Short pause. They eat.)

JANE *(To Benjamin, to say something)*: Tim's an actor too, Uncle Benjamin.

BARBARA *(To Tim)*: Are you?

BENJAMIN: What play are you in now?

TIM: Nothing right now. I'm doing this workshop. For my friend, Joanne. Working with her students. *(To the others)* Bard has a beautiful theater.

BARBARA: A very famous architect—

BENJAMIN: What play are you going to be in?

TIM: I don't know. I do a lot of television. I'm in a—pause.

(He "smiles.")

BARBARA *(To Tim)*: We have a theater in town.

TIM: I'm not really looking to be in a play.

BARBARA: I wasn't suggesting—

TIM: I didn't mean—

JANE *(Over)*: Barbara, Tim isn't interested in—

BARBARA: I know that. Of course I know. He's . . .

(Then:)

Uncle Benjamin always turned his nose up at our little theater too.

TIM: I wasn't . . .

BARBARA *(To Benjamin)*: Even when Marian auditioned to play the blind person in that mystery? You wouldn't help her. She telephoned him all the way to London, and do you remember what you said?

BENJAMIN: I don't remember.

BARBARA: You said, it's not as much fun as it looks.

(Short pause.)

TIM *(To Benjamin)*: Sir, I saw your reading at the Y a couple of months ago.

BARBARA: You were there?

TIM: I was.

BARBARA *(To Jane)*: Weren't you still with your husband then?

JANE: Not really . . .

(Off, from the kitchen, the dog begins to whine.)

RICHARD *(Standing up)*: I think the dog needs water . . .

JANE: Maybe he needs to go out.

BENJAMIN: Is that Oliver?

(This stops everyone.)

RICHARD: No, Uncle, that isn't Oliver.

BENJAMIN: Where's Oliver? *(Smiles)* He always eats what I don't want. He always sits here . . . *(Starts to stand)*

JANE: Uncle Benjamin . . . That is not Oliver. *(She looks to the others)*

BENJAMIN: Where's Oliver?

(Jane looks to Barbara.)

BARBARA: I've told him. Ten times.

RICHARD: Oliver is dead, Uncle. You had to put him to sleep. He had cancer. He was in a lot of pain.

BENJAMIN: When?

RICHARD *(After a glance at Barbara)*: Last week. And that's why I'm here, I've brought you a new dog from the city.

JANE *(The dog)*: Toby. A friend of Richard's—

RICHARD: He's getting married. She's allergic. He's very well trained. You were just petting him. In the kitchen. You seemed to like him. We told you all this.

BENJAMIN: Where's Oliver??

BARBARA *(Then, the frustration comes out)*: Oliver is dead, Uncle Benjamin!

RICHARD: Barbara, please—

BARBARA: You want to take care of him! Go ahead. If I'm not doing it right.

JANE: He's sitting right there. *(Seeing she is hurt)* I'm sorry. You're a saint. You really are.

BARBARA: I don't want to be a saint. *(To Tim)* He keeps forgetting, and so each time—it's like he learns it again for the first time. Over and over . . .

(Short pause. Benjamin looks down, upset.)

JANE *(To Barbara)*: He had Oliver for—how many years?

BARBARA: Sixteen.

JANE *(To Tim)*: He'd take him to rehearsal. Travel with him. *(Pause)* Should I bring in Toby?

RICHARD: No.

(Pause.)

BARBARA *(Going to Benjamin)*: You have his collar next to your bed.

(She rubs his back, kisses the top of his head.)

(Quietly explaining) And Richard came up to bring us a new dog. That's what today's all about. And Jane happened to be in the area, so . . .

JANE: And Tim.

BENJAMIN: Who's Tim?

(Barbara points him out.)

RICHARD: And it worked out to be a good day to— Hardly anyone's going to be in the office today. I don't want to be there today.

JANE: His boss is going to win an election today.

RICHARD: So nothing's going to get done there . . .

(A bark from the kitchen.)

I'll see what Toby needs. *(Stops)* He's never been out of the Upper West Side. So—another New Yorker in Rhinebeck. *(Laughs; to Barbara)* Just what you need.

(Richard goes off to the kitchen.)

JANE *(Quietly to Barbara)*: Boy, you really have your hands full.

(The lights fade.)

Acting and Forgetting

A short time later. Benjamin, Barbara, Jane and Tim. Richard has yet to return.

TIM: Mr. Apple . . . ? Could I ask you something?

BARBARA: What?

JANE *(To Barbara)*: It's all right, Barbara.

BARBARA: What's he going to—?

TIM: About your reading, sir. At the Y. A few months ago? Friends of mine had seen you the night before, and they told me it was a must-see. Especially for actors.

JANE (*Answering a much earlier question, to Barbara*): I didn't even know he was there, until after.

TIM: Of course we all knew about your illness. The heart attack. And—the memory. I think that was one of the first things we all said to ourselves, when we heard . . . (*He turns to Barbara*) He knows he's had the heart attack?

BENJAMIN: Yes.

TIM: We said . . . what's an actor—if he can't remember? (*Smiles*) But—then to see you at the Y, reading the Oscar Wilde—it was—you were—incredible . . . You weren't just reading, you were—reading it fresh, for the first time. And so it had the sense that you couldn't make a mistake—if you made one, it wasn't really a mistake. If you fumbled . . . That was part of the performance.

(*Then:*)

I've wanted to say that, sir. After all, that's every actor's dream, isn't it?

BENJAMIN: What is?

TIM: I suppose—to forget.

(*Benjamin looks at him.*)

To forget that you've learned lines, forget that you've rehearsed, forget that you're performing a play. My actor friends and I came up with a whole new definition—just from watching you—for what we've been attempting to do all of our lives. Do you want to hear it?

(*Benjamin nods.*)

Great acting—is simply willed amnesia.

BENJAMIN: Mmmmmmm.

(He looks off in thought and smiles. All look at him.)

Yes, I think that's very important.

(Richard returns.)

RICHARD: I took Toby outside—
JANE: Sh-sh.
RICHARD *(To Barbara)*: Where do you keep little plastic bags?
JANE: Be quiet.
RICHARD: What's going on?
TIM *(To the others, continuing)*: To forget that you are civilized. Scripted. So something true perhaps, something real is seen.
RICHARD: What?
JANE: I don't understand.
BENJAMIN: Yes. To be without judgment. And so without inhibitions. Is that what you mean?

(The others are very interested now, as Benjamin has been engaged.)

TIM *(After a look at the others)*: I think so.
BENJAMIN: "Why am I saying this?" "Why did I do that?" "Why do they laugh or don't laugh?" We only limit ourselves— by remembering.
JANE: As actors you mean?

(No response.)

As actors?
BENJAMIN: It's a complete contradiction of course.
RICHARD: What is?
TIM *(Explaining)*: Acting.

BENJAMIN: You have to in fact be aware of what you're doing, very consciously *and* not consciously. But I think that is the experience of freedom. When you are really doing it all without self-judgment, without inhibitions. It's how you discover things.

TIM: So your acting has— *(To the others)* Sorry, but I've been so curious about this—

BARBARA: No, no—

RICHARD *(Over this)*: Please . . .

TIM *(To Benjamin)*: So you are aware that your acting has changed, since the illness? Your amnesia?

BENJAMIN: Yes.

TIM: I'd seen you many many times on stage. And have so admired you. But I have to say, this reading at the Y was something different.

BENJAMIN: Perhaps amnesia— *(Explaining to the others)* which is what I have, I'm told.

JANE: We know.

BENJAMIN: Gives one the capacity to respond—freshly, spontaneously, to whatever happened to you.

BARBARA *(Quietly)*: This is the first time he's ever talked about this.

BENJAMIN: It's a state of being where you will not—and this is not a particularly original thought but it's worth making—where you will not be bogged down with your past. Literally, it's not only can you not remember—I can't tell you what I did last week or earlier this morning. Is it still morning?

RICHARD: It's nearly eight at night, Uncle.

BENJAMIN: Anyway, not remembering—there's an advantage to that—obviously certain disadvantages—but the advantages of that is that each day is completely free. You're not thinking, Can I do better than I did last week? Each day is a free day, and you take it as it comes. And you'll find what you want to find in it. You'll learn what you want to learn. And to that extent it's true that I never feel apprehensive now. About myself, I mean. I don't mean about Barbara and Marian . . . And . . . I don't feel apprehensive about myself. I don't have any concerns—am I going to do this as well as I have, and so forth.

(Short pause.)

JANE: And this is so useful to your acting.
BENJAMIN: It's useful.

(Pause.)

BARBARA: I have a question.

(Benjamin looks at her.)

Uncle, when you sit alone outside in the garden or on the porch swing? You look like you are lost in thought. Into your own world. What do you think about?
BENJAMIN: Oh. Many many things. I think about the day that's ahead.
BARBARA *(After a glance at the others)*: Do you despair?
BENJAMIN: No. I don't think I ever have. I've never felt myself to be desperate at all.
BARBARA: Do you have moments when you are frustrated?
BENJAMIN: I don't think I do. I think I possibly should have more. I don't seem to get into situations now where I'm frustrated. I seem not to.
BARBARA *(She is speaking very quietly, a tension in the room, one could hear a pin drop)*: Are there times when you look around and wish you could remember?

(A couple of dog barks from the kitchen.)

BENJAMIN: No. There aren't. Not that I'm not aware of the absence of things in my memory, but apart from . . . *(Tries to remember, but can't)* No I mean, I might try to remember something and be annoyed that I can't remember it. And why can't I remember it. But that's comparatively short-lived. Not that I wish I had a better memory or had a memory about this. I don't. No. No, I don't feel frustrated in that sense. Not at all. Actually, I think I'm happy. *(He smiles)*

(Silence.
  Marian enters from the kitchen.)

MARIAN *(Entering)*: Sorry to be late.

(The others are startled, jump. Jane screams.)

BARBARA: You scared us.

(Then:)

It's Marian. Look who's here, Uncle Benjamin.
BENJAMIN: Marian.
RICHARD *(Holds his chest)*: My god . . .
MARIAN *(To Richard)*: What did I do? Is that the new dog in the kitchen?
BARBARA: Marian, sh-sh. Benjamin is in the middle of telling us—what he's been feeling. I asked him if he despaired. He doesn't. He doesn't despair. We've wondered about that.
MARIAN: He doesn't?
BARBARA *(To Benjamin)*: What else do you want to tell us, Uncle? *(To Marian)* It's been so interesting. *(To Benjamin)* Tell Marian too.

(No response.
  Marian goes to Benjamin, who eats.)

MARIAN: Uncle, tell me too.
BARBARA: He said he's happy.

MARIAN: Are you happy, Uncle?

(No response.)

BARBARA *(To the others)*: Marian comes by almost every day to see Uncle Benjamin. *(To Benjamin)* Doesn't she? She wants to hear too.

(Benjamin continues to eat.)

RICHARD: I think maybe—he's done for now.

(Short pause.)

JANE: How are you Marian?
MARIAN: Sorry I'm late.
JANE *(To Marian)*: Even as a kid you were always creeping up on us.

(They hug.)

MARIAN *(Hugging)*: I don't remember ever "creeping."
JANE: Maybe you only "creeped" up on me.
MARIAN: I wasn't "creeping." Richard, what did I do? I'm sorry if I interrupted—
RICHARD: You didn't do anything.
BARBARA: We started without you.
MARIAN *(About Tim)*: Who are you?
JANE: You ask like he's a burglar.
MARIAN *(To Jane)*: I did not.
TIM: Tim—
RICHARD: This is Tim. Should I get you a plate, or do you want to—? He's doing a workshop.
MARIAN: What does that mean?
RICHARD: He's an actor.
JANE: Don't just stare at him, Marian.
MARIAN: I'm not staring—

JANE: Tim, this is my other sister, Marian.

TIM: Nice to meet you—

MARIAN: Nice to meet you— *(Looks to Barbara)*

BARBARA: "Tim."

MARIAN: Barbara, he's young.

BARBARA: That's it, Tim. There are no more of us.

RICHARD: Thank you god . . . Take a plate, Marian. We didn't
wait . . .

(The lights fade.)

Marian

*A short time later. All but Marian are sitting. Perhaps they have sat
down in different chairs, with plates, drinks, eating. Marian stands,
serving herself.*

MARIAN *(Answering a question)*: Adam's poll watching.

BARBARA *(Explaining to Tim)*: He runs the Democrats here.

MARIAN: He doesn't "run" them. But he's busy tonight. He said
he might try and drop in after the polls close. But I doubt it.

(Short pause.)

JANE: Is it going to be as bad as they say?

MARIAN *(About Richard)*: At least his boss is going to win.

TIM: Do we think they'll take both houses?

RICHARD: I was telling them a funny story—

BARBARA: Don't. Please.

MARIAN: What? What funny story? I think tonight we're going
to need all the funny stories we can get.

(She smiles.)

RICHARD: The punch line goes something like—"Fuck Kirsten Gillibrand and the horse—"?

MARIAN *(Upset)*: For Christ sake—when are you going to grow up?!

BARBARA *(Over this)*: I told you not to—

MARIAN: Why is that funny, Richard?! You want her to lose? You want them to win everything?

RICHARD *(To himself)*: "And the horse's name is Chuck."

MARIAN: I really don't understand you. *(To Barbara)* Thank god Adam's not here. *(To Richard)* You know he calls you a whiner.

JANE *(Smiling)*: Does he? *(To Richard)* Did you know that?

MARIAN *(To Jane)*: And you too sometimes.

JANE *("Whining")*: When do I whine?

RICHARD: I think of myself as—objective. As—critical. A social critic.

MARIAN *(To Barbara)*: When did he give up?

RICHARD: What have I given up? What is there to give up on? *(Smiles)*

MARIAN *(To Jane)*: Barbara said she didn't even know you were spending the week up here. And if Richard hadn't told her, we'd never have known.

JANE: We were settling in.

MARIAN: Bard College is just down the road.

JANE: I know where Bard is. I'm working hard on my book.

(Short pause. They eat.)

MARIAN *(To Jane)*: How's Billy?

RICHARD *(Before she can answer)*: He's lost. He doesn't know what he's doing. Helpless.

JANE: He's thinking of applying to law schools.

BARBARA: You didn't say that—

JANE *(To Barbara)*: I'm not "pushing him." *(To Marian)* How's Evan? Will we see her—?

MARIAN: She might drop by. I told her her uncle was here . . . *(Gestures to Richard)*

28

JANE: What about me?

MARIAN *(To Jane)*: Mostly she just goes in and out.

BARBARA: That passes. *(To Jane)* Doesn't it?

(Jane shrugs.)

MARIAN: If we don't support people like Gillibrand, no matter what we may think of her—and I sort of like her . . . I've met her. She's okay. But—we need to win, Richard. It's not about "like" anymore.

JANE: I'd have voted for Gillibrand.

(Marian looks at her.)

I've been up here. It was too late for an absentee ballot. *(To Tim)* Wasn't it?

BARBARA: I thought you said you voted for Cuomo.

JANE: Did I? *(To everyone)* Did I? I guess I *feel* like I did. *(Then)* I would have . . .

*(She eats.
     Benjamin starts to stand up.)*

MARIAN: Where are you going, Uncle Benjamin?

BENJAMIN: Where's Oliver?

(They all look at each other. Then:)

MARIAN *(Impatient)*: Oliver is dead. You put him to sleep. We couldn't ask Barbara to keep cleaning that mess up—

BARBARA: That wasn't why we put him—

MARIAN: He's dead, Uncle.

(Benjamin looks around, and sits.)

(Calmly to the others) He forgets. You have to remind him.

BARBARA *(To say something)*: The bean salad and the dessert are Marian's. She brought them over earlier.

TIM: It's very good . . .

(Barbara looks at Tim; he buries himself in the eating.)

MARIAN *(To Richard)*: And how are your kids, Richard?

RICHARD: They're good. They're not teenagers yet.

BARBARA: And your wife?

MARIAN: She has a name, Barbara.

BARBARA: I didn't mean— How's Pamela?

RICHARD: I just spoke with her. Before dinner. I called. She sends her best to all of my many many sisters . . . Tim, do you have sisters?

TIM: No.

(Short pause. The sisters wait for Richard to say something.)

RICHARD: I'm not going to say anything. Certainly nothing that could get me hurt.

MARIAN: We spoiled him, Tim.

RICHARD *(To Tim)*: I've got the scars to prove it. *(Starts to pull up his shirt)*

BARBARA: Not while we're eating. Where did you grow up?

(This makes all the siblings smile.)

JANE: He teased us mercilessly.

RICHARD *(To Tim)*: That is a complete lie—

JANE: Shut up.

MARIAN *(To Tim)*: We taught him everything. *(Beginning to name the things they taught him)* To keep the toilet seat down.

JANE: What else?

BARBARA: I think that's it. That's all that mattered to us. *(Smiles, then back to the subject; to Richard)* Is Pamela home now for good?

RICHARD: We've worked things out.

BARBARA: Good.

(Then:)

(To Tim) She was away.

RICHARD *(Without looking at anyone)*: I'm going to be leaving the office. I've taken a job with a big firm. It's time. The kids are going to be going to college . . .

MARIAN: What? *(To Barbara)* Did you know about this?

BARBARA: No.

MARIAN: Did you, Jane?

(Jane nods.)

BARBARA: Jane and Richard talk, Marian.

(Short pause.)

MARIAN: Because of Pamela??

RICHARD: Shut up.

MARIAN *(To Jane)*: Because of her? Is this how you worked things out? You love your job. *(To Barbara)* He's now worked for how many Attorneys General?

(Short pause. They eat.)

BARBARA *(To Marian, as they digest this news about Richard)*: Jane and Tim got to Rhinebeck early and she showed him around town.

MARIAN *(To Jane)*: Putting off coming here?

JANE: No. No.

TIM *(To help Jane out)*: It's a sweet village. I love the wooden signs.

MARIAN: We live here.

TIM *(After a look at Jane)*: I didn't mean—

MARIAN: On weekends in the summer, you New Yorkers come here and saunter in the middle of the street—like it's some amusement park. And so we're supposed to just stop our cars so you can walk . . . ?

(Then:)

There are more registered Democrats than Republicans in this village now. That is a big change since I came here.

TIM: Is it . . .

MARIAN: We have the first openly gay elected official in all of Dutchess County. Kathy. She's the town highway super-intendent.

TIM: That's—good.

MARIAN *(To Jane)*: I thought Tim would be interested in that—being in the theater.

(Pause.)

TIM: So—then the Democrats will win—here?

MARIAN *(Eating)*: There were a lot of old people in line to vote. That's never a good sign. People aren't thinking . . . There's a lot of anger.

RICHARD: I'm angry.

MARIAN: Are you? I'm talking about the crazies, Richard.

RICHARD: I don't think they're crazy. I think they're just pissed off. I think they're looking at society—a government, and I'm not saying just this government, it's been like this for decades, it's just coming to a head. A government that's always saying: "We're here to give out things." So every-one line up, push in line, cut in line, get your head in the trough! That's not very inspiring!

TIM *(To Jane)*: What is this?

JANE: Sh-sh . . .

MARIAN: So—that's your excuse for quitting your job? You're fed up? Do you even believe that yourself, Richard? Or is that just how you justify buying a bigger apartment so your wife would come home and leave that other guy?

BARBARA: Marian . . .

(Short pause.)

JANE *(To Richard)*: Are you and Pamela getting a new apartment?

RICHARD: I don't want to talk about this.

JANE: How did you know?

MARIAN: She complains about their apartment. She's always after something else.

RICHARD: That's not the reason.

MARIAN *(To Richard, as she eats)*: So right now, it is very useful for you to be angry, Richard.

(They eat. The lights fade.)

American Manners

A short time later.

TIM *(To the others, glancing at Jane)*: It's all about manners. A kind of social history of American manners. *(To Jane)* Right? They're interested.

BARBARA: She never wants to talk about her books.

TIM: She says—

JANE: Tim.

TIM: They want to know. She says that by studying manners— which after all are just customs—such as, say, how people greet each other, how— *(Gestures around the room and to the table of food)* they eat together. Their etiquette. That it's a way of getting to the heart and soul . . . of us. Right?

RICHARD: I guess then it's like—tell me if I'm on the wrong track, Jane.

JANE: Why is everyone suddenly so interested in my book?

TIM: It's a very interesting book.

JANE: It's not even a book yet.

RICHARD *(Continuing)*: It's like—a way of taking one element of behavior—which society has organized, the culture has, the country has organized—and if we look close enough, examine it thoroughly enough, put it under the microscope, we maybe see what's behind it, what real purpose it serves. And get some insight into—us.

BARBARA: America?

RICHARD: I think that is her point, yes.

(Then:)

Is it?

(Jane hesitates, then puts down her plate.)

JANE: What I'm after is: I want to describe or dissect how Americans—court? And marry. How they raise their children. Treat their old people. Dress. Decorate their homes. Eat and entertain. How they spend their money—not on what, but how they address that action, how they think about it, talk about it. How they behave at ceremonies. How they mourn their dead. All of these customs—manners are ways in—to an understanding. Conventions have had to be agreed upon—why are they necessary? What are they protecting? Hiding? I don't know what.

BARBARA: What do you mean—hiding?

JANE: If you get people to agree to behave in a certain way, then you are trying to get them not to behave in another way—or, and this I'm getting more and more convinced of as I research this—or, what are they trying to disguise?

(Short pause.)

I haven't settled on a structure. I'm mostly doing individual essays, and hoping it all makes a whole. *(Smiles and shrugs)* We'll see.

RICHARD: When's it due?

JANE: Pretty soon. A first draft. That's why I'm up here working.

MARIAN: Oh. That's why.

(She "looks" at Tim.)

RICHARD: And it's Random House?

(Jane nods.)

JANE: They really liked the pitch. It's in the air now—all this. Once the *Times* started that whole Style section some years ago—I think that gave this sort of thing a real legitimacy—as news. There have been a couple of books already. How we see ourselves. Or better, how we wish to see ourselves or be seen. Or rather what we want others not to see in us. What we are pretending to be? What are we hiding?

(Looks to Benjamin who is listening to all this as he eats.)

I even thought of doing an entire chapter—about a dinner party. *(Gestures: "like this")* Actually, I was thinking of inviting a group of friends to dinner—a doctor I know, a friend who teaches, my yoga instructor, someone in my building, and so forth. And then analyzing that. Beginning with the generally agreed—where we put our silverware and why. Simple, mundane things we don't even think about. The napkins. The order of the meal. The chair arrangement. Who sits first. That's more interesting. Who chooses where who sits. That's very interesting. Who talks first. Then what is talked about. Among strangers. Among friends. What isn't talked about.

(Short pause.)

BARBARA *(Suddenly)*: You're not thinking of using—? *("us")*
JANE: No. No, of course not.

(Then:)

I could if you—
MARIAN: Please. No. Don't.
BENJAMIN *(To Jane)*: I don't understand what you are saying.

(They all look at him.)

BARBARA: Jane's writing a book, Uncle.
BENJAMIN: I heard that. I just have amnesia; I'm not an idiot.
RICHARD: The book's about etiquette.
MARIAN: How—we talk to each other.
BENJAMIN: And that's an interesting book?
JANE: I hope so.
BENJAMIN: How people talk to each other? Don't we know that? Won't that just seem boring?
JANE: I hope not.
TIM: Jane's come across a number of interesting historical kinds of manners. That are very—revealing, she thinks. Things people did—customs—I'd never even heard about. I'm not sure what they say about us—
JANE: Maybe nothing. Maybe something.
RICHARD: What do you mean, "historical"—?
TIM *(To Jane)*: Where's that book you found? You had it in the car.
BARBARA: What book?
TIM *(Getting up)*: I'll get it from the car.
JANE: Tim—
TIM: They'll be interested.

*(Tim heads off through the kitchen and outside.
Pause.)*

BARBARA: A whole chapter about people having dinner? Now I'm going to be self-conscious for the rest of the evening.

JANE: I promise you, Barbara, there are no hidden cameras, and all iPhone microphone apps are off.

BARBARA: Good.

JANE: No one is listening.

MARIAN *(To Barbara)*: What did she just say was off?

BARBARA: I don't know.

BENJAMIN: What are we doing?

RICHARD: We're waiting for Tim. He's going to read something to us. Something that's very very interesting.

JANE: Don't build it up.

BENJAMIN: Who's Tim?

(The others look at each other.)

RICHARD: Tim is Jane's new boyfriend.

MARIAN *(Hesitates, then to Jane)*: He doesn't look at all like your husband.

RICHARD: He's younger.

MARIAN: He looks a bit like you, Richard. There's a definite resemblance. *(Smiles)*

JANE: Why are you smiling?

MARIAN *(To Benjamin)*: Tim's an actor, Uncle Benjamin. But I've never heard of him.

JANE: He's been in a lot of shows. When do you go to New York anyway?

MARIAN: I teach.

JANE: I know.

MARIAN: I do the books for Adam's lawn business.

JANE: I know.

(Short pause.)

BARBARA *(To Jane)*: What does that say?

JANE: What?

BARBARA: What does that tell you? What you two just said to each other. You said you could analyze—

JANE: Nothing. It tells you nothing. Not everything does, Barbara.

BARBARA: I am so self-conscious now.

(Tim has returned with a book.)

TIM *(The title)*: *Bundling.* We found this in a funky bookshop in Livingston. In a barn for about seventy-five cents. What?

MARIAN: We were talking about you.

BARBARA *(To Jane)*: When did you go to Livingston?

JANE: I don't know. *(To Tim)* A couple of days ago?

BARBARA: I thought you didn't have a car until . . .

JANE: We borrowed one. We went to a bookshop. For my work.

BARBARA: If you'd already borrowed a car, you could have also come here.

RICHARD *(To change the subject)*: How old is that book? It looks very old.

(Tim opens it and looks.)

TIM: "1871." They didn't know what they had.

MARIAN: And you didn't tell them? They're trying to make a living.

TIM *(He keeps going)*: It was published in Albany.

RICHARD *(To Barbara, teasing)*: "And fuck Albany and . . ."

MARIAN: What?

TIM: It's all about bundling.

JANE: I'm now thinking of doing a whole chapter on bundling.

RICHARD: What is—?

BARBARA: I think I know— When a man and a woman—

TIM: Here. There's a definition: "Bundling: a man and a woman lying on the same bed with their clothes on; an expedient practiced in America on a scarcity of beds, where, on

such occasions, parents frequently permitted travelers to
bundle with their daughters."

(It sinks in.)

RICHARD: What??
BARBARA: That's what I thought it was.
RICHARD: I've never heard of this.
BARBARA *(To Richard)*: I have. *(To the others)* I have.
TIM: It says this definition is from *The Dictionary of the Vulgar
Tongue*. It's sort of—pornographic, this book.
RICHARD: Let me see—
JANE: It reads like some sort of bundling "rule book."
MARIAN: May I see?

(Tim continues to look through the book.)

TIM: How you weren't supposed to take off *all* your clothes—
you kept on your underwear.
JANE: And even what happens if the woman gets pregnant.
BARBARA: What happens?
TIM: The man's "obliged" to marry her. And if he doesn't and
doesn't "abscond," then he's excommunicated.
JANE: So the church seems to be involved too.
BENJAMIN: Are there any pictures?
TIM: No.
JANE: Read them the poem, or song, or whatever it is.
MARIAN: What poem?
JANE *(To Tim)*: It's toward the back . . .
TIM: Here it is . . .
JANE *(To the others)*: Sh-sh. Listen.

TIM *(Reads)*:
Since bundling very much abounds . . .

JANE: It's from the very late 1700s.

TIM *(Reads):*

> . . . abounds
> In many parts in country towns,
> No doubt but some will spurn my song . . .

JANE: It's actually a song.

TIM *(Reads):*

> And say I'd better hold my tongue . . .
> Some maidens say, if through the nation,
> Bundling should quite go out of fashion,
> Courtship would lose its sweets; and they
> Could have no fun till wedding day.

RICHARD: Case made. I vote for bundling.

(Laughter.)

BARBARA: Me too!
MARIAN: You? You're an old maid.
BARBARA: What the fuck does that mean?
RICHARD: She's had boyfriends, Marian.
BARBARA: Don't defend me.
RICHARD: What did I do?
BARBARA: Keep reading.

TIM *(Reads):*

> It shant be so, they rage and storm,
> And country girls in clusters swarm,
> And fly and buz, like angry bees,
> And vow they'll bundle when they please.

(Reactions: "Ohhh . . .")

> Some mothers too, will plead their cause,
> And give their daughters great applause—

BARBARA: Not Marian.

MARIAN: Be quiet.

BARBARA *(Getting even)*: She thinks her daughter's become a slut.

MARIAN: Shut up!!

(Short pause.)

TIM *(Reads)*:

> And tell them, 'tis no sin or shame
> For we, your mothers, did the same.

I'll skip . . . *(Turns a page)*

MARIAN: It's so easy to just start reading into things that we know nothing about. From a long time ago. There weren't enough beds. Barns weren't heated—

TIM *(Reads)*:

> Some really do, as I suppose,
> Upon design keep on some clothes.

MARIAN: There you go.

TIM:

> But then she'll say when she lies down
> She can't be cumber'd with a gown,
> And that the weather is so warm,
> To take it off can be no harm . . .

RICHARD: Marian, she's stripping . . .

TIM:

> But she is modest, also chaste,
> And only bare from neck to waist,
> And he of boasted freedom sings,
> Of all above her apron strings.

BARBARA *(To Richard before he can say anything)*: Shut up.

TIM:

> I leave now for others to relate,
> How long she'll keep her virgin state.

(He looks up.)

RICHARD: Marian still thinks they're just being polite. "Move over daughter, give the stranger a little room."

MARIAN: They've got their clothes . . . Some of their clothes on. I'm not saying things didn't happen. But that couldn't have been the point . . . We just don't know.

RICHARD: It sounds to me like that was *precisely* the point. Tim, my sister here believed to the bitter end that Monica's dress must have been stained by Coca-Cola. *(Laughs)* Or was it Dr. Pepper?

MARIAN: Shut up! I never said that. I never did. Why are you making fun of me? What have I done to you? And that was over ten years ago.

RICHARD: I hate to see you get hurt. And Tim, she was really hurt.

JANE: Read the rest.

(Short pause.)

TIM *(Reads)*:

> But you will say that I'm unfair,
> That some who bundle take more care . . .
> For some we may with truth suppose,
> Bundle in bed with all their clothes.

BARBARA *(To Marian)*: There . . .

(Short pause.)

TIM:

> But bundler's clothes are no defence,
> Unruly horses push the fence.

(He closes the book. Short pause.)

RICHARD *(To Marian)*: "Horses push . . ." Marian, you know what that—?

MARIAN: I know. I know.

(Pause.)

RICHARD *(To the others)*: What did I do?

(Jane takes the book from Tim and hands it to Marian.)

JANE: Here.

RICHARD: How come she gets the book first?

JANE *(To the others, about the book)*: Is it some potentially wonderful insight into the underbelly of those times? A possible peep hole? For historians? Does examining a custom like this—maybe open up—

RICHARD: "Open up." Is that the best choice of words?

(Off, a phone begins to ring.)

JANE *(Ignoring him)*: Open up new avenues for understanding—people? At least some people. Our ancestors.

MARIAN *(To Barbara)*: Your phone is ringing.

BARBARA *(Getting up, to Jane)*: What do you think it shows?

JANE: I don't know. I just know from our own lives—we hide things. I know I do.

BARBARA: What do you hide? *(She goes off)*

JANE *(Calling after her)*: By being polite. I think we all do. With our manners. *(She turns back to the others)* We pretend we're one thing because—that's what's expected, I suppose. Or we're embarrassed or scared of what we—feel. What we need. What we want. Obviously our ancestors built an entire "rule book," for this "custom"—and if you peel it away—what you find is—

43

RICHARD: Sex?

(Marian looks at an uncomfortable Tim. Off, Barbara has picked up the phone; the ringing stops.)

JANE: I suppose, manners are ways of disguising what is basic to us. We all know it's there, but we don't want to admit it. "Sex." Love. Survival. Hunger. Maybe power, authority. Control. Or what we fear. I don't know. That's what I meant earlier about the dinner party. Who speaks first, and so forth. What else is going on? Strip it all away— what is underneath?

(The lights fade.)

The Republican

Lights up. A minute later. Jane is looking to eat something else. The others are as they were; Barbara still off.

BENJAMIN *(To Jane)*: You're not eating the chicken?
JANE: I'm vegetarian.
MARIAN: Since when?
JANE: For about two years. So is Tim.
BENJAMIN: He's eating the chicken.
JANE: And I don't know why he is.
TIM: I'm fine. I'm okay.
MARIAN: I think Barbara has a pasta salad in the refrigerator.
TIM: I'm fine. Please.
JANE *(Sitting again; to Tim)*: You didn't have to eat the chicken. You don't have to be so polite.

(Barbara returns.)

BARBARA *(To Marian)*: That was your husband. Uncle Benjamin, you haven't voted.

BENJAMIN: What?

BARBARA: That's what he was calling about. They're trying to drag in everyone. I told him you hadn't. *(To Marian)* Adam's sending someone over to walk him to the polls.

(Benjamin starts to stand up.)

JANE: Who are you going to vote for, Uncle Benjamin?

BENJAMIN: I don't know. I'll see who I like.

MARIAN: There will just be names. Vote Democrat.

BARBARA: They have those awful new machines. Tell him how to use the new machine. *(To the others)* What was wrong with the old ones?

MARIAN: They'll tell him. You just color in the bubble wherever it says Democrat, Uncle. Following the line with your finger. That's what I did. "Democrats," Uncle.

JANE: Why don't you write it on his hand?

MARIAN: Give me your hand.

BENJAMIN: What are you doing? I'm going to vote for whom I want to.

MARIAN: You're going to vote Democrat. Or you're not going.

BARBARA: You're going to vote for Schumer and Gillibrand and Cuomo.

MARIAN: They don't need his vote. Murphy—that's going to be close. Make sure you vote for Scott Murphy.

BENJAMIN: Who's that?

MARIAN: He's our congressman, Uncle Benjamin. Vote for him.

BARBARA: He's the one with the red hair and big family. In the TV commercials? You said you liked him.

MARIAN: And everyone else. I don't know who the hell they are, but vote for them. Ask Adam, he'll tell you who you're voting for.

(Benjamin stands up.)

BARBARA *(Gesturing back to the kitchen)*: Where's the dog?

RICHARD: What?

BARBARA: The dog. He's not in the kitchen.

RICHARD: What do you mean he's not—

TIM *(Smiling, raising his hand. Richard looks at him)*: He was scratching at the door. He wanted to go out. When I was getting the book. *(Gestures to the book about bundling)* I let him out.

RICHARD *(Standing, incredulous)*: You let him "out" where?

(The doorbell rings off.)

MARIAN: That's your escort, Uncle.

TIM: Into the backyard. There's a fence.

RICHARD: There's a fence—not a gate. It's open to the street. For Christ sake, Tim—!

TIM: Then why have a fence?!

JANE *(To Richard)*: Don't blame him, he's your responsibility—

RICHARD: Shit! . . .

(Richard runs out into the kitchen to search for the dog.)

TIM: I should help him.

JANE: It's not your fault—

(Doorbell again.)

BARBARA: Let's go, Uncle Benjamin. They're in a hurry.

(Barbara leads Benjamin off.)

JANE: And Uncle Benjamin goes off to vote . . . *(To Marian)* They got here fast. Must really be desperate.

MARIAN: We vote at the town hall. Just around the corner. They'll have him back in two minutes.

JANE *(To Tim)*: Everything is so simple here.

TIM: I knew there wasn't a gate. We came in that way. I saw that. I should look for him . . . *(Stands)*

(Off, the dog barks.)

JANE *(Grabbing Tim's arm)*: The dog's back. No harm done. See? *(Patting Tim)* He needed to go out. *(To Marian)* What is so confusing—is that he doesn't look—physically that different. Uncle Benjamin. So I keep forgetting—that he can't remember.

(Barbara returns.)

BARBARA: That dog's been skunked.

(Reactions: "What?" "Oh god." "What does that mean?")

MARIAN: Do you have tomato juice? *(Standing)* I have cans—
BARBARA: I have it. Richard's already doing that.
TIM *(Confused)*: Tomato juice?—
MARIAN: You pour tomato juice—cans of it— The only thing that really gets rid of the— Christ, you can smell him in here.
JANE *(Smelling him)*: I smell him.
TIM *(Smelling)*: My god . . . Does Richard need—?
BARBARA: No.
TIM *(To anyone)*: I feel terrible—

(No one is listening to him.)

MARIAN: He's sorry he went out for a pee now, I'll bet. And he's a city dog, isn't he?
BARBARA: The man who came to pick up Uncle found him on the steps, he said he looked scared shitless.
TIM: It was my fault—
JANE: You don't have to keep apologizing. And you don't have to eat the chicken.

(Short pause.)

If it makes you feel better, go help Richard.

TIM: I'll just see if he needs another pair of hands . . .

(Tim goes out to the kitchen.
   Jane stands and looks over the food, still deciding. She is near Benjamin's seat. She moves his plate. Barking off from the yard.)

JANE: He . . . seems worse.

MARIAN: Who?

BARBARA: Richard? He does seem out of sorts, doesn't he?

MARIAN: Pamela's put our brother through quite a lot, I'm sure.

JANE: I meant—Uncle Benjamin.

BARBARA: Oh. Does he?

JANE: Maybe because I haven't been around him. So maybe it's me. But he was always so . . . I remember him having all this energy. Could do eight shows a week, and then something, a talk, a reading on his day off. Like a bull.

BARBARA: I think he's happier.

JANE: I sort of doubt that.

(Tim returns.)

TIM *("Smiling")*: He says he doesn't need any help.

(Short pause. Tim is uncomfortable.)

JANE *(Explaining to Tim)*: We were just talking about Uncle Benjamin.

TIM: I was worried you were talking about me.

(He smiles. They ignore him.)

BARBARA: He seems happier to me. He was a very wound-up man. Also, I thought, tense. There was aggression in there, inside him. An anger that he couldn't get out. Now—it's out. It's gone.

JANE: Because he can't remember?
BARBARA: I suppose. I don't know.
JANE: Because he can't remember what he was angry about?
BARBARA: Maybe.

(Short pause.)

TIM *(To Barbara)*: How long ago exactly was the heart attack?

(Barbara lets Jane answer.)

JANE: Couple of years.
BARBARA: He wasn't happy for a while. That took some time—
JANE: I know that.

(Then:)

BARBARA *(Looking at Benjamin's plate, to Marian)*: He likes your bean salad. He's eating it. I'll give him some more . . .

(She begins to serve him some more beans.)

TIM: Jane told me, he was in a "home" for a while.

(This stops the sisters.)

MARIAN *("Smiling")*: I wouldn't call that—a home.

(Short pause.)

Our uncle had to be protected from himself, Tim. He did a lot of bad things. When he came out of the coma— he was upset. And so we had him committed. We all got together . . . We all decided. In fact, we sat right here at this table.
BARBARA: The worst day of my life.

49

MARIAN: Then we went to see the place. There's Uncle Benjamin . . .

(Marian tries not to cry, looks to Barbara.)

BARBARA: Right away you know, this is wrong. Didn't we? He's got a brain injury, not a mental illness. He shouldn't be tied up. *(To Jane)* Did I tell you this, Jane? *(Barbara turns to Tim)* One day, Tim, I arrive and Uncle Benjamin is kicking in his door. He said—someone had stolen— something. A checkbook.

JANE: You've never told me this.

BARBARA: He couldn't understand why he was forgetting and losing things and what was happening to his mind. "Oh let me not be mad." *(She looks to Tim and smiles)* You know where that's from. *(Continues)* So, first, Tim, he constructs a world out of his imagination, where he's being— the victim. Then—next, it all became a play to him. The other patients—he criticized their acting, remember?

JANE *(Smiling)*: He did. I remember that.

BARBARA: Then drugs kicked in, and after a while—it seemed forever—

MARIAN: Seven months . . .

BARBARA: He could remember he'd had a heart attack. He could remember that he had no checkbook . . . At least, he'd accept this if we told him.

JANE *(To Tim)*: And then he came here.

(Short pause.)

BARBARA *(To her sisters)*: When I sit with him, sometimes it's as if he's trying to put the pieces endlessly back together. Endlessly doing this puzzle in his head. I ask him about this. And he says, "I'm just counting."

MARIAN *(To Jane)*: Sometimes he sits outside and you hear him just saying: "yes, yes, yes."

BARBARA *(Smiles)*: Or—"oopsie doopsie doo." *(Shrugs)* "Oopsie doopsie doo."

JANE *(Repeats)*: "Oopsie doopsie doo."

(Richard appears in the doorway, his shirt soaking wet.)

RICHARD: I hosed him off outside, but now he smells of tomato juice.

TIM: Richard, I really am sorry.

JANE: For Christ sake, Tim, you let a dog out to pee! You did nothing to apologize for! *(To Richard)* I'm learning things about Benjamin I didn't know . . .

BARBARA *(To Tim)*: He was playing Gaev when it happened.

TIM: Really?

MARIAN: Not actually during—

TIM: I understand.

(Richard sits.)

RICHARD: Our sister, Barbara, is a saint, Tim.

BARBARA: Not true. His investments more than pay for this. I'm now a kept woman. *(Smiles)* It's good for me to have him here. It's good to have all of you here. Jane's been avoiding us.

JANE: That's not true.

BARBARA *(To change the subject)*: And how are you doing, Richard? Your sisters are worried about you, too.

(No response. He looks to Jane.)

JANE *(To Richard)*: I didn't say anything.

BARBARA: When do you start this new job?

RICHARD *(At the table)*: Are we done? Should we have dessert?

BARBARA: Marian made dessert. Pumpkin pie and vanilla ice cream.

JANE: Did you make the ice cream? Do you still do that?

MARIAN: No.

RICHARD: Maybe we should take some of this back into the kitchen . . .

MARIAN *(To Richard)*: You're not going to tell us about your new job?

RICHARD: So what are you worried about? It's not about giving up, Marian. I can do a lot of good there.

(She smiles.)

Don't smile like that. I always hated that smile. I'll be doing pro bono. That's in my deal. I was recruited. Mr. Cox himself. It's exciting. As I've told Jane—I'm being groomed. At my age. *(Smiles)*

MARIAN: And I never liked that smile.

BARBARA: What do you mean? Who's Cox?

RICHARD *(Ignoring her)*: Groomed for exactly what, I'm not sure. But—if you can believe it, State Attorney General has even been mentioned. I've told them I am no politician. Just ask my sisters. *(Smiles)* But it's flattering. This is not a big thing, Marian. I'm changing jobs. I need a change. I really do.

(Then:)

Mr. Cox is a senior partner in Patterson, Belknap—

MARIAN: Is that the "Richard Nixon–son-in-law" Cox?

RICHARD: Yes.

MARIAN *(To Barbara)*: Who runs the state Republicans? . . .

JANE: Richard's being groomed to be a Republican.

(Pause.)

That's what I think. That's what I've told him.

RICHARD: I'm being hired to be a lawyer. I'm a good lawyer.

MARIAN: A Republican, Richard?

RICHARD: For Christ sake, I'm changing jobs— And what if I was? *(Shrugs)* Javits was a Republican. Mayor Lindsay—

MARIAN: Paladino.

RICHARD: You know I don't mean— There's a fine tradition—

MARIAN: Who? Bloomberg?

RICHARD: I'm not talking about—

MARIAN *(To Tim)*: We don't have elections anymore, Tim—we just have money contests.

RICHARD: Why are you saying this to Tim?

TIM: I don't mind.

MARIAN: Fucking Bloomberg. I liked him too. Once. A man with so much money—they seem incorruptible. That was the argument that got me. The problem is—we're corruptible by a man with lots of money. So a Republican like Bloomberg.

RICHARD: No.

BARBARA: We don't have to talk about this.

MARIAN: This is Pamela's doing—

RICHARD *(Upset)*: This is not about my wife!

JANE: We can clean up later.

RICHARD: You really don't have the right to judge her. Maybe I was at fault too. Could that be possible?

MARIAN *(To her sisters)*: I think she's got him into therapy.

RICHARD: Shut up!!

MARIAN: The party of Javits is long gone, Richard. Don't kid yourself. You're being used. Who's being naive now? Who's going to be hurt now?

RICHARD: You don't understand.

MARIAN: And there's going to be a new Attorney General. He seems fine. We just voted for him.

JANE: I didn't.

RICHARD: He's an Albany politician.

MARIAN: Give him a chance. Maybe he's different.

RICHARD: The politicians like him. Because he's a politician. I don't owe you this, but . . . let me try to explain.

(He hesitates.)

MARIAN: We're listening.

RICHARD: When Eliot—resigned? That was a god-awful week. I'd almost gone to the governor's office with him. I went up two, three times in the transition? You can't believe the jokers who are up in Albany. You can't imagine the incompetence, greed, the stupidity . . . Eliot maybe came on a little too strong, sure. True. But all of us—we'd have walked off a cliff for him.

(Then:)

It was worse for those who went to Albany of course. But it was bad for the rest of us too. We were crushed. Betrayed? *(Shrugs)* I don't know. And then Andrew— *(Smiles)* For Andrew everything is politics. Celebrity politics. What gets noticed. What makes the impression. And so, he couldn't forgo the opportunity. And he denigrated Eliot. Just sat on his carcass and ate . . . I'll never forgive him for that. *(Shrugs)*

MARIAN: Spitzer's got a TV show now. Have you watched it?

RICHARD: I can't.

But then, I suppose they're all shits. Remember Grandpa always telling us—they are all crooks.

MARIAN: He was talking about Chicago. Everything was always crooked in Chicago.

JANE *(To Tim)*: Tim, another uncle, not Benjamin, he got a job in the parks department—and everyone in the family had to promise to vote for the Democrats. To get his job, and then keep it. *(Shrugs, to Marian)* How did they know how everyone votes?

MARIAN: Rhinebeck for one is not Chicago.

(Short pause.)

RICHARD: No. But the whole thing—it needs something. Something to happen. To change where we're headed . . .

MARIAN: Another Republican? Is that what's needed, Richard? If that's the case, then let's just wait another— *(Looks at*

her watch) Forty-five minutes and we'll have a whole lot
more of "them."

(Doorbell rings.)

BARBARA: That's probably Benjamin back from the vote. *(She
hurries off)*
JANE: Must not have been any line. Is that a good sign?

(She is gone.)

RICHARD *(To Marian)*: So our enemy is "them"? You love to say
that, don't you? "Them." As for me, I always get a little
suspicious when it's "them." "Them" tea partiers. *(Smiles)*
"Them" crazies. "Them"—
MARIAN *(Upset)*: Don't you fucking condescend to me, Richard!
RICHARD: What have I done? *("Innocently")* Tim, what have
I done?
JANE *(To a confused Tim)*: Stay out of this.
RICHARD: I'm just trying—perhaps foolishly—to get you to
open your goddamn small town self-righteous closed
"liberal" mind!
MARIAN: Fuck you.
RICHARD: Language.
MARIAN: Fuck you. I'm so sick of your smugness, Richard. It's
not cute anymore.
RICHARD: I didn't think it was—
MARIAN: Get off your fucking ass and quit smirking at every-
thing.
RICHARD: I'm smirking? I didn't think I even knew how to smirk.
MARIAN: Fuck you!
RICHARD: You should have been the lawyer with that gift for
argument.
MARIAN: Fuck you! Fuck you!
RICHARD *(To the others)*: And she teaches second graders?!

(Barbara enters with Benjamin behind.)

BARBARA: I leave for one second. We could hear you on the porch. If I want to hear stupid arguing I can watch television. Not here.

(Short pause.)

RICHARD *(Under his breath)*: "Them" . . .
JANE *(To Benjamin)*: How was the voting? Did you color in the right bubbles?
BENJAMIN *(In a sudden panic)*: The "right" ones?
JANE: I mean the correct ones.
RICHARD: Did you vote Democrat, Uncle?
BENJAMIN: I don't know . . .

(He sits, looks at Barbara for help.)

BARBARA: I wasn't there.

(Short pause.)

RICHARD *(To Barbara)*: How's Toby?
BENJAMIN: Who's Toby?
BARBARA *(Stops)*: I think we closed the kitchen door.
RICHARD: I better check . . .
TIM *(To no one)*: I can check!

(As Richard heads off:)

RICHARD: Don't people close doors in the country?

*(He is gone.
    Short pause.)*

BARBARA *(Calls)*: I'm sure we closed it!

(They look at each other. Then:)

MARIAN *(To say something)*: It was very crowded earlier. The town hall. A lot of old people . . .

JANE: So you said . . .

MARIAN: At least we have Benjamin's vote.

(Then, as they watch Benjamin eat:)

Maybe.

(The lights fade.)

Clearing the Table

A short time later. Richard has not returned. All except Benjamin have finished eating; their plates rest on their laps or on the floor or one of the tables.

JANE *(To Benjamin)*: Do you remember playing Gaev? In *The Cherry Orchard?*

BENJAMIN *(Eating)*: No. I don't remember that production at all, unfortunately. I have a poster of it.

BARBARA: I put it up in his room.

JANE: That was a good idea.

BARBARA: Might help him—

JANE: Yes.

BENJAMIN: I've met people who remember seeing it.

(The siblings look at each other.)

MARIAN: You have? And you remember them?

BENJAMIN *(Without answering the question)*: But I don't remember being in it, saying any of the lines. I'm immensely proud of the play. I couldn't tell you any of the lines. Probably if my memory were not affected by my illness I could remember more. Perhaps not.

(Short pause.)

JANE: I thought you were wonderful in it.
BENJAMIN: I would love to do it again. Someone has to ask me I suppose. Actors have to be asked, don't they?
JANE: Tim's an actor, Uncle.
TIM: Can I ask you something? *(To the others)* Jane and I were talking about this in the car on the way here . . . *(To Benjamin)* Is there a point where your memory stops? Do you remember some things, and then it just . . . ?
BENJAMIN: I think the only trouble I have remembering—I don't remember the heart attack, and everything after that. But I can remember . . . I did a reading.
TIM: I saw that. I was there.
BENJAMIN *(To Barbara)*: Of Oscar Wilde?
BARBARA *(Smiling)*: That's right.
BENJAMIN: And I remember on the back of the program were all the parts I'd played. And I can certainly remember some of them.
TIM: Which ones?

(Pause.)

MARIAN: Sometimes, Uncle, I think you tell us what you think we want to hear. And then we probe . . .

(She looks at her siblings.)

JANE: Do you remember playing the piano?
BENJAMIN: I do remember playing the piano. I don't play it very much now.
MARIAN: Then sometimes you do play now?

(She looks to Barbara, who shakes her head.)

Barbara has a piano.

BENJAMIN *(Ignoring her comment)*: I was a good pianist. I was an amateur. If I was playing something I knew and understood well, I was really good. And people would take pleasure in it. I was lucky because I started the piano very young.

JANE: You also liked to sing.

BENJAMIN: I did.

JANE: You used to sing to us when we were kids. Do you remember doing that?

BENJAMIN: Of course.

BARBARA: Do you remember what you'd sing?

(They wait.)

MARIAN *(To Tim)*: He was around a lot. He helped raise us. Especially me and Jane.

BARBARA: Especially them.

JANE *(Smiling)*: I remember you singing "Surrey with the Fringe on Top." *(To Tim)* This was even before Dad left. And tell us stories. He has wonderful stories.

BARBARA: I remember— *(Softly sings:)*

Sweetly she sleeps, my—*Barbara*—fair . . .

(Explaining) He'd change the name—

JANE AND THE OTHERS:
Her cheek on the pillow pressed . . .
Sweetly she sleeps while her flaxen hair,
Like sunlight streams o'er her breast.

MARIAN *(Over this, singing)*: "All Through the Night." I remember you singing that. I remember falling asleep to that.

MARIAN AND THE OTHERS *(Singing)*:
> Sleep my child and peace attend thee,
> All through the night,
> Guardian angels God will send thee,
> All through the night.

BARBARA AND THE OTHERS *(Singing)*:
> Sweetly she sleeps my Janey fair,
> Her cheek like the first May rose,
> Sweetly she sleeps and all her care
> Is forgotten in soft repose.

JANE: Do you want to sing something to us now, Uncle?

(Richard returns.
No response.)

(To Tim) And Mother said whenever he could, he'd come.
(To her sisters) I remember seeing him more than Dad. *(To Benjamin)* And I always loved it when we visited you . . .

(Short pause as the sisters notice Richard.)

What have you been doing out there, Richard? We missed you.

RICHARD: I stepped outside to get some air.
   I got to watching these young couples walking down the street. Well, younger than me. And I suddenly realized they must be on their way to vote.

BARBARA: We vote just around the corner.

MARIAN *(Looking at her watch)*: The polls are still open.

RICHARD *(Smiles)*: They seemed—young.

BARBARA *(To Marian)*: That's good, isn't it? That they're young?

TIM: How's the dog?

RICHARD: Asleep. I left him some water. He's had a very busy day.

JANE: Richard, we've been trying to get Uncle to sing for us, like he used to.

RICHARD: I'd like that too, Uncle. What do you remember singing to us?

I think I was this big— *(Very small)* —and Uncle was the only one who could get me to calm down. And get me to sleep. By singing . . . What are you going to sing?

(No response. They look at Benjamin.)

JANE *(To Tim)*: When Dad left us, Uncle Benjamin became our father.

MARIAN: Not exactly.

TIM *(To Jane)*: You told me.

JANE *(To her sisters)*: I hardly remember Dad.

RICHARD *(To Benjamin)*: Do you remember when we visited you over Thanksgiving?

JANE *(To Tim)*: He was in a show. In New York. I was like five?

RICHARD: And Mom drove all the way from Chicago with us?

(To sisters) Did we sleep somewhere on the way?

BARBARA: I don't know. I don't think so.

MARIAN: Where was Dad?

JANE *(Over this)*: Do you remember any of that, Uncle Benjamin?

(He nods.)

What do you remember?

(No response.)

You don't want to tell us? He has secrets.

(Short pause.)

BARBARA: How are we doing? Anyone want any more? Tim?

TIM: I'm fine, thank you.

JANE *(To Tim)*: There's more chicken. *(Looks at Benjamin)* He looks like pictures of our father. Barbara's lucky, she gets to have him here all the time.

BARBARA: Yes, I do.

JANE: I didn't mean—

BARBARA: He does suddenly remember things sometimes. I don't know where they come from. A couple of weeks ago he suddenly— *(To Marian)* I told you this— *(To Jane and Richard)* —suddenly remembers putting on shows with Dad when they were boys.

RICHARD: What?

JANE: I've never heard about this. Dad?? He hated plays.

BARBARA: In their backyard. In a tent with flashlights. *(Shrugs. To Benjamin)* Remember telling me that?

BENJAMIN *(New thought)*: I remember . . .

(This gets their attention.)

All of you coming to visit me in New York at Thanksgiving.

RICHARD: He does remember.

BENJAMIN: And I took all of you and your father and mother to the Rainbow Room. And then to a show. *(Smiles)* At each place setting at the Rainbow Room was a little orange-and-black candle in the shape of a turkey that each of you took home with you.

MARIAN: That wasn't us, Uncle Benjamin. That was Uncle Fred and his children. That wasn't our Thanksgiving. *(To the others)* I talk to him all the time—to get him to remember things. *(Then to Benjamin)* Benjamin—why did our father leave us?

RICHARD: Marian—

MARIAN: He doesn't answer. Maybe some day he will. What do we know? What do we think we know? *(To Tim)* Tim, when our mother was ill, Barbara sat night and day with her, trying to get her to tell her things—

BARBARA: That's not why—

MARIAN: So she could write them down. But she said, when I die, just ask Benjamin, he knows all the secrets. He knows everything . . .

(They all look at Benjamin.)

Why Father left. Where he went. Who paid for us to go to school?

RICHARD: Father paid—

MARIAN *(Dismissive)*: We don't know that. We know what we were told. *(Talking through Tim)* Tim, when Father visited Barbara . . . She was the only one he ever visited. I think we all resented that. She was teaching then on Long Island. And he found her. He took her to lunch. *(To Barbara)* You said he looked successful?

BARBARA: His shirt was ironed.

MARIAN: And you went to the cafeteria. And he told you he was going to write us all a letter and explain. We never got a letter. And then—

BARBARA *(To Tim)*: He put a folded twenty-dollar bill in my hand. Kissed me on the cheek and said one more thing, before vanishing. He said, "Barbara, I know you're my child, but I'm not so sure about your brother and sisters . . ."

(Pause.)

Is everyone done? Should we wait to have dessert?

JANE: Why would we wait to have dessert? *(To Tim)* Marian's pumpkin pie . . .

(Long pause as all except Benjamin stand to clean up the table, etc.)

RICHARD: Sit down, Tim. Sit. You're a guest . . .

(Tim sits.)

JANE *(To say something, as they pick up the dishes)*: Tim just visited *his* father. He lives in Texas.

BARBARA: Texas. I don't know anyone who's ever lived in Texas.

RICHARD: You're not from Texas?

TIM *(Shaking his head)*: My father retired there.

MARIAN: I've never been to Texas. I've been to Virginia. I've been to Florida. *(She heads off with plates)* So what's Texas really like?

(She is gone.)

JANE *(Shouting off)*: He said it was very Southern.

BARBARA: What does that mean?

(Barbara goes off.)

TIM *(To Richard)*: They do wear cowboy hats, but there are no prairies. There are pine forests actually . . .

RICHARD: In Texas? That's not how I picture it.

JANE *(Picking up, etc.)*: He said he was in a restaurant waiting for the plane in Shreveport, Louisiana—I love saying that. *(Bad Southern accent)* "Shreveport, Louisiana." And everyone in that restaurant was not only fat, they were obese.

(She heads off with plates. As Richard follows her off:)

RICHARD: That doesn't surprise me.

(Tim and Benjamin are left alone for a moment. They look at each other. Then:)

BENJAMIN: Who are you?

(Marian and Barbara return for more dishes.)

BARBARA: Decaf? Should I make a pot of decaf too?

(Richard and Jane are right behind them.)

RICHARD: I'd like decaf.
BARBARA: Anyone else?

(No response.)

MARIAN *(To Richard)*: Your dog still smells of skunk.

(As they pick up more plates, etc.:)

JANE: Tim said that the moment they heard he was from New York? And—an actor? Down in Texas?

(The others stop and listen.)

First they wanted to know if he was famous.
MARIAN: And he isn't.
JANE: He could just feel the hatred. They hate us.

(As Barbara goes off with dishes to the kitchen:)

MARIAN: Well we hate them. *(She follows Barbara off)*
JANE: You looking forward to Marian's pumpkin pie, Uncle? *(She goes off)*
TIM *(To Richard)*: I passed a car repair shop—this was in Texas? It had handwritten signs: "Guns for Sale." Like you're selling lemonade.
RICHARD: That doesn't surprise me.
TIM: Or just: "Guns!" exclamation mark.
RICHARD: Like: "Jesus Saves!"

(The women come out together, talking, carrying the pie, plates and ice cream.)

BARBARA *(To Jane)*: How did he know that those Texans hated us? I assume you all want vanilla ice cream?

JANE: It's how they—just say things. In that ridiculous accent. You know, how they'd ask a question—how they heard people in New York walk so *(Bad accent)* "fast." And just the way they said "theater" or "play." It was like they were talking about shit.

(They begin serving the pie and ice cream.)

MARIAN *(To Richard)*: And now you're one of them.

RICHARD: One of what?

MARIAN: A Republican.

JANE *(To Tim)*: How many churches did you see in Texas? *(To the others)* He told me he stopped counting.

RICHARD: I try and make sense of things for myself. I try like hell not to just let my buttons be pushed.

MARIAN: And we let our buttons just be pushed? *(She smiles)*

(The pie and ice cream is served.)

BARBARA: Is that too much ice cream on your pie, Uncle Benjamin?

(No response. The women have sat down. Everyone starts in on the pie.)

MARIAN *(Taking a bite)*: So—we just let them push our buttons . . .

(They eat. Short pause. Then:)

RICHARD: "Sarah Palin."

(All hell breaks out: "Oh my god!" Marian even drops her plate of pie and ice cream. Barbara starts to go and help Marian.)

MARIAN: I'll pick it up.

JANE: Let me cut you another piece?

BARBARA: Did it break?

(She cleans up the mess.)

RICHARD: It's like I stuck a pin in a voodoo doll.

MARIAN: For Christ sake, Richard. What is there to say? What can you say?

RICHARD: Tim, I'll talk to you because I don't think my sisters will even listen.

JANE: Why drag Tim in?

RICHARD: Palin—is the creation of people like them.

MARIAN: I'm not listening to this.

RICHARD: Run away. Go ahead. *(Continues)* The creation of people—like us. Me too at the time. We remember all those outrageous things. "Drill, baby, drill." Writing on her hand. Not knowing anything. But—if we go back to the weekend when McCain chose her? I think he chose her on a Friday. By that night, and I don't think she'd really actually said anything yet—but by that night, we'd made her the devil. Demonized. Ridiculed. Lied about. Ripped apart. Rumor-mongering about her Down syndrome child not being hers. Soon the feeding frenzy about her daughter's pregnancy? Attacks on her accent. For her hair, her clothes. Her state? For being a woman?? Didn't that bother any of you women at the time? There seemed to be such a rush of hatred—this need to crush her. It was beyond ugly. And, eventually, made me sick to my stomach.

(Then) Of course the irony was that this particular woman pretty much thrives on that, on attacks like that— and so, she became, in front of our eyes—Sarah Palin. Because on the other side, they're thinking anyone that hated, anyone who bothers them—us—that much, must be pretty darn good. Pretty darn great. She must be a star!

There was that "progressive" reporter renting the house next to her—to what? Spy on her in the shower?

Imagine if someone had done that to Obama? Think what we'd say. Think what we'd believe.

What I'm saying is—how come we cut off—turn off—our sense of right and wrong, fair and unfair, just and unjust—just in order to win. Or under the banner of: winning.

What have we become?

MARIAN: Sarah Palin was not ready to be Vice President of the United States.

RICHARD: No, she wasn't.

MARIAN: That was the point being made.

RICHARD: No, it wasn't. That day wasn't about her competence. Or her knowledge. Of course that came into it later, eventually. But no—this was about crushing someone. Destroying someone. And relishing that. That's what I saw. This is something different.

And this is about various groups and organizations with nice-sounding names which feed upon our insecurities and frustrations, so we will give them money. *(Short pause)* *"They're* racists." *"They're* bigots." "But you"—they tell *us*—"*we*—are good."

MARIAN *(To her sisters)*: Am I the only one upset?

(No response.)

(To Richard) Have you ever even bothered to look at a conservative website? And see what they're saying, how they're raising money?

RICHARD: Why is it that every time I question what we've become—with my friends, people at work—I'm met with the same: "But they're worse." Since when has not being worse become what we are?

MARIAN: I don't believe I'm hearing this.

BARBARA: If we don't win elections, Richard, what can we get done? You want to be Ralph Nader?

MARIAN: Good thing no one's listening to this.

RICHARD: I am not defending Sarah Palin. I am criticizing us.

MARIAN: I don't see the distinction.

BARBARA: And their side doesn't do the same thing?

RICHARD: I've said—"they" do.

BARBARA: So what's your point?

RICHARD *(Quietly)*: Our elections are a mess. I think that's obvious.

JANE: And—thanks to the Court—even worse now.

(Her sisters look at her.)

(Explains) Richard and I agree about this. We talk about this. He's been good to talk to. I suppose one big reason I came today was maybe to talk about this. It builds up and then what happens? You feel like you can't even question . . . That that's some sort of heresy. I figured, maybe as a family, we could talk . . .

(Then) I didn't vote. I didn't want to.

RICHARD: I didn't vote either.

BENJAMIN: I did. Didn't I?

BARBARA: Yes.

JANE: We want to win. But what are we winning?

(Then:)

MARIAN: What do you want to say? What do you need to say? We're family . . .

JANE *(After a look at Richard, very quietly)*: When Obama got to the Senate, do you remember what he tried to make his signature issue?

(No response.)

(Answering) Campaign finance. Others thought he was muscling in on their territory, but he pushed forward. It's what he believed in. He understood its importance.

BARBARA: And then he abandoned—in his election. I know. I know.

MARIAN *(Shrugs)*: So he broke a promise. *(Shrugs)* He changed his mind. He was raising a shitful of money.

RICHARD: That's right. A shitful. Well said.

MARIAN: And the Republicans were trying to do the same—

JANE: No they weren't, Marian. At least not the one and maybe only Republican who believes in campaign finance reform. He took public financing. And then we outspent him five to one or something. We swamped him.

BARBARA: But Obama won.

JANE: Yes.

(Then:)

(To Marian and Barbara) Should we stop?

(Short pause. They shake their heads.)

RICHARD: When I went up to Albany those few times for Eliot—a friend up there took me aside one day and said—there are three types of politicians here. About a third want to do some good. They usually don't last long. A third are here to have sex. They last a little longer. And a third are here—to get rich. And they're the ones in control. Everyone knows this. Look at any piece of legislation and you see the fingerprints of money.

TIM: I agree with that.

(The others look at him.)

BARBARA: You do?

(He looks around the room. Then, to Jane:)

TIM: Can I . . . ?

(She nods.)

I wonder if we got together, say, in a year. How many Wall Street boards the soon-to-be retired senator from Connecticut will be on? Or how many Wall Street clients his consulting firm that he's sure to start up will have.

JANE *(To Barbara)*: He's the head of the finance committee—

BARBARA: I know.

JANE *(To Marian)*: He's written the new rules for Wall Street. *(Smiles)*

MARIAN: Obama was getting money from normal people. Five dollars, ten dollars . . .

RICHARD: True.

MARIAN: How is that corrupting? It was sort of like a kind of election—

JANE: What kind of election? Where your vote counts only if you give money?

MARIAN: Normal people giving him money.

JANE: And getting money from Goldman, Bank of America— more money from Wall Street than any presidential candidate had ever received before. That too is true. We forget that. We don't want to face that. Money—from people who know which side of the bread to butter.

(Marian laughs.)

What's funny?

MARIAN: There are so many more important problems this country now faces than campaign finance.

RICHARD: Are there? I always thought of elections as the trees which bear the fruit. They tell us everything about ourselves. Not just who we want. But what we are. And to always remember, that for a politician—they are something else. They are hurdles, obstacles, things to overcome and ride out. But for us—the rest of us—shouldn't elections be our voice?

TIM: They appointed a place holder in Delaware for Biden's seat, to wait for Biden's son. That blew up in their face.

(He stops himself. Then:)

They changed the law in Massachusetts, when Teddy was ill and Romney was governor, so if Teddy died, they have to have an election. That blew up their face. Illinois, Obama's own seat blew up. Pennsylvania—pressing the guy not to run against Specter. Boom. The White House pushing Caroline Kennedy on us? Protecting Gillibrand from—us? So on and so on.

(Short pause.)

I'm sure the Republicans have been much worse. But these guys are still bad . . .

RICHARD: Marian, I admire all the work you do. Your commitment to your town. To Rhinebeck. I admire the teas you have for the Democrats. The phone banks. All the work your husband does. I'm not trying to denigrate that . . .

MARIAN: I'm surprised at you, Jane. Very surprised.

JANE: Well, I guess we don't really talk . . .

MARIAN: People are out of work. That's what all this is about. If they had jobs everything would be different.

JANE: Would it? *(Short pause)* What do you think, Barbara?

(Barbara looks at the others.)

BARBARA: We're just talking? We're not arguing about anything.

RICHARD: No, no one's arguing.

BARBARA: I have been thinking of writing a short story.

MARIAN: You haven't written in years—

TIM *(To Jane)*: She writes too—?

JANE: She used to write great stories. She had a story in the *Atlantic*. How old were you?

MARIAN: She was twenty-two.

BARBARA: I had this idea. I hadn't wanted to write for a long time. One of my AP students, she was writing about Afghanistan. And looking for books about war—poetry, novels, plays. That got me reading the Greeks for the first time in I don't know how long. Euripides. It helps to be older to read Euripides. *(Smiles to herself)* I remember seeing you in some Greek play, Uncle.

TIM *(To Benjamin)*: Do you remember?

(He thinks, says nothing.)

BARBARA: I came across a play I'd never read—*Helen*.

(No one knows it.)

About Helen of Troy and how she hadn't been taken to Troy, that hadn't been her—that was an apparition created by a god. She'd been kept hidden on an island. A soldier from the wars washes up on this island and sees her, and realizes what's happened, and that all the deaths, all the destruction, the rapes, the pillaging, everything, all of that, had been for nothing. It had all been a kind of test—by the gods, to see what sort of people they were. How they handled their—rage.

(Smiles) It seemed reading it, to be maybe the smartest thing I'd ever read about war. How they all went to war—the Trojan War—the epitome of war—because of something only imagined, not real, only in their minds.

(Short pause.)

I started to think, what if a character, a woman, on a ship, in, say, the Caribbean, is washed overboard and ends up on an island where she meets all the people who died during 9/11. And they're not dead. Because it was their apparitions we saw on that day, that we'd seen die in the fires and in the collapse. Now all these people had been spirited away, safe and sound, onto this island. I wondered if I could make a similar point, that it all had been a test to see what sort of people we are, and how we handle—being hurt. I'd have the woman realize, like the soldier, that it had all been for nothing, the hundreds of thousands on all sides dead, those young boys and girls whose faces we watch in silence on the *NewsHour*, the billions and billions spent, year after year after year—which could have been our national health care, our schools, our poor, our children. Nothing, because when you think about it—it's hard to figure out—what have we gained. What it's all been for . . .

(Short pause.)

Of course I know people did die. I know that there are people who want to kill us. And I know I want to be protected from them. But how we reacted to . . . It all feels so out of proportion. Doesn't it?

(Short pause.)

MARIAN: Isn't Obama trying to fix that? He's doing all he can. He's tried talking to the Muslims . . .
TIM: And added tens of thousands of more American soldiers.
BENJAMIN: When did that happen?
RICHARD: It's still happening, Uncle.
MARIAN: There's a timetable—
RICHARD: For what?
JANE: I wish to god I sometimes couldn't remember.

(Then:)

TIM: When I was in the Shreveport airport . . .

JANE *(Bad accent)*: "Shreveport."

TIM: Last week. It's a very small airport. An armed guard, with a machine gun, stopped my rent-a-car on my way in, and made me open the trunk. *(Shrugs)* Shreveport. Going through security? It's a really tiny airport. There was no line. I was the only person. And there were nine—nine uniformed security people at that post. What are we doing?

(Short pause.)

At noon—inside the airport, they now play the national anthem over the intercom. This since 9/11 I was told. And everyone—everyone has to stop what they're doing, stand, and most people put their hand to their heart. Someone yells at you—or worse, I think—if you don't. Why does that seem so wrong?

BARBARA *(Quietly)*: When he began, he was the anti-war candidate.

MARIAN: I know. I know.

TIM: He was anti–Iraq War. He said Afghanistan was the right war.

MARIAN: Is it now?

(They are surprised by Marian.)

I'm not convinced. I'm not. About all the other things. But if we're being honest . . . We are being honest? And we're just talking?

RICHARD: Yes. Yes.

MARIAN: This war makes no sense . . .

(Pause. Jane looks at Richard and Barbara.)

JANE *(Quietly)*: How did it happen?

TIM: I think as a candidate he just didn't want to appear weak.

MARIAN: He couldn't do that. Such a young man. A black man. He had to. I know. I know.

TIM: He never would have been nominated . . .

MARIAN: No.

But now? What he's afraid of now? What are we doing?

(Pause.)

BARBARA: He's a very good man.

JANE: I believe that too. I think we all do. That's not the point.

MARIAN: Who wants to do the right things. *(To Richard)* You disagree?

RICHARD: I think that is complicated. I think he wants to do good things for this country. I think he's honest. I think he has a big heart—whether he shows it on his sleeve or not, doesn't matter to me.

JANE: Me neither.

BARBARA: Me too . . .

MARIAN: I don't need to see him emote.

JANE: I think he has surrounded himself with the wrong people.

TIM: I agree.

JANE: That chief of staff? I hated all that giving the finger, macho stuff.

BENJAMIN: What?

JANE: Thank god he's gone.

RICHARD: He gives people the finger, the chief of staff. He shouts and screams and swears. That makes him tough? Why did he choose him?

JANE: He's back in our hometown.

RICHARD *(More names)*: Geithner. Summers. He's going too. But it took too long.

(The others agree.)

You just always get this feeling that they are protecting something. Not us. What? A system they know and believe in? Maybe. *(Shrugs)* Their friends?

76

TIM: "There's no such thing as shovel-ready."

BENJAMIN: What?

JANE: The stimulus, Uncle. What we were told. Maybe what he was told.

BARBARA: Maybe it's because this is the first president who has been younger than us. Maybe that's our problem.

(No response.)

RICHARD: He's been running this country like he's the president of a university. Congress, they're the deans. And I suppose—we're the students . . . That's not good. But it is what he knows . . . *(Shrugs)* He's trying hard.

JANE: And why does he seem so scared to ask anything from us? It's all—"we're going to give you things." We know that doesn't work. Why doesn't he ask?

RICHARD: Is a country led by its leaders, or its leaders by us?

TIM: Before becoming a senator, what actually had he done?

BARBARA: Part-time teacher. *(Looks to Richard)* Part-time lawyer. Part-time legislator. *(To Jane)* Writer . . . What did we know about him?

But I don't fault him. Not him . . .

RICHARD: No.

JANE: No.

BENJAMIN: Why not?

(Pause.)

RICHARD: Maybe we voted for him to feel good about ourselves.

(The others look at him.)

To feel we were good people, people without prejudice. To have all that over and done with. And just feel good . . .

(The lights fade.)

Gaev

A short time later. They still have their dessert plates, but the coffee has been forgotten.

BARBARA *(To Jane)*: It's in the bookcase in the kitchen.

(Jane goes off. The others look at Benjamin.)

MARIAN: She's getting a book, Uncle. One of yours.

TIM: Actors have to be asked. You said that, Mr. Apple. We're asking.

BARBARA: You were telling Tim about your Gaev.

(Jane returns with a book, which she hands to Tim.)

JANE: It was right on top. Tim can read the other characters' lines.

RICHARD: Or maybe Marian. We were talking earlier, Marian, about that time you tried out for the Rhinebeck theater? *(Miming)* To play a blind girl?

MARIAN *(To Barbara)*: Why were you talking about that? *(To everyone)* That was really embarrassing.

TIM *(Handing Benjamin the book)*: Here . . . From there, Mr. Apple . . .

(Benjamin takes the book.)

BENJAMIN *(Reads Gaev, as if for the first time)*: "The harder you pray, the more trouble you know you're in. I've wracked my brains for a way out. All I come up with are fantasies that aren't going to happen. Maybe suddenly we inherit a fortune—out of the blue. Maybe Anya marries a rich man.

Maybe I go to Yaroslavl and try my luck with my aunt, who is very, very rich."

TIM: Varya says, "If only God would help us!"

JANE: Why don't you stand up, Uncle.

(He doesn't stand, just looks closely at the book.)

MARIAN *(To Tim)*: Why did you choose this?

TIM: It's the most Gaev has to say in the play.

BENJAMIN *(Reads to Jane as his "Anya")*: "Sweetie. My child. You're not my niece—"

(The others look at each other.)

". . . you're my angel. On Thursday I was at the district court, a lot of us were there, we were talking and one thing led to another and someone was saying that he knew someone else who might take a note signed by me and loan me enough to pay the interest we owe the bank."

TIM *(Reading)*: "God help us."

BENJAMIN: "I'll go back on Tuesday. That should do it. We'll pay the interest. I'm certain. I swear on my honor, on anything you want—this estate will not be sold. I swear on my happiness! Let's shake hands. May I rot in hell if I let it be auctioned. I swear—by everything I hold dear." *(He looks up)* I don't remember any of this. What's going to happen to them?

*(He turns the page.
    Off, the dog begins to bark.
    Pause.)*

BARBARA *(To the others)*: You're sure you don't want coffee?

JANE: We should get back to Bard. And Richard has a two-hour drive.

RICHARD *(About the dog)*: He's probably hungry.

BARBARA *(To Richard)*: You can sleep here.

JANE: I'll do the dishes . . .

BARBARA: That all can wait.

RICHARD *(About the dog)*: He threw up in the car. On the way up.

BENJAMIN: What's that?

BARBARA: That's Toby, Uncle.

BENJAMIN: Who the hell is Toby?

JANE: He's—your new dog.

BENJAMIN: What are you talking about? Where's Oliver?

(They hesitate. Then:)

BARBARA: I think I saw Oliver resting out back.

JANE *(Continuing)*: I've had some wine. I wasn't supposed to. I'm the driver.

TIM: You had like a half of a glass.

JANE: I know. Still—I won't be able to work.

BARBARA: It's nine. The polls have closed. Should we turn on the TV?

BENJAMIN: That stupid dog is going to upset Oliver. He's not been well you know.

RICHARD: Really?

TIM: Should we pick up?

(Tim is picking up plates.)

BARBARA: Tim, you're the guest. Richard . . .

(Richard takes the plates from him.)

RICHARD *(To Jane)*: So—American manners: a world revealing itself around the dinner table . . .

JANE: Or buffet?

RICHARD: Or buffet.

MARIAN *(To Richard with a salute)*: Mr. Republican . . .

RICHARD: I promise you all that when I'm home with my friends in New York—I'll still laugh at all the Sarah Palin jokes, trash the "goddamn" Tea Partiers, and make fun of John Boehner. Which isn't hard to do.

MARIAN: No. But it's enjoyable.

RICHARD: And so forth and so on. No one will know.

MARIAN: They'll know when you've become a real Republican.

RICHARD: How will they know?

MARIAN: The horns. *(To everyone)* Adam says, if the polls were right, our brand-new Republican senator from Idaho is now—Mr. Crapo. Senator Crapo.

(Laughter.)

And our brand-new Republican from Arkansas? Boozman!

(Laughter.)

RICHARD *(As he goes off to the kitchen)*: I think it's pronounced Crāpo. So are we now just going to make fun of their names? Uncle, I'll go get Toby for you . . .

BENJAMIN: I don't need a dog. I've got a dog.

RICHARD: Well, he wants to see you.

(He heads off. Marian starts to follow him. Jane stops her.)

JANE: We didn't talk about health care?

MARIAN: Don't get me started on that Rube Goldberg mess . . .

(As Marian goes:)

JANE *(To Marian)*: So explain to me again—why can't we buy drugs from Canada?

BARBARA *(Picking up a plate)*: Are we going to turn on the TV and watch the returns or not?

JANE: I'm going to do your dishes.

BARBARA: No you're not. I need something to do . . .

(Richard returns.)

RICHARD *(To his sisters)*: Toby shat all over the kitchen.

BARBARA: Jesus Christ.

(Barbara hurries off. Jane follows.)

JANE *(From off)*: Oh my god. Toby! Bad dog.

RICHARD *(To Tim)*: I hate picking up dog shit. And this isn't the hard stuff either . . . He must have eaten something when you left him outside, Tim.

TIM: Maybe just being out of the city . . .

RICHARD *(A look at his watch; calls out)*: I have to go!

MARIAN *(Coming back out)*: Jane's going to tie him to a tree outside. He needs to be hosed down again. *(To Benjamin)* He rolled all in it.

BENJAMIN: I don't care.

RICHARD: Marian . . .

MARIAN: I know you need to go. I'll clean up the kitchen later. Just watch where you walk.

(Distant barking from the backyard.)

RICHARD: Uncle, good to see you . . . *(Turns to Tim)* Tim . . . *(He slaps him on the back)* We'll get together in the city. You too, Uncle. Come to the city. We'll see a show—

(Barbara has snuck up behind Richard. Tim and Marian see her, but she gestures for Tim to keep quiet and for Marian to join in. And now Barbara attacks her brother, tickling him.)

What the hell are you doing? Stop that!

(Marian joins the attack.)

Stop. Marian!! Stop this! Stop it, damn it!

(Jane comes in.)

Jane!

JANE: Me too!! *(She joins in)*
MARIAN: Where's Toby?!
JANE *(As they try to tickle him)*: He's tied to a tree . . . I've washed my hands.

(They are all chasing him.)

RICHARD: Uncle Benjamin, stop them.
JANE *(To Tim)*: We used to do this every time he got too big for his britches . . .
BARBARA: Won a big case.
MARIAN: Or got into Princeton!

(They surround him, tickle him.)

RICHARD: Tim! Tim! Help!
TIM: I think I'm supposed to help. Three women against—
BARBARA: Oh you think so—

(She goes to attack/tickle Tim, Jane interferes.)

JANE: He's not family. He's safe.

(And the brief burst is over. They huff and puff, look at each other. Suddenly, smiling Richard goes to tickle Marian. She doesn't resist, then suddenly she is crying.)

RICHARD: What? What?
MARIAN *(Trying not to cry)*: Sometimes it all feels so hopeless . . .
RICHARD *(Hugging her)*: Don't go there. Don't go there, please . . .
BENJAMIN: Why is she crying?

(Short pause.)

JANE *(To Tim)*: We should go . . . Toby's outside. He needs to be hosed.

(Barbara nods.)

I could do it if you—
BARBARA: No. No, I'll put on old clothes. Go.
TIM: Marian. Barbara. Thank you.
BARBARA *(To Jane)*: You did wash your hands?
MARIAN: When are we going to get together again like this?

(They hesitate.)

RICHARD: Soon.
BARBARA *(Hugging Richard good-bye)*: Is that a promise?

(They have begun to shake hands with Tim.)

MARIAN: Love to Pamela. Good luck with the new job.
BARBARA: And the apartment.
RICHARD: We're going to wait on that. Save some money first.
    Though Pamela's looking . . .
JANE *(To Richard)*: We're parked next to each other. We'll say
    good-bye out there . . . *(To Tim)* Are we forgetting any-
    thing?
TIM: I've got the book.
JANE: Bye.
RICHARD: Bye, Uncle Benjamin. Don't forget Toby.

(Richard, Jane and Tim leave.)

BENJAMIN: Don't forget who?

*(Short pause. The dog is heard barking from the yard. Marian
begins to roll up her sleeves and head for the kitchen.)*

BARBARA *(Stopping Marian from going into the kitchen)*: I'll put
    on old clothes . . .

(Barbara picks up. Marian looks at Uncle Benjamin.)

MARIAN: Uncle Benjamin? I could play you one of those songs . . . That you used to sing. *(To Barbara)* Would you mind? I'll come back and help . . .

*(Barbara shakes her head.
    Marian helps Benjamin up.)*

Stand up. You're done eating. Come with me, Uncle Benjamin.

BENJAMIN: Where are we going?

MARIAN: To Barbara's piano . . .

BENJAMIN: Why?

BARBARA: She's going to play us a song, Uncle Benjamin.

MARIAN *(To Barbara)*: Leave some of that for me . . .

*(In the distance, the dog barks. Marian and Benjamin go off.
    Barbara folds up the card table.
    Then from the next room: music from the piano, and we hear Marian singing as she plays.)*

While the moon her watch is keeping,
All through the night.
While the weary world is sleeping . . .

(Benjamin begins to sing with Marian.)

MARIAN AND BENJAMIN *(Off, singing)*:
All through the night.
O'er thy spirit gently stealing,
All through the night.

MARIAN *(Calls)*: I think he remembers the song, Barbara!

BARBARA *(Surprised)*: Does he?

(As Marian prompts him:)

BENJAMIN *(Singing)*:
>Visions of the night revealing,
>All through the night . . .

MARIAN AND BENJAMIN *(Singing)*:
>Though I roam a minstrel lonely,
>All through the night.
>My true harp shall praise sing only,
>All through the night.

(As she listens, Barbara joins in.)

MARIAN AND BENJAMIN *(Off)* AND BARBARA *(Singing)*:
>Love's young dream, alas, is over,
>Yet my strains of love shall hover.
>Near the presence of my lover,
>All through the night.

(And Barbara, with the folded-up card table, heads off.)

END OF PLAY

SWEET AND SAD

A Conversation on September 11th
The Tenth Anniversary of 9/11
2011

For Oskar and The Public Theater

PRODUCTION HISTORY

Sweet and Sad was commissioned by and first produced at The Public Theater (Oskar Eustis, Artistic Director; Joey Parnes, Interim Executive Director) in New York on September 11, 2011. The director was Richard Nelson; the set and costume design were by Susan Hilferty, the lighting design was by Jennifer Tipton, the sound design was by Scott Lehrer and Will Pickens; the assistant director was David F. Chapman, the production stage manager was Pamela Salling, the stage manager was Maggie Swing. The cast was:

RICHARD APPLE	Jay O. Sanders
BARBARA APPLE	Maryann Plunkett
MARIAN APPLE PLATT	Laila Robins
JANE APPLE HALLS	J. Smith-Cameron
BENJAMIN APPLE	Jon DeVries
TIM ANDREWS	Shuler Hensley

In December 2013, the complete series of *The Apple Family* was presented at The Public Theater in rotating repertory. *Sweet and Sad* was revived with Sally Murphy playing Jane and Stephen Kunken as Tim.

The Apples:

RICHARD APPLE, a lawyer, lives in Brooklyn.

BARBARA APPLE, his sister, a high school English teacher, lives in Rhinebeck.

MARIAN APPLE PLATT, his sister, a second grade teacher, lives in Rhinebeck.

JANE APPLE HALLS, his sister, a nonfiction writer and teacher, lives with Tim in Manhattan.

BENJAMIN APPLE, his uncle, a retired actor, lives with Barbara and Marian in Rhinebeck.

TIM ANDREWS, an actor, lives with Jane in Manhattan.

TIME

The play takes place between approximately two P.M. and four P.M. on the afternoon of Sunday, September 11, 2011.

PLACE

Rhinebeck, New York: a small historic village one hundred miles north of New York City; once referred to in an article in the *New York Times* as "The Town That Time Forgot." A room in Barbara Apple's house, which she shares with Benjamin and Marian, on Center Street.

NOTE

Play one: *That Hopey Changey Thing* is set on November 2, 2010 (the night of the midterm elections). Before the play begins, Uncle Benjamin Apple, a well-known actor, has had a heart attack, which sent him into a coma. When he regained consciousness, he had serious amnesia. By the beginning of the play, he has retired, and moved into his niece Barbara's home in Rhinebeck, New York.

The strong can forget.

—Saul Bellow, *Herzog*

A wooden table and three wooden chairs. A few short-stemmed flowers in a small glass vase on the table. Rugs. Beirut's "Scenic World" begins.

Barbara enters with a tablecloth, which she lays over the table. Soon, Marian and Benjamin bring in plates, silverware, glasses, etc., which they set in the middle of the table. Barbara leaves. Marian goes off in a different direction.

Then Richard enters and sits at the table with Benjamin, both with coffee cups. Marian returns and joins them at the table. The Beirut fades, and from a CD playing in the next room, we hear the Kyrie from Duruflé's Requiem.

Lights come up on them listening.

The Kyrie

Music plays. Pause.

RICHARD: It's very beautiful.
MARIAN: It is . . .

(They listen. Benjamin starts to stand.)

Where are you going?
BENJAMIN *(Holding out his hand)*: Could I have a cigarette?
MARIAN: You just had one. No.

*(He gives her a look and sits back down.
Richard watches this. The music plays.)*

RICHARD: Listen to the music, Uncle. *(About the music)* How
often do they rehearse?
MARIAN: Once a week. At night. Tuesday nights.

(She smiles, listening.)

RICHARD: What?
MARIAN: The pianist. He never wears shoes. He plays barefoot.
Barbara says he's always there.
RICHARD: Why doesn't he wear shoes?
MARIAN *(Shrugs)*: I don't know. I don't know. Listen to this.

*(They listen. Marian looks at her brother, reaches out and takes
his hand and holds it.
Then:)*

Barbara says—it's a phenomenal feeling, singing in a group
that size.

RICHARD: How big is the—?

MARIAN: Hundred and twenty maybe. Hundred and thirty? And all ages. Not just from the community, but Bard students too. You should come up and hear one of their concerts, they perform in a beautiful new theater. Right on the campus.

RICHARD: Where they do the summer—? *("festival")*

MARIAN: Same place . . .

RICHARD: Have you been to one of these concerts, Uncle?

MARIAN *(As Benjamin turns to her; answering for him)*: He has.

RICHARD: This is from last Christmas, you said?

MARIAN: Their Christmas concert . . . *(To Benjamin)* You were there.

  She says she feels like she's part of something. Something big. Or bigger.

RICHARD: I can imagine that.

MARIAN: The conductor's a very nice man. Smart. He makes it fun.

RICHARD: I wish I could sing. So what's stopping you? You should join. Barbara's right.

MARIAN: Maybe.

RICHARD: You sing.

MARIAN: I don't know.

RICHARD: You should get out.

MARIAN: I get out, Richard. *(Points out)* The altos . . . *(She looks at him)*

(The sound of car doors closing interrupts.)

That's them. That's Barbara's car. I have to turn that off.

(She is up.)

RICHARD: Why do you have to—?

MARIAN: And— *(Looks around, then gesturing toward the living room)* Hide in here—

RICHARD: What? Why—?

MARIAN: Hide. Hide! Come on, Richard. Uncle, sh-sh. Don't say anything.

RICHARD *(Getting up)*: My car's out front.

MARIAN: You said it was a rent-a-car. Hide! Wait, take your cup. Please. I want to see their faces . . .

(Marian hurries off into the living room. Benjamin and Richard share a look. Benjamin hands him his cup.
The music suddenly goes off in the other room. Marian hurries back in.)

(Hurrying through) Hide! Will you just hide? Get in there!

(She pushes Richard off into the living room, then hurries off into the kitchen.
Greetings off in the kitchen; Benjamin is alone, confused. The lights fade.)

Richard

Moments later, Barbara, Marian and Jane enter from the kitchen, talking. Benjamin is sitting at the table.

JANE *(Entering)*: Sorry we're so late.

MARIAN: That's not your fault—

BARBARA *(This explains everything)*: Amtrak . . .

JANE *(To Marian)*: You look good.

MARIAN *(To Barbara)*: What did she expect, Barbara? *(Makes a funny "sad" face)*

JANE: I meant, I like the blouse. I didn't "expect" anything.

(Marian is smiling.)

BARBARA *(To Benjamin)*: You know who this is, Benjamin.

JANE *(To Marian)*: Why are you smiling like that?

BARBARA: Say hi to Benjamin.

JANE *(To Benjamin)*: It's so good to see you, Uncle. It's been a while, hasn't it? How are you doing? *(To Barbara)* He's looking great. *(To Benjamin, a joke)* I think the word is "dapper." *(She gives him an awkward kiss on the cheek. To Barbara)* Is this what he's going to wear for the reading?

BARBARA: He's going to change. He's got a suit.

MARIAN *(Playfully, messing up Benjamin's hair)*: He's hungry. So he's grumpy.

BENJAMIN *(To Marian)*: Stop that.

JANE: Are you hungry, Uncle? Tim and I can't wait to see you "perform."

BARBARA *(To Benjamin)*: It's Jane.

BENJAMIN: I know it's Jane.

MARIAN *(To Barbara)*: He doesn't know who she is. *(To Benjamin)* She's our sister, Uncle Benjamin.

BENJAMIN: I know who Jane is. When are we going to eat?

MARIAN: He likes to eat early. Too early, I think. *(To Benjamin)* They're late. The train was late.

BARBARA: And the reading's—

JANE: That's at five? We have time. We're not that late.

MARIAN *(To Barbara)*: I kept everything warm in the oven . . .

JANE *(To Benjamin)*: We haven't seen you act since—for ages! *(To Barbara)* The last time, was that at the Y?

BARBARA *(To Benjamin)*: When you did your Oscar Wilde at the Y in New York.

MARIAN *(Interrupting)*: Sh-sh!

BARBARA: What are you doing?

MARIAN: Both of you, sh-sh.

(They are confused.)

BARBARA: We're talking. *(Continuing to Benjamin)* Jane and Tim have come up to see your reading, Uncle.

MARIAN: Sh-sh! I have a surprise!

BARBARA: What surprise?

BENJAMIN: And Richard.

JANE: What?

MARIAN: Benjamin!

BENJAMIN: And Richard's come up. He's here.

(Barbara and Jane are confused.)

BARBARA: Richard?

JANE: What do you mean? What are you talking about? Richard's not here.

MARIAN: Uncle—

BENJAMIN: He's here. *(To Marian)* Isn't he here? *(To Jane and Barbara)* He went in there. *(Points, then calls)* Aren't you in there, Richard?

*(Richard comes out.
Jane is stunned.)*

RICHARD: Surprise . . .

JANE: What is he doing here?

MARIAN *(To Benjamin)*: Why did you tell them?

JANE *(To Richard)*: What are you doing?

BARBARA *(Over this, to Marian)*: When did he get here?

MARIAN: I wanted to surprise you. *(Explaining)* He just walked in. Didn't even knock. I turned around—I just screamed.

JANE *(To Richard)*: Why are you here? *(To Barbara)* You said he couldn't come.

BARBARA: He called this morning. I didn't tell them, Richard.

RICHARD: It's good to see you too, Jane.

JANE: I didn't mean— *(As she hugs him)* I'm just surprised. That's not your car—

RICHARD: Pamela's taking the kids somewhere . . .

MARIAN: It's a rental.

BARBARA *(To Marian)*: He told me not to tell you. All of a sudden, he says he wants to come to the reading.

MARIAN: You knew he—?

BARBARA: I wanted it to be a surprise . . . *(To Jane)* Jane, my turn. *(As she hugs him)* I'm happy to see you.

JANE: So am I.

MARIAN: It was a surprise.

BARBARA: Good! It worked.

JANE *(To Richard)*: You could have driven us up. We took the train—

RICHARD: I didn't know—

BARBARA *(For him)*: He decided at the last minute. He told me this on the phone. He wanted to come . . .

(The lights fade.)

Tim and Jane

Lights up a moment later.

JANE: That train was so late, Uncle. You must be starving.

BARBARA *(To Marian)*: Give him a cigarette. That's what he wants.

MARIAN *(Giving Benjamin a cigarette)*: Everything's ready. We can eat now—

(Jane watches Benjamin take the cigarette.)

We don't let him smoke in the house.

BARBARA: Marian doesn't . . .

(They watch Benjamin go off with his cigarette.)

MARIAN: That's not true.

JANE: When did this start?

(After Marian looks to Barbara:)

MARIAN: You didn't know that he's smoking now? *(Shakes her head; then to Barbara)* Why do you always want to keep everything quiet?

BARBARA: I don't always want to keep—

MARIAN: Like it'll go away. We should talk, Jane. About Benjamin. You too, Richard.

JANE *(To Richard)*: Do you know about this?—

RICHARD: No.

MARIAN *(Over this)*: And you try and say anything to her about this and she just goes quiet. See what I mean? There. See what I live with? She always used to do that.

RICHARD: I don't remember Barbara doing that.

MARIAN: Maybe just with me and Jane. A sister thing. Jane remembers.

RICHARD *(To Jane)*: Do you—?

(Jane doesn't.)

BARBARA: I thought we were going to eat.

JANE: Can we fit around the table?

BARBARA *(Heading off, calling back)*: Richard's here . . . We'll use the card table. We can do a buffet. It'll be more comfortable. If that's all right with everyone . . .

RICHARD *(Joking)*: I didn't mean to cause a problem.

JANE *(Joking)*: Why stop now?

MARIAN *(To Barbara)*: Are you asking me?

BARBARA: Is that all right, Marian?

(She is gone.)

MARIAN: Benjamin smokes almost a pack a day now. Barbara says he used to smoke in his twenties. She remembers this . . . She thinks something just—I don't know. *(Snaps her fingers)* And now he's back in his twenties so he's smoking.

(Marian heads off.)

(Happily shouts to Barbara) Barbara, Richard's here!
JANE *(To "the world")*: So am I . . .

(Jane and Richard are alone.)

RICHARD: He's now smoking. *(To Jane)* I can take you back.
JANE: We're staying the night.
RICHARD: Right.
JANE *(Then)*: Tim's with me.
RICHARD: Barbara said that.
JANE: What did she say?
RICHARD: That—Tim would be here.
JANE: We dropped him off in town. He wanted to—buy some
    wine.
RICHARD: I stopped there too.
JANE: We're together. Again.
RICHARD: I heard that somewhere. We do share two sisters.
JANE: And what do they say? I'm curious.
RICHARD: No one's criticizing you, Jane. I like Tim.
JANE: I'm sorry I haven't called . . . It's been—crazy.
RICHARD: Have you been up here—recently?
JANE: No. You?

(Richard shakes his head.)

Marian looks pretty good. She's teaching. I was surprised
    when I heard she'd moved in. Weren't you?
RICHARD *(Shrugs)*: They shared a room for a while as kids.
JANE: I guess I forgot that.

(Barbara enters lugging a card table.)

BARBARA *(To Jane)*: Tim's here.
RICHARD: That's no longer news.

BARBARA: He's in the kitchen.

RICHARD *(To Barbara)*: Can I help with that?

JANE: What can I do?

BARBARA *(Shrugs)*: Bring in things.

JANE: I'm very sorry to hear that Uncle's smoking. *(She starts to go off)*

BARBARA *(Setting up the card table)*: He got lost this week.

(This stops Jane.)

JANE: What? What do you mean?

BARBARA: That really upset Marian. He went off to the CVS— for cigarettes. It's just down the street—

RICHARD: I know the CVS.

BARBARA: I get a call from one of my students . . .

(Marian returns with a tray of bowls—vegetables, potatoes, etc.)

She thinks she's seen my uncle about a mile and half down Route 9. *(Looks at Marian, then)* We drive down and there he is walking, just walking.

MARIAN *(Setting out the bowls)*: I'm glad you're worried too, Barbara.

BARBARA: Of course I'm worried.

MARIAN *(To Richard and Jane)*: He sneaks out to Foster's. He won't admit it—

BARBARA: Marian—

MARIAN: I have a friend who's a waitress . . . He sits at the bar.

JANE: What's wrong with that?

MARIAN: Buys people drinks. People he doesn't know.

RICHARD *(Trying to make a joke)*: How does he know he doesn't know them?

MARIAN: They take advantage of him, Richard.

(Tim enters with two bottles of wine and some glasses, his hands full.)

TIM: Where do you want all this? *(Greeting)* Richard! They just told me—

RICHARD: Tim! *(To the others)* Tim's here.

JANE: That was quick.

BARBARA *(To Tim)*: On the card table. First, let me put the tablecloth on . . .

(She flaps open the tablecloth.)

JANE: You bought two bottles.

TIM: You asked me to. Red and white.

MARIAN: We just got Benjamin—finally—drinking the nonalcoholic . . . *(To Richard)* He really doesn't know the difference.

JANE *(To Marian)*: I doubt that very much.

TIM *(Hands still full)*: Richard, I'll shake hands in a minute—

MARIAN *(Over this)*: He doesn't, Jane.

JANE: We are celebrating his show, Marian . . .

BARBARA *(Under her breath)*: That's what I said . . .

MARIAN: It's not a show. And I certainly wouldn't call it celebrating, Jane. So we should be encouraging him to get drunk? He doesn't need any encouragement for that . . .

(Marian goes off into the kitchen.)

JANE: I'll bring in things. *(She heads off)*

RICHARD *(To Tim)*: I put a bottle in the fridge.

It's alcoholic too.

BARBARA: I'll get another tablecloth, this one has a stain.

(She heads off. The men are alone.)

RICHARD: I didn't think I could come— A last minute thing.

TIM: That's what Barbara just— A nice surprise. *(Shows Richard that his hands are still full)*

RICHARD: They could make you hold that all day. I know my sisters.

They like being waited on.

TIM *(Awkward joke)*: If that's the worst that can happen to me.

(He laughs, Richard doesn't.)

RICHARD: What do you think can happen to you? We all like you, Tim. You're welcome here. Let me help you.
TIM: I got it. I'm fine.
  Rhinebeck hasn't changed. Looks the same.

(Barbara returns with another tablecloth for the card table.)

RICHARD: And really nice to be out of the city. Especially today.
TIM *(With emphasis)*: Especially today.

(Jane carries in two chairs.)

RICHARD *(To Jane)*: I could have done that.
JANE: Then why didn't you?

(From off, church bells—playing a hymn.)

TIM: Are those church bells? They're lovely . . . This is such a charming town. You're lucky to live here, Barbara.

(Marian returns with bowls, etc.)

RICHARD *(To Jane)*: Should I get my bottle?
JANE: What's wrong with Tim's two bottles?
BARBARA *(Setting up the tablecloth, to Tim)*: Those aren't real bells, by the way.
TIM: What do you mean?
MARIAN: It's the Dutch Reformed—they play CDs of bell music through loud speakers in their steeple. Barbara hates that.
TIM *(Innocently)*: Why do you—?
BARBARA: We'll set out the salad here too. *(Then back to the bells)* Why should they be allowed to blast us with their CDs? I mean, if they were bells and real people were ringing

them—okay. I get it. But they're just stupid CDs. At Christmas it's the worst. Like you're living inside a mall. Who the hell do they think they are? I mean, if I stuck a speaker out of my goddamn window and played it whenever I wanted to play it, they'd come and arrest me . . . *(She goes off)*

MARIAN: See . . .

(Short pause as they set out the rest.)

Thank you, Tim.

TIM *(He now goes to shake hands)*: Richard, good to see you.

RICHARD: And you. *(To his sisters, a bad joke one more time)* Tim's here.

(As Barbara and now Benjamin return with another chair, more bowls, etc.)

What else can I do?

BARBARA: What "else"? What have you done?

JANE: Getting hungry, Uncle Benjamin?

BARBARA: He likes to eat lunch now at eleven.

MARIAN: And I don't know why you let him do that.

RICHARD *(To be useful, moving chairs)*: Why don't we have Benjamin sit there. Tim, Marian—there. Barbara—

JANE: It's Barbara's house. You're really going to tell her where to sit? Why do you always do that? *(To Tim)* Why do men do that?

TIM *(On the spot)*: I don't know.

BARBARA: It's also now Marian's house, Jane.

(Awkward moment.)

I mean, she's not a guest. She lives here too.

(They start to serve themselves.)

RICHARD: You remember Tim, don't you, Uncle?

MARIAN *(To Benjamin)*: He's the actor. You like him. He's from New York.

BENJAMIN: Always a pleasure to see you, son. I used to live in New York. *(To the others)* Of course I remember him.

(The others exchange doubtful looks.)

(To Barbara) Didn't I live in New York?

(Barbara nods.)

TIM: It's great to be up here, sir. Out of the city. *(To Richard)* Especially today.

MARIAN *(To Jane)*: I'm so glad you two are back together. I never liked your husband.

(This stops the conversation for a moment.)

What did I say?

JANE: It is nice. It is very nice . . . For me.

(She smiles at Tim.)

TIM *(After a prompt)*: And me too.

JANE: Richard, how's Pamela?

RICHARD: She's good.

MARIAN: I'm so sorry she couldn't come too. *(To Barbara)* Aren't we?

(No response.)

(To Richard) She couldn't come, right? *(To Barbara)* She's always so busy.

RICHARD: She's doing things with the kids.

She told me to say hi from her to my lovely lovely sisters . . .

(Short pause.)

MARIAN: Say hi back.

BENJAMIN *(As he goes to the card table)*: Can I get anyone else a glass of wine?

MARIAN *(Trying to stop him)*: We have your favorite wine in the kitchen, Uncle. Let me get it for you—

BENJAMIN: I want this wine. I'd like a change.

(They continue to serve themselves.)

TIM *(Serving himself)*: Look at this. Turkey. Coleslaw. Is this chicken salad? *(To Barbara and Marian)* You two have gone all out . . .

MARIAN *(To Tim, pointing)*: Lima beans and carrots . . . *(About a casserole)* This is vegetarian, Jane . . . Or are you over with that?

JANE: I'm not "over with that."

BARBARA *(Suddenly worried)*: We didn't rush the dinner, did we? *(Explaining)* The reading's at five . . . *(Looks at her watch)* And you heat things for too long . . .

TIM *(After a look at Jane)*: No, no . . . I'm ready to eat.

MARIAN: And Benjamin was getting very hungry.

(They look at Benjamin.)

BARBARA: I didn't mean to rush us . . .

JANE: You didn't, Barbara. We were late.

After the reading maybe we can take a walk around the village a little. I'd enjoy that. And we are staying the night.

(They serve themselves.)

Tim couldn't wait to come up here. He loves this village.

RICHARD: You're not thinking of getting a weekend place up here, are you?

JANE: Where would we get that kind of money, Richard? We're not all expensive lawyers.

BARBARA: You don't strike me as the weekender type, anyway.

TIM *(To Barbara)*: What is the "weekender type"?

MARIAN: Don't get Barbara started . . .

(They continue to serve themselves.)

(To Barbara) Sunday night, the weekenders are pretty much gone by then. So it'll be nice. *(To Jane)* For your walk.

A lot of city people were up this weekend.

(Short pause as they continue to fill their plates.)

BARBARA: I hate it when the moment you walk into a house— they serve the meal.

JANE: Barbara, it's fine. What else could we do?

RICHARD *(To say something)*: How late was your train?

TIM: I'll have a roll . . .

JANE *(Looks to Tim)*: Forty, fifty minutes—?

BARBARA *(To Tim)*: When Marian first moved to Rhinebeck? She was the first.

TIM: I know.

BARBARA: She was waiting on the platform at Rhinecliff and the guy from the ticket office was there, and she asked him for the time? *(To Marian)* What did he say?

JANE *(To Tim)*: I've heard this—

RICHARD *(To Tim)*: I've heard it too . . .

MARIAN: They've heard this.

BARBARA: Tim hasn't. He said, "Honey," he called Marian honey, Tim. "Honey, I threw away my watch the day I joined Amtrak."

(Tim laughs.)

JANE *(To Tim)*: I'd told you that story . . .

(And they have all taken seats and are about to eat, when: The lights fade.)

Up the Hudson

Lights up a moment later. As they eat:

TIM *(Eating)*: I love the train.

JANE *(Surprised)*: It's expensive.

MARIAN: Everything goes up.

BARBARA: And Sunday's the worst. It can be cheaper other days.

TIM: I think that's one of the most beautiful train rides in America.

BARBARA *(To Tim)*: You should ride that train with Richard sometime—he's the expert.

RICHARD: What are you—? *("talking about")*

BARBARA: He's like a tour guide—

MARIAN *(Over this, adding her two cents to Tim)*: Like a docent.

BARBARA: Look there. Look at that. Where they tied a chain across the Hudson to stop the British.

MARIAN: In the Revolutionary War.

BARBARA: Bannerman's Castle. West Point.

RICHARD: Jane knows all that too.

BARBARA: Not like you do.

JANE *(To Richard)*: I've read one book. I told you about one book—

BARBARA: Or like Richard used to. *(To Tim)* Richard used to love that river.

RICHARD *(Eating)*: I still do.

BARBARA: Good. He used to go back and forth to Albany a lot when he worked for the Attorney General's office. Or have you forgotten that?

MARIAN *(She knows the answer)*: Now you don't go back and forth?

RICHARD: No.

MARIAN: I suppose now you just have to walk to Wall Street to meet with your rich clients. *(Looks at Barbara and smiles—that made the point)*

RICHARD: I do pro bono work as well. I can live with myself.

(They eat.)

I gather from Marian, she's thinking of joining your community chorus, Barbara.

BARBARA *(Surprised)*: When did she tell you that—?

MARIAN: I'm thinking of it. You've wanted me to think about it.

TIM *(To Jane)*: What?

JANE: Barbara's in a chorus at Bard. Marian, are you thinking of joining?

BARBARA: I've been trying to get her—

RICHARD *(Over this)*: She was playing a CD of your Christmas concert. When I arrived—

MARIAN *(Trying to make it a joke)*: Snuck in on me.

BARBARA *(Very interested)*: She was? You were?

JANE *(To Marian)*: Why don't you? You have a good voice. Sounds like fun, doesn't it? You should get out.

MARIAN: I get out.

RICHARD: I said the same thing.

BARBARA: I've tried to get you to listen to that CD a hundred times.

JANE: I think it's a great idea.

MARIAN: I get out. School's started. I teach every day. I went to church this morning.

BARBARA: She's getting out now.

(They eat.)

TIM *(To Marian)*: How was today's service in church? Do they do anything special up here today?

BARBARA: There's our concert tonight—

TIM: I meant in church. And did anyone watch any of it on TV this morning? I thought the garden they made looked quite beautiful . . . Those rows and rows of trees. Serene and peaceful. That is, once all this noise dies down.

JANE: I thought so too.

RICHARD: They're making it so only a certain number of people at a time can . . .

JANE: You book online.

BARBARA: Makes sense. *(Answering the earlier question)* Benjamin and I went with Marian to church . . .

MARIAN: What she's trying to hint at is—I made them go with me. Which is not true. I can go by myself. I go lots of places by myself. *(To Barbara)* I've seen Adam. I'm not hiding from him.

(They eat.)

I'm not.

BARBARA *(Continuing to Tim)*: And they did something very special in church today, Tim. It was really very nice, wasn't it, Uncle? Very simple.

BENJAMIN: What? I don't know.

BARBARA: You liked it. All the names? *(To the others)* If someone had lost—someone, a friend, a friend's friend, certainly a family member, a loved one—in the towers or I suppose one of the planes . . . You could have their name read out. It was a pretty long list. I was surprised. *(To Marian)* Weren't you surprised? All the way up here.

(They eat.)

JANE: So—was Adam there?

MARIAN: Is this all going to be about me?

JANE: Was he there? I'm just asking. Barbara?

(Barbara nods. Jane looks to Richard.)

RICHARD *(To Jane)*: I've written him twice. I've tried calling him. Marian knows this.

MARIAN: I'm right here.

RICHARD: He should pay something. And it shouldn't be up to Marian to make him.

BARBARA: Talk to Marian.

MARIAN: I know what he's—

RICHARD: Barbara's told me, Marian, you're still paying half of the mortgage. You know, that makes no sense. You're not being—"independent," you're being silly. And I'm not saying you have to fight him. Just that it should be fair . . .

MARIAN *(To Jane)*: I don't want Richard doing anything. He knows this. Can you tell him that?

JANE: He's a lawyer. He's your brother.

MARIAN: And what do *you* get, Jane?

JANE: That's different.

MARIAN: Why is it different? Why is she different?

BARBARA: I'm sorry, Tim.

TIM: No, no, it's . . .

JANE *(To Marian)*: Alfred paid for Billy's school. That's all I cared about. That's all I've asked for. And that was a lot. We just want to help you . . .

(Short pause. Jane eats.)

MARIAN: Where is Billy now?

JANE *(Eating)*: Philadelphia. They say, that's a good place for young people. Stay out of New York. It's too unreal now. Too rich. Too many kids with trust funds. *(Eating)* I have a friend who works in Chelsea, in a gallery there, and the kids, the girls—the receptionists—the clothes they wear. Well, I couldn't afford them. None of us could.

BARBARA: Maybe Richard.

JANE *(Smiles)*: Maybe him.

RICHARD: I'm saving for two college educations!

JANE *(As she eats)*: Where do they get the money? It must seem unreal. Especially to impressionable kids. *(Turns to Tim)* Tim says it's maybe the one good thing that's come out of the recession.

RICHARD: What is, Tim?

JANE: To be reminded that rich people aren't heroes, just because they're rich. For years now that's been hard to explain to kids. To my son. *(Smiles to herself)*

RICHARD *("Under his breath" to Tim, a joke)*: She speaks for you now?

JANE: Rich people just look so appealing— But then for at least a minute, *(To Tim)* right?

RICHARD *("Under his breath" to Tim, teasing)*: Say "right."

BARBARA: Richard—

TIM *(To Jane)*: Right.

(Richard laughs.)

JANE: Our kids got a chance to take a real good close look at some of those people. And see for themselves—is that what they want to become.

But then again, all that's maybe already passed. That's depressing. Uncle, you're not the only person around with amnesia. It's disgusting. *(Eats)* And they're getting away with it.

(Pause.)

MARIAN: So Alfred paid for Billy's school. Good. And I'm glad Billy is doing so well.

JANE: I didn't say— He doesn't have a job—

MARIAN: And how are your children, Richard?

(The others realize the weight behind this.)

RICHARD: They're—fine, Marian.

MARIAN: Good. I'm glad. That's so nice to hear. *(Standing)* Excuse me. I think we need more— *(Looks around)* potatoes . . .

(She takes a bowl and goes into the kitchen. The moment she is gone:)

RICHARD: Jane—

JANE: I'm sorry I didn't mean to start talking about Billy. I'm sorry. I'm sorry. I wasn't thinking. Where is my head?

BARBARA: You can't just stop talking about your kids.

JANE: You said she's getting out of the house now. And she's teaching . . . That's all good, isn't it?

RICHARD: I could try and see if I can talk some sense into Adam this afternoon. Just go knock on his door.

(Barbara shakes her head.)

What if he's at the reading? Should I just say nothing? He is getting away with—

JANE *(To Richard)*: What a son of a bitch.

RICHARD: I agree.

JANE *(To "Tim")*: And now Barbara is living in her own basement.

BARBARA: My choice, Jane. There's a bathroom down there.

RICHARD *(To Barbara)*: And for how long?

BARBARA: For as long as she wants. As long as it takes. It takes time . . . Give her time—

JANE: We were brought up to be women who stood up for ourselves—

(Barbara sees Marian returning with the potatoes and stops the conversation. Short pause.)

MARIAN: Richard, I thought today was the day every year you always spent with your old buddies. It was a "thing" you did.

BARBARA: More than a "thing," Marian.

MARIAN: I didn't mean—

RICHARD: I do. I did. We had our breakfast. Same place. Same toasts. Same "buddies."

But we— It felt different today. From other anniversaries. And it was getting very crowded down there. And loud . . . Anyway, we just stayed a little while. Hence—I could come here.

(Raises his glass to them.
Benjamin gets up.)

BARBARA: Are you done?
BENJAMIN: No.

(He looks off.)

MARIAN: Your cigarettes aren't in your room.
BARBARA: Remember, Marian is keeping them for you. Marian, he can have another cigarette.
MARIAN *(As she doles out a cigarette)*: And make sure you use the ashtray.

(Benjamin starts to go to the kitchen.)

BENJAMIN: I use the ashtray.

(They watch him go.)

MARIAN *(Calling after him)*: Sometimes you just flick them . . .

(They eat.)

BARBARA: The mornings are his best time. The best for me too. He's funny. He helps us out in the kitchen, doesn't he? It's when we have our conversations. Our talks. As the day wears on, he gets more and more . . . quiet.

You wonder: Is he watching us? Judging us? That's what Marian—
MARIAN: I do not.
BARBARA: Sometimes. Or just listening? Or is he somewhere else?
MARIAN *(About Benjamin)*: Shouldn't he have a sweater?
BARBARA: He's fine. *(Then, to Richard)* So it was just too crowded for you?

RICHARD: Downtown?

JANE: We met a couple on the train—they were escaping the city too, like you, Richard.

RICHARD: I wasn't—"escaping."

JANE: You could see it in their faces. They didn't have to say anything. *(She eats, then)* It was a beautiful ride up. It's a beautiful river. Tim brought along a kind of guidebook and was reading me things on the train.

(Marian gets up and pours herself a glass of wine.)

BARBARA: About the Hudson?

RICHARD: Taking my job, are you?

TIM: I wasn't—

RICHARD: I'm joking.

JANE: Like all of American history has flowed down that river . . .

MARIAN: A lot. Not everything. Don't exaggerate.

TIM: Pretty much.

BARBARA *(Taking Marian's side, giving examples of history the Hudson wasn't connected to)*: Slavery—the Civil War. *(To Marian)* I agree with you.

RICHARD: He's praising your river.

MARIAN: Praising or sentimentalizing?

TIM: Actually—the underground railroad, right up the Hudson—

MARIAN: The Gold Rush then.

RICHARD: The Mills Mansion. Mr. Mills made all that money selling picks and shovels in the Gold—

TIM: Not everything. But . . .

RICHARD: It is a neat river.

(Pause. They eat.)

JANE: How late is the Roosevelt Home open on a Sunday? It is open today? Tim hasn't been.

RICHARD *(To Tim)*: You haven't been?

JANE: Today's not a holiday?

RICHARD: The wine store was open.

JANE: He's wanted to see it.

MARIAN: We have the reading. It's not open that late.

JANE *(To Tim)*: Tomorrow then. When does it open?

RICHARD *(Eating)*: You walk into that museum, and, Tim—you can walk right into the part that starts with his first term. And—I swear, you will be moved. Amazed. They did this and this and this . . . *(Snapping his fingers)* Changed the whole damn country. Sort of gives you hope. That things can change. "Hope and Change." Where have I heard that before?

BARBARA: Richard—

RICHARD: That's—if there's the will. If it's not all just about "splitting the difference" and—getting reelected . . .

BARBARA: Richard. Is this really the day to talk politics?

(Short pause.)

RICHARD: I'm not going to say any more, Barbara . . .

(They eat.)

We were talking about the Hudson . . .

(Then:)

I just read an interesting book. A lot of it's set on the Hudson. About General Lafayette's return to America.

JANE: When was that?

RICHARD: Years after—as an old man. 1820s. The book's by his secretary. It's his secretary's journal. Congress one day up and decides to invite Lafayette back. As a national celebration, I suppose. They felt they needed one at the time, I guess. To remember! *(Smiles)* So he returns. He's broke now.

TIM: I didn't know that.

RICHARD: He'd been nearly guillotined in his own country.

The highlight of this trip—is a boat ride up the Hudson.

TIM: How far up?

RICHARD: Albany. *(Eats)* And everywhere along the shore, every town, every hamlet, wants to celebrate him. Thousands and thousands line the riverbanks. Eighty-year-old men—those who had fought alongside the young Lafayette, and who had risked everything to create this country—they pile into boats in their old uniforms, row out to the general to pay their respects. Fireworks light the sky, bands can be heard from the shore.

(Benjamin returns in the middle of this, and heads back to the table.)

Reading this book, lying in my bed one night, I found myself—imagining the scene. The general and his old pals—sit around on that boat, and after a few drinks, he asks his old comrades in arms: So how has democracy grown in the years I've been away? Are your politicians serving the people?

BARBARA: Richard.

RICHARD *(Over this)*: Is business fair? Elections, are they honest?

BARBARA: Richard . . .

BENJAMIN *(Confused, to Richard)*: What—?

BARBARA: Nothing, Uncle. Nothing.

RICHARD: The same old thing, Uncle. "Hope and Change." Let's talk about something else.

(The lights fade.)

Ghosts

Lights up. A short time later. As they eat, Tim has just begun a story.

TIM: First you walk up these, this stairway—nothing's been changed, touched for fifty, sixty years.

BARBARA: Like what?

TIM: The names on the doors. On the bubbly glass. Old little firms. An accountant. Someone else—casting agent I think. The stenciled names are still there. Anyway, we get to the top of the theater—to Mr. Belasco's apartment.

BARBARA *(To Benjamin)*: I didn't know they lived in their theaters.

BENJAMIN: Oh yes.

RICHARD *(To Benjamin)*: You remember that?

JANE *(To Barbara)*: Some did. Many did. They had fancy apartments. Tell them about the apartment.

TIM: Most of it's been—stripped; god knows where it's all gone. But there's a safe. A locked safe. Just sitting in the first room we go into. Then . . . Well the ceiling is quite low. Belasco was a very short man.

(Jane smiles at the others; they are interested.)

JANE *(Prompting Tim)*: The collar.

BARBARA: What?

TIM: He used to turn his collar around and so he looked like a priest.

BARBARA: That's weird.

MARIAN: Why would he do that?

RICHARD *(To Tim)*: You were doing a play in this theater.

TIM *(Nods)*: It's all changed now. It's all been renovated.

JANE: He was called "The Bishop of Broadway."

BARBARA: That's creepy.

JANE: It gets worse. Or something. *(Prompting)* The bedroom . . .

TIM: There's a big wooden structure. Carved dark mahogany I think. Very gothic. In this—the bedroom. It looks like a confessional you'd find in a Catholic church. But larger. Then our stage manager, he'd been given a tour himself. Now he's showing us. He shows us a door to a very small elevator—which goes down to the stage. And a little window—you can look down on the stage through this window from this bedroom. And so he'd—Mister Belasco—he'd phone down to *his* stage manager, having chosen a girl out of the chorus. She'd then be put in the tiny elevator up to his apartment—and the first thing she'd see was this large confessional—which, well, it was large enough for a small bed.

RICHARD: Christ . . .

JANE: He'd obviously, like a priest, open the little shuttered window, look through at the girl in the bed . . .

BARBARA: Wow. *(To Benjamin)* Is that how theater was in your day, Uncle?

BENJAMIN: I hope so.

(They laugh.)

JANE: Did you ever do a play at the Belasco?

BENJAMIN: I don't remember.

(Jane looks to Barbara.)

BARBARA: I don't know.

TIM: Anyway, that's a very long story just to explain . . . *(Now the story he wants to tell)* We're in tech. Late one night. The director calls it quits for the day. We all go. Then I'm at Joe's and I realize I've left my sweater—my cashmere sweater—back in the theater. The stage door guy lets me in. The theater's dark, just the ghost light's on. I feel my way along the seats—I remembered leaving it in the back. That's when I heard . . .

(Pause for effect.)

MARIAN: What?

TIM: The elevator. The little elevator. Which we'd been told couldn't work anymore. Hadn't worked for years. Just this . . . *(He makes the sound)*

MARIAN: You're sure it was—

TIM: That's what I told myself. Must be a dimmer or something . . . Something left on. "Hello?" I say. Nothing. I keep working my way through a row of seats, trying not to bang my shin—when I look up and there is a dim light coming from the stage-left box.

There's a woman there. She's crying. She has a scarf, which covers a lot of her face.

MARIAN: You could hear her . . . ?

TIM: Yes. I could hear her. I find my sweater—it'd fallen between two seats—and lean over. And as I lean I feel a hand on my shoulder.

(Marian reacts.)

RICHARD *(To Marian)*: Are you all right?

TIM *(Continuing)*: I swear to god. That's what I feel. There is no one there. But I felt it. Felt someone's fingers . . .

She wasn't in the box anymore.

JANE: And then he hurried like hell out into 44th Street.

(The others relax.)

RICHARD: I'll bet you did. *(Laughs)*

JANE: Supposedly, one of these chorus girls—something had happened in that bedroom and she'd died. In his apartment. *(To Tim)* Five, six other people?

(He nods.)

Have seen her too. He learned this. Once he told some friends about it, and they'd heard the same story. She's always crying.

TIM *(Teasing Jane)*: I can still feel her fingers . . .

JANE *(Ignoring him)*: Now that they've renovated . . .

RICHARD: So she's moved on?

JANE *(Laughs)*: Probably.

TIM: Or went to L.A. for pilot season and never came back.

(Tim, Jane and Benjamin laugh.)

MARIAN: I didn't understand . . .

TIM: I'm sorry. How did I get talking about—?

JANE: I don't know.

RICHARD: Barbara—

BARBARA: I was telling Tim about the show Benjamin and I saw. It was at the Belasco.

RICHARD: That's right. I remember.

BARBARA: Richard, you got us the tickets. What was the show? *(To Benjamin)* You liked it.

BENJAMIN: Did I? You're always telling me what I've liked and didn't like. What I've done. *(To the others)* It's a very curious relationship to have with another person.

RICHARD: Is it. Not for me. I have Pamela.

(The sisters like this, laugh.)

BARBARA: You shouldn't talk like that about your wife.

RICHARD: It was a joke.

BARBARA: You shouldn't joke . . .

RICHARD: Then why are you laughing?

BENJAMIN *(To Tim)*: Tim?

(This gets their attention.)

Tim??

(The others nod.)

Are you in a play now? You're an actor?
BARBARA: He is an actor too, Uncle. Like you.
MARIAN: I think Tim told us he did mostly TV.
TIM: Actually, I'm . . . What? *(Turns to Jane)*
MARIAN: You don't know? You have to ask her?
BARBARA *(To Richard)*: She's worse than Pamela.

(Laughter, except for Richard.)

JANE: Be quiet. Tim's got himself a—
TIM: Jane, they don't want—
JANE: A very good gig now—at a restaurant.
RICHARD: At a restaurant? What do you mean?
JANE: Right below where we live now at Manhattan Plaza.
(To Tim) Can I tell them?

(He nods.)

Really nice people. A lot of other terrific actors . . . So
when one of them gets an acting job, they let you out. And
then . . . They take you back.
RICHARD: That sounds convenient.
TIM: It is.
JANE: Tim does a lot of readings too.
TIM: They pay like shit. Excuse my French. But they keep
you—limber.
MARIAN: Limber? Don't you sit in a reading?
JANE: Actually, maybe you all could help us figure something
out.
TIM: Jane—
BARBARA: Figure out what?
JANE: Maybe it'll help to talk about it.
BARBARA: About what?
JANE: Tim's been offered— *(To Tim)* You want to tell them?

TIM: You can tell them.

JANE *(Then)*: Another restaurant/bar has been trying to poach him. *(She smiles at Tim)* He's that good a waiter. More hours. A set schedule. He's not sure whether he should take it.

TIM: I'm an actor.

JANE: It's a very tough . . . The economy . . . The theater especially . . . You can imagine. You have to be employed—his union says—a certain number of weeks to get the health insurance. He hasn't worked that many weeks. This bar, they have some benefits.

RICHARD: If it's the high deductible crap—that's worthless. Do you know?

TIM: I don't know. I don't know anything about health insurance.

BARBARA: You should know—

JANE *(To Tim)*: You haven't asked—

RICHARD: You need to find out. You need to know what questions to ask.

TIM: I don't think I'm going to take it. So . . . *(Looks at Jane)*

JANE: That's not what you said this . . . *(To the others)* We go back and forth. He's a wonderful actor. I can't take my eyes off of him when he's on stage. Can I?

(She kisses him on the cheek.
  Then:
  They eat. Short pause.)

BARBARA: How's your book, Jane? You haven't said a word about that.

BENJAMIN: What—?

RICHARD: Jane's magnum opus on American manners . . .

JANE: Don't make fun.

RICHARD: I wasn't making fun. It sounds like a brilliant book. I'm waiting to read it.

JANE: It's almost done. It's with an editor. They're thinking about it.

TIM *(Trying to help)*: She sent it to her son to read. She's dedicating it to Billy.

MARIAN: Are you? That must make him . . .

JANE: He hasn't read it yet. He's busy. *(To herself)* Children . . .

TIM *(Trying to help)*: Jane's trying to sell one chapter as an essay to *Playbill*.

BARBARA *(To Richard, explaining)*: That's the little magazine they give you free—

RICHARD: I know. I have gone to the theater. When I can't avoid it.

TIM: An article about audiences. How things haven't changed. It's very funny.

BARBARA: Why is it funny? . . .

TIM: Tell them about the German conductor.

JANE: They don't want to hear—

BARBARA: What German conductor?

TIM: He's giving an outdoor concert in New York in something like—1850? And as soon as he starts, people start talking. One guy makes a lot of noise lighting up his cigar. So—what does the conductor do? He stops the orchestra, looks out into the audience and says to the man— *(Turns to Jane)*

JANE: "Go on, sir, don't mind us." It's not that funny.

BARBARA: Just like with cell phones today.

JANE: That is my point.

TIM: What's changed?

JANE: People have been rude for—forever.

RICHARD: I think it's gotten worse. Do you ever go to the movies?

TIM: She has a lot of little stories like that. About audiences.

JANE: Tim told me one. It's in the article.

TIM: I heard an older actor tell it. Whether it happened or—

BARBARA: What?

(Tim looks to Jane.)

JANE: It's your story.

TIM *(Then)*: A very established actor—like yourself, Benjamin. He takes another much younger actor under his wing. And he's explaining about audiences to this young man. He says, "Son—"

RICHARD: What's his name? The older actor. Is he famous?

JANE: It doesn't matter.

BARBARA: Pass around the turkey. *(To Marian)* We bought too much. There's plenty of turkey.

MARIAN: I told you—

JANE: Tim's trying to— I thought you wanted to hear this.

(They quiet down.)

BENJAMIN: Was I famous?

MARIAN *(After a look around the table)*: To all of us, Uncle.

JANE: Tim . . .

TIM *(Continuing)*: "Son," the older actor says, "pretend for a second you're in, say—London during the Blitz. And the Germans are attacking, women and children are dying, the city's on fire. And you walk into a theater—"

RICHARD: The theaters were open during the Blitz?

JANE: Yes, they were.

TIM *(Continues)*: "And you hear an actor give this speech, this way:" *(He stands)* "'Once more unto the breach, dear friends, once more; or close the wall up with our English dead!'"

BENJAMIN: I know that.

BARBARA: Where's it from?

(They wait. He doesn't answer. Then:)

TIM *(Continuing)*: The older actor asks the younger one, "How would that make you feel, hearing that?" And the young man says, "It would make me feel like I'd want to fight, and beat those Nazis!"

(Food is being passed around.)

BARBARA *(Explaining)*: The young man's an actor too.

JANE: He said that.

MARIAN: Is he?

TIM: The older then says, "Now let's pretend we are in, say, America during another war—the Vietnam War. And people are protesting, and, you know, innocent women and children are dying over there. And you walk into a theater—"

BARBARA: There was theater then, Richard.

RICHARD: I know, I remember.

TIM *(Continues)*: "And hear the same actor—" *(A joke to Jane)* He must be on tour—

(She laughs.)

"Give the same speech, the same way: 'Once more unto the breach, dear friends, once more; or—'"

BENJAMIN: "'—or close the wall up with our English dead!'"

BARBARA: He remembers.

JANE: Tim just said it.

BARBARA: Still, he remembered that.

RICHARD: Good for you, Uncle.

TIM *(Continuing)*: "And now—how does *that* make you feel," the older actor asks. And the young man says, "That sounds just loud, and thoughtless."

(For the first time during this story, everyone is paying full attention.)

The same words. The same actor. The same way. —What is different? *(He looks around at the others)* What's different?

BENJAMIN: The audience.

(The others are amazed and pleased.)

JANE *(Nodding)*: The audience. What we, the audience, bring when we come to theater—what we might be feeling that

day. What might have happened to us. That is a big part
of what a play is.

(They continue to eat and dish out seconds.)

RICHARD: Is that really true?
JANE: We may think we're just sitting back, watching—but in
a way we're as much a part of what is happening in that
theater, as any actor on the stage . . .

(They eat.)

TIM *(Serving himself)*: I did a show in Boston around 9/11?
There was a song, a joyous, funny song in the show, called
"Wake the Dead." On September 10th, the audience
cheered and laughed. On September 12th, they wept.
Same song . . .

(The lights fade.)

More Ghosts

Lights up a moment later.

JANE: We're also writing a screenplay together.
BARBARA: About—?
JANE: We keep changing our idea. But it'll be something for
Tim to act in.

(She looks to Tim who nods.)

MARIAN *(Trying to be "funny")*: I think you should write a movie
about a lawyer who leaves his job helping ordinary peo-

ple, and goes to work for the rich. And starts watching
FOX. And hating teachers . . . *(Smiles)*
RICHARD: You know me better than that. Don't put me in a box.

(Short pause.)

BARBARA: The reason I brought up going to the theater—
MARIAN *(Interrupts, to Tim)*: I believe in ghosts. I believe that
girl or woman was there. And she touched you.
BARBARA: Marian . . .
TIM: It felt real.
MARIAN: I've seen a ghost. I've heard her. I've talked to her. I've
felt her hand on my shoulder.

(This has stopped the room.)

BARBARA: Are you talking about Evan?

(The others don't know what to do.)

MARIAN: I know—I know it's in my head. But who says ghosts
can't be in our head? I call her cell phone. Two, three
times a week, don't I? *(Looks to Barbara, who is about to say
something)* Sometimes more.
RICHARD *(To Barbara)*: I didn't know that.
MARIAN: Adam still pays for her phone. Maybe because he calls
her too? *(Smiles)* So I call, to hear her message. I hear my
daughter's voice. I talk. And more often than not, I think
she hears me . . .
JANE: I'm sure she does, Marian.
MARIAN: Don't patronize me.

(Short pause. No one knows what to say.)

(To Tim, as if the most natural thing in the world) I only say
this because we were talking about ghosts . . .

TIM: I'm sorry if I—

MARIAN: You didn't do anything.

(Short pause.)

BARBARA *(Pushing forward)*: As I was saying, the reason I brought up going to the theater with Benjamin—which led to—the ghost in the theater, very interesting story, Tim. Well, it's because Marian and I—

MARIAN: What?

BARBARA: Uncle Benjamin. What we've been doing with you.

MARIAN: You, not me. You're the one doing this.

BENJAMIN: Doing what?

RICHARD *(To Benjamin)*: Don't you know?

BARBARA *(To Marian)*: You're helping. We're doing this together.

JANE: What?

BARBARA: We've been asking Benjamin questions—mostly about his life, and his career as an actor—and recording them.

MARIAN: She asks him questions—

BARBARA *(Over this)*: And Marian transcribes them.

MARIAN: You do most of that too.

BARBARA: Not true. We do it together.

JANE: Are you thinking of writing a book?

BARBARA: We're just asking questions. We'll get the notes if you'd like. And show you. You might be interested. Marian, maybe you could get it?

MARIAN: You're asking? *(Stands up)* She never asks you to do anything. *(To Barbara)* You know how hard that is to live with? *(As she goes)* I'm kidding.

BARBARA: It's on the desk. *(Calls)* And bring the tape recorder! There's a tape in it. *(To the others)* I was transcribing earlier . . .

(As soon as Marian is gone:)

TIM: I haven't known what to say about her daughter. So I haven't said anything. I am so sorry.

RICHARD: That's probably best, Tim.

JANE: I don't know.

TIM: Jane and I weren't together when she died.

JANE: They know that. You sent a lovely note. He read it to me.

BARBARA: And Marian appreciated the gesture. *(Making a joke)* At first she didn't know "who the hell Tim was?" Then I told her and she appreciated it.

BENJAMIN: What are you talking about?

BARBARA: Evan, Uncle. Marian's daughter, Evan . . .

(Marian returns with a large notebook and a small tape recorder.)

JANE: So—what sort of questions?

BARBARA: You'll see. *(Taking the notebook)* Thanks.

RICHARD: You going to play that?—

BARBARA: It's hard to hear. Most of the time I have to hold that up to my head. *(Opens the notebook)* This is the part you wanted them to hear, Uncle.

BENJAMIN: Did I?

BARBARA: Tim, will you read Benjamin? You're an actor.

(She hands a copy of the transcript to Tim. She keeps a second copy for herself.)

(Reads) Question: "Why is it important to you to be an actor."

TIM *(To Jane)*: I'm interested in this.

BENJAMIN: Me too.

TIM *(Reads)*: Benjamin answers: "Well, it's the most absorbing—" Do you want to read it yourself, Benjamin?

BARBARA: Why don't you do that?

TIM: Come here, sit down. Sit here. Come on.

133

(Benjamin sits and is given the transcript.)

(Points out the place in the transcript) "Benjamin." There.

BARBARA: We want you to read yourself. *(To the others)* We'll let him play himself. *(To Marian)* We haven't done it this way.

MARIAN: No.

BARBARA *(To Benjamin, pointing out the place)*: Go ahead. There. Where I'm pointing. Question: "Why is it important to you to be an actor." And you answer:

JANE: Go on, Uncle.

BENJAMIN *(Reads)*: "It's the most absorbing, thoroughly absorbing work that I could do. That I can do. I have at times thought of other things that I could do, and have done; I've thought about many things, from—including being a doctor—but I never took any medical education."

(Richard laughs.)

BARBARA: He's obviously bullshitting. Aren't you, Uncle?

BENJAMIN: Am I?

BARBARA: I think you are.

RICHARD: I agree.

(Benjamin looks up at them.)

BARBARA: Keep reading.

BENJAMIN *(Reads)*: "I've thought of running for election. For Congress. I don't think there is any possibility in which I should likely be elected."

(The others laugh.)

JANE: I'd vote for you, Uncle!

BENJAMIN *(Reads)*: "Most politicians seem to have amnesia but won't admit it. They don't remember any of the promises they've made."

(He laughs.)

(To the others) That's very funny. I like that. He's funny.

JANE: You know he is you, Uncle?

BENJAMIN: I know.

(Laughter.)

RICHARD: You'd fit right in.

BARBARA *(Reads)*: "So you would be the honest politician?"

BENJAMIN: Yes. Yes.

BARBARA *(Points)*: That was a question. I'm reading. Here.

BENJAMIN *(Reads)*: "I don't say it's a pressing ambition. I'm not going to address it, unless someone comes and offers me the chance, then I'd probably take it. I would love to be a member of Congress . . ."

BARBARA: Me. *(Reads)* "Uncle, you were telling me why you are an actor." This is interesting. *(Reads)* "What do you bring to a role that is particular to you?"

TIM: Good question.

BENJAMIN *(Reads)*: "I suppose I bring my history, my childhood, upbringing and maturity, and, strangely enough, perhaps I've reached a point in my life where I bring a total confidence—I don't mean a total confidence in the way I play—but in my necessity."

RICHARD: What does he mean?

MARIAN: What do you mean by that, Uncle? Do you remember?

BENJAMIN: I think . . .

(They wait for him to answer. Then:)

BARBARA: Me. *(Reads)* "Would you bring the history of your illness—that's part of you now. And your amnesia, that is you, would you bring that into a role, do you think?" *(Helping him)* We turn the page.

BENJAMIN *(Reads, very interested in this himself)*: "I think I would. And I think I would with great satisfaction, pride—bring that history and show how I have survived it. And have actually learned from it. And help others to learn from it."

JANE *(To Barbara)*: Is he bullshitting?

BENJAMIN *(Answering)*: No, I don't think he is.

RICHARD: Are you sure?

BENJAMIN: It sounds to me like he isn't. I believe him.

BARBARA: Question. *(Reads)* "What have you learned from it?"

BENJAMIN *(Reads)*: "I think I've learned from it the—the limitless capacity of myself, and, therefore, I would say of a human being, to recover, to overcome—not to be scathed, robbed of . . . I do actually believe, I don't know if this is true—all illnesses can be recovered from, except of course death. Which of course isn't an illness . . ."

JANE: He's not bullshitting . . .

BARBARA *(To the others)*: We record in the mornings. He's at his best. I told you that.

BENJAMIN: Could I have my wine?

(Barbara gives him his wine.)

MARIAN: Is this bothering you, Uncle? We can stop.

BENJAMIN: No. No.

BARBARA: Me. *(Reads)* "When you're doing your Oscar Wilde performance that we've seen you do in New York this past—the reading you did at the Y. Are there times that you forget that you are you?"

TIM: That's a fantastic question.

BENJAMIN *(Reads)*: "What do you mean?"

BARBARA *(Reads)*: "Do you become someone else? For instance, do you become Oscar Wilde in prison?" Pause.

BENJAMIN *(Reads)*: "I think I do. Become someone else. I mean I actually do become Oscar Wilde."

JANE *(To Richard)*: Telling the truth?

(Richard shrugs.)

BARBARA *(Reads)*: "As a person today, you seem very calm and easygoing, you don't—there's not a lot of—you know—emotional things that I see. Big happiness, big sadness, you seem very very calm. Are you acting?" *(She looks up)* Another pause. Benjamin you didn't answer.

Me again. *(Reads)* "But on stage you show so much emotion, you know—you're like a different—like it just takes over."

BENJAMIN *(Reads)*: "Yes. It's not that I haven't got the capacity to feel and remember great emotions, um, I suppose that this period of my life corresponds—well not exactly to the period where Wilde was in prison . . ."

BARBARA *(Reads)*: "But it is *like* being in prison? Your amnesia."

BENJAMIN *(Reads)*: "In a way."

BARBARA *(Reads)*: "It's interesting to me that you connect the two. I don't want to put words in your mouth, but, in a way, playing Oscar Wilde in prison has been a chance for you to express emotions that you feel?"

(Short pause
He reads to himself.)

Read it out loud, Uncle.

BENJAMIN *(Reads)*: "Very much so. Very much so."

JANE: My god—

BARBARA: I know. I know. But he's not done.

BENJAMIN *(Continues)*: "As I say, I do believe—I don't mean to say I give the best performance that could ever be given—but I am Oscar Wilde when I do . . ." *(He reads to himself)*

BARBARA *(Gently)*: Out loud, Uncle.

BENJAMIN *(Reads)*: "Not that I'm . . . No, in that sort of literal sexual sense that I've ever had that intensity of experience of love for a young man. I have had, not . . . well I suppose you could call it homosexual, certainly not homosexual in the sort of physical, complete sense, but I have had an intense—intense love—for a man, a young man—"

(He is reading this just to himself now.)

"—I was young at the time—who was more or less my own age, somewhat older, but about three or four years older. So I can to that extent I can—I certainly feel no stranger to the idea of . . . loving a man intensely . . . I suppose it would be properly called, if you were asked to define it in sexual terms—a homosexual love. I don't mean a complete homosexual affair, but homosexual love. So I mean I have, as it were, that in common with Oscar Wilde."

(Benjamin suddenly stands, looks around.)

Can I smoke in here?
MARIAN *(Giving him a cigarette)*: No, Benjamin . . .

(He starts to head off with his copy of the transcript. Stops.)

BENJAMIN *(To Barbara)*: Thank you. This is so interesting.

(Benjamin heads outside through the kitchen. They watch him go. Barbara turns on the tape recorder. Bad crackling sound of a piano. She stops it.)

BARBARA: I have just asked him if he wants to play me something on the piano. We've asked him this a hundred times, haven't we?
MARIAN: We have.
BARBARA: Marian's here. He sits down at the piano and he says—

(She turns on the tape recorder—a garbled voice. Barbara laughs.)

JANE: I couldn't understand.

(Barbara stops the tape recorder.)

MARIAN: He said he's not used to this keyboard. *(Smiles, shakes her head)* He hadn't played forever, and this is what he says . . .

BARBARA: And then . . .

(She starts the tape recorder. We hear Benjamin playing nicely, but not perfectly, Schubert's Trout.*)*

JANE: That's him?

(The lights fade.)

Adam

Seconds later. The music on the tape recorder is still playing, but the phone in the kitchen has begun to ring.

JANE: I'll get it, Barbara. *(She starts to go)* Anyone need anything? Tim knows this piece. Some day you should hear him sing.

(She goes off. They listen.)

BARBARA *(To Tim)*: You know this?

(They listen. Then Tim suddenly sings and sings well:)

TIM *(Sings)*:
  In einem Bächlein helle,
  Da schoss in froher Eil
  Die launische Forelle
  Vorüber wei en Pfeil.

(The others are taken aback.)

I trained as a singer. I do musicals . . . I'm an actor and a singer . . . It's the *Trout*. It's well known.

(Jane returns.)

JANE *(Entering)*: It's Adam.

MARIAN *(Over this)*: I'm not here. *(She stands to go off to her bedroom)*

JANE: Don't run away. He's just on the phone. He's going to the concert. He just wants to let you know that. He wants to know if that's okay.

(Marian doesn't say anything. The music on the tape recorder plays.)

Is that okay? *(To Tim)* Were you just singing— *(As she waits for a response)* He says everyone's going. *(To Barbara)* What else is on the program tonight?

BARBARA: A group of kids playing fiddles. You know—Suzuki. They're cute. They wear little red bandanas. A few other singing groups. It's very—community. My students put this together.

TIM: Did they.

JANE: Marian, what do I say? He's asking.

RICHARD *(Suddenly standing)*: Let me talk to him . . .

MARIAN: No, Richard!

BARBARA: Please—

RICHARD: For Christ sake, Marian—you paid for most of that house. You built his fucking lawn business. And now you're in Barbara's bedroom? And she's in her fucking basement?!

MARIAN *(Yelling)*: No, Richard, no!

RICHARD *(Over this)*: Where are we—the Middle East? Stand up for yourself. If you can't, that's where a brother comes in. *(He heads off)*

MARIAN: Richard!! *(Looks at the others)* What's he going to do?

*(Barbara shuts off the tape recorder. The music stops.
Benjamin has passed Richard on his way in.)*

JANE: Enjoy your cigarette, Uncle? You know those are bad for
you. Why start smoking now?

BENJAMIN: I've always smoked.

JANE: No, you haven't.

BENJAMIN: I remember always smoking.

JANE *(Half to herself)*: We remember what we want to remember . . .

BARBARA *(To Benjamin)*: Sit down. You haven't finished your
dinner. Marian, could you pass the potatoes and—

(Marian suddenly gets up.)

MARIAN *(Heads for her bedroom, stops)*: I asked Richard not to
talk to him . . . Why can't he listen?! *(She hurries off)*

BENJAMIN *(To Tim)*: I started smoking when I was twelve years
old.

TIM: That's a really long time.

BARBARA *(To Jane)*: She saw Adam at church this morning. He
didn't used to go to church, that's what she said.

JANE: What's he doing—stalking her? *(To Tim)* Adam said all
these really nasty things to her. Blamed her. I don't think
I've told you everything.

BARBARA: Sorry, Tim.

TIM: I'm fine. It must have been just awful.

JANE *(To Barbara)*: I don't care if Adam was upset. What he
said to her was unforgivable.

BARBARA: Evan was his daughter too. What's worse than losing
a child? I don't know.

TIM: I can't imagine anything worse.

BARBARA: See, even Tim—

TIM: "Even—"?

JANE: That doesn't justify what he said to her.

BENJAMIN *(Confused)*: What?

JANE: We're talking about Evan's—"accident," Uncle. He blames our sister.

BENJAMIN: For what?

JANE: For not answering her fucking phone! Marian didn't hear her phone. And so she's to blame . . . Never mind, Uncle. It's all in the past. It's done. Forget it.

BENJAMIN *(Eating, to Barbara)*: What did Adam say?

BARBARA: Nothing, Uncle—

BENJAMIN: I don't understand.

JANE: Adam found Marian's cell, Uncle, in her purse. And there were some messages—

BARBARA: Three.

JANE: —from Evan, that she hadn't listened to. So she didn't hear her phone in her purse? Big fucking deal, Adam. *(To Tim)* He acted like a complete asshole to her. "Why the fuck didn't you answer your phone?" Like she killed her daughter!

BARBARA: Jane—

JANE: That's what Marian heard! I don't want to see him tonight. I don't ever want to see the son of a bitch. *(To Tim)* How many times do I not hear my phone? It's not like she did it on fucking purpose?

BARBARA: She did.

JANE: Did what?

BARBARA: Not answer when Evan called. On "fucking purpose."

JANE: I don't understand. That's not what you told me when—

BARBARA: They'd had a fight that morning. Evan and Marian. So she wasn't answering Evan's calls.

(Jane is taken aback by this.)

I didn't know this either until about a month ago. I haven't seen you in a month—

JANE: On purpose?—

BARBARA: They'd had a fight. Not an uncommon thing between the two of them. You know that. Mothers and daughters, I guess. Some are more difficult than others. And so that day, she had decided she wouldn't answer Evan's calls. So it's not that she didn't hear them, like we first thought.

That's why Adam . . . When she told him. I suppose he—got angry. Understandable. Isn't it? All this just came out one night—when we were still sharing my bedroom. She needed to talk . . .

(Silence.)

She chose—not to answer her daughter.

JANE: Well, they'd had a fight.

BARBARA: And then she killed herself. Why? *(Shrugs)* Anyway, I agree, Adam shouldn't have said half of what he said. It wasn't fair. And he knows that now. He's apologized to me—a hundred times. She won't talk to him. He keeps trying. *(Gestures toward the kitchen and the phone call, shrugs)* Poor man. I've told them both that their daughter had many problems. I had her in high school . . . They'd done their damnedest. But they're not going to listen to me.

JANE: No.

BARBARA: They're just going to beat themselves up.

(Richard returns.)

RICHARD *(Entering)*: He's going to give her some money. A monthly check—the bastard didn't say how much.

BARBARA: She won't take it, Richard.

RICHARD: It's her goddamn money . . . Do you know how many years she kept his stupid lawn business afloat?

JANE: Richard, Barbara was just—

BARBARA: Don't.

RICHARD: What?

JANE: Nothing.

RICHARD *(Hesitates, then)*: She could get herself an apartment.

BARBARA: She doesn't want an—

RICHARD: What about you?

BARBARA: She's welcome here. I like having her here.

RICHARD *(Sitting, to Jane)*: On the phone she keeps complaining about what it's like living with Marian.

BARBARA: I mouth off. Don't take me seriously—

JANE *(To Barbara)*: You do?

BARBARA: I don't mean it—

RICHARD: We can imagine what it must be like. *(To Jane)* Can't we?

JANE: I couldn't live with Marian.

BARBARA: It's just fine. The house is big enough.

RICHARD: It isn't, Barbara. *(Getting up)* Where is she?

BARBARA: Stay in here, Richard.

(He looks at her, then sits back down.)

RICHARD *(To Jane)*: He tried to give me all this bullshit about— how I just didn't understand.

JANE: Maybe you don't.

RICHARD: What do you mean? Of course I understand. I told him, I damn well understand. She's my sister. *(Starts to stand again)*

BARBARA: Stay in here. She'll come back when she's ready. You know Marian.

(He sits back down.)

And Richard, maybe she doesn't want you to help her. Maybe she needs to do this herself. Let's leave her alone.

(Richard looks at her.)

Eat some more. We made too much.

(The lights fade.)

Evan

Lights up a short time later.

JANE: How is your eye, Richard?

BARBARA: What's wrong with your eye?

RICHARD: Nothing.

JANE: A little vein in his left eye—it what? Popped?

BARBARA: What does that mean?

JANE: That he now has blurred eyesight in his left eye.

BARBARA: Have you seen a doctor?

RICHARD: Of course I've seen a doctor. I'm fine.

BARBARA: Why didn't you tell me about this?

JANE: He's had two laser surgeries. They didn't help. He tries to compensate—watch how sometimes he closes that eye.

(Barbara studies Richard.)

He's not going to do it when you stare at him. He asked if it could have been caused by stress. And his doctor—"oh yeah." He told me he thinks he knows the exact moment when the vein popped.

BARBARA: So it's like a stroke?

RICHARD: No.

JANE *(Over this)*: During a conversation with one fat-ass Wall Street client.

BARBARA *(Very concerned)*: Richard . . .

RICHARD: It'll get better.

JANE: It's not going to get better. You told me that.

BARBARA: Twenty years in the Attorney General's office and you're the picture of health, and ten months in this place and he's having strokes.

RICHARD *("Smiling")*: There's a lawyer in the firm, his brother had something like this, and he'd been wearing glasses all of his life, and after just one surgery, he not only fixed the blurriness but no longer even needed glasses. *(Trying to make it all a joke)* Says it's really helped his golf game. So you never know.

BARBARA: You've taken up golf?

RICHARD: No.

BARBARA *(To Jane)*: Thank god.

(Benjamin pours himself another glass of wine.)

Don't drink too much. You're acting today.

JANE *(Getting up)*: I'm going to see how Marian is. Maybe she shouldn't be alone, Barbara.

BARBARA: She's . . . *(Starts to stop her, then)* Go ahead.

(Jane goes off.)

(To herself) Go ahead . . .

(Short pause.)

TIM *(To say something)*: You have a farmer's market.

BARBARA: What??

TIM: A farmer's market. In the village. In the parking lot.

BARBARA: Yes. Yes, we do.

TIM *(Explaining)*: I—passed it . . .

(Barbara looks at her watch.)

RICHARD: Benjamin, do you need to prepare in any way?

BENJAMIN: For what?

BARBARA: You'll have to change your clothes.

(Benjamin starts to stand.)

You still have time.

BENJAMIN: I don't have to change my clothes?

BARBARA: Not yet.

TIM *(Another try)*: What a good idea, Barbara—to get your students involved today.

BARBARA: It was their idea—they wanted to do something. They're now my seniors and so—they were—six, seven, eight years old when it happened? It's interesting what they remember. But it's been a part of who they are . . .

At first I think they had in mind—something more— "exciting"? *("Smiles")* Like they saw when we killed Bin Laden. I said, I think this is about more than that.

I assigned a poem—the one Benjamin, you're going to read—and to write an essay on—today. On the anniversary. On how we remember things. How we should remember. And two of my best students came up with this idea for a community concert. Instead of writing a paper. It was their idea.

TIM *(Smiling)*: Sounds like they just didn't want to write a paper. *(To Richard)* That's how I was—

BARBARA: No. No. You're wrong.

The school at first didn't want to open the auditorium on a Sunday . . . but . . . It is a day you feel like you want to share with . . . with others. Do you feel that way?

TIM: I'm happy to be here—

BARBARA: Even just sitting in an audience with others . . .

TIM: It sounds like a wonderful thing. I'm looking forward to it. And to you reading this mysterious poem, Benjamin.

RICHARD: Why is it mysterious?

TIM: They haven't told us what it is.

RICHARD: What's the poem, Barbara?

BARBARA: You'll have to wait until tonight. *(Standing)* Anyone still eating?

RICHARD: I might be done. And I might not be. Sit down.

(She sits.)

Funny, it's one of those days, isn't it—where it comes in and out of your consciousness. Your head. The anniversary. This morning—with my friends. It was all about that. And then I forgot all about it. Then, it's back . . . *(Then to Tim)* It's why Barbara came. To Rhinebeck. She came after the attacks. So I'll bet today you're having—

BARBARA: There were a lot of reasons.

RICHARD *(Over this)*: She just picked up and left Manhattan.

BARBARA: I wasn't the only one.

RICHARD *(To Barbara)*: Did you know I sent in a memorial plan?

BARBARA: What do you mean?

RICHARD: For the competition. I didn't tell you? I must have told Jane. Anyone could submit one.

TIM: I remember that.

RICHARD: Thousands of people did, I think. *(He smiles)* I called mine a "peace garden." Later I read that something like four hundred submissions called theirs "peace gardens" . . .

TIM: What was it?

RICHARD: A garden maze . . . Places where you'd be in groups and then sections where only one person could fit, so you'd be alone . . . *(Shrugs)* I just wanted to do it. It felt good to do.

BARBARA: On TV it looked nice. What they ended up with. *(To Benjamin)* We watched a little this morning. Before we went to church. *(To Tim and Richard)* Lots of trees. Pools—in squares where the towers were.

RICHARD: Sort of. Not quite in the exact . . . Close enough.

BARBARA *(To Benjamin)*: The waterfalls? Remember? The bagpipes . . . Those school kids in their bright blue jackets? He liked the jackets.

RICHARD: We made them turn off the TVs in the bar this morning. So we weren't watching. But somehow a full minute before—the exact time—we all knew. We felt it. There wasn't a sound. Then just the bells.

(Jane returns.)

JANE: She doesn't want to talk. She doesn't want company. She's lying on your bed, Barbara—

BARBARA *(Over this)*: Her bed.

JANE: Reading *Harry Potter*. *(Shakes her head, shrugs)* What are you talking about?

TIM: Richard submitted a plan for the Ground Zero memorial.

JANE: I think I knew that.

BARBARA: He didn't win.

JANE: I knew that.

TIM: I think if someone had asked me, I'd have said—why not just a big statue to Philippe Petit. That would be my memorial.

BARBARA: Who's—?

JANE: The French guy who tightrope walked between the towers.

RICHARD *(To Tim)*: What does he have to do with—?

TIM: It's when the Trade Center—for a lot of people, I think, when it became—human. Up till then everybody hated those buildings. And—became glorious. My father was here then, doing something—a friend called him: "You're not going to believe this, get the hell downtown." Dad said he just watched this guy—between the two—walking. And it was beautiful. Like he'd conquered something inhuman, and tamed it for everyone. And made it human.

RICHARD: There was the guy who crawled up one of them—

TIM: That's right. I forgot about him. That's sort of the same thing.

RICHARD: So you'd have nothing about the attacks, the victims—

TIM: I don't know. I just think it would be inspiring. Philippe Petit. It could be . . .

RICHARD: One of my buddies this morning at our breakfast— he had an idea. As crazy as yours.

TIM: I don't think mine's—

RICHARD: He'd seen a show in Chelsea, an artist who'd done— what he called "candy spills." That's just what they were. Little wrapped candies, sort of spilled in a pile on the floor. And what you're supposed to do is—take one and eat it. And slowly then, over time, it'd all be gone. The pile is gone.

He said the artist intended it as a memorial—for people dying of AIDS.

JANE: What do you mean? I don't understand—

RICHARD: I know. He said, the goal was to make the world sweet again. *(Smiles)* And have everyone participate. And—and this was most important—he said the artist wanted to make art that would disappear. That memorials are not in the past or the future, but now. And so my friend, he was trying to convince us that the best memorial for 9/11 would be one that would have an end.

(Short pause.)

JANE: Tim has a friend, a gay director. *(To Tim)* You know who I mean? This made me think of him. Graham. *(To the others)* Years ago—in the eighties, at the height of the AIDS crisis for gay men, he's asked to organize a fundraiser. *(To Tim)* You asked him—

TIM *(Continuing the story)*: What sort of show could he do? And Graham says he's going to find the most attractive "hot" boys he can, and have them strip. And—be sexy as hell.

I said—isn't that in sort of bad taste? Given how people are dying? You know what he said? That there are young boys right now, who totally associate the act of sex with—death. And isn't that wrong, he asked. How more wrong could you be? Sex is not death—the exact opposite. And so he wanted to memorialize the dead and the dying—with sex. With life.

RICHARD: So he put on a strip show?

TIM: Yeah. *(As a joke)* And raised a hell of a lot of money.

JANE: You won't believe how much money—

(They laugh. Short pause.)

RICHARD *(To Jane)*: Barbara was saying that the kids who are organizing today—they were six or seven then . . . So pretty much their whole life . . .

JANE: Billy was twelve . . . I've asked him what he remembers.

RICHARD: What does Billy remember?

JANE: Well, I know he doesn't tell me everything.

He said he remembers when I came to pick him up at school—there was a man, a father—his suit completely covered in dust. And how the man was checking his watch—to put down the "correct" time on a sheet in the school office. To sign his son out and take him home. I think what Billy was saying is that it seemed so normal on the one hand, and so—something else—on the other. At the same time. Unsettling for a kid. *(Shrugs)* And—this: I don't have any memory of this at all. About two years later, Billy just came out with this—how when we had stopped at an ATM, walking uptown—Billy says there was a long long line—and no one in that line was saying anything to anyone; no one was looking at anyone . . .

(Short pause.)

BARBARA: Where were you, Tim?

TIM: In Boston. Doing a play.

BARBARA: You said. That song—

TIM: Trying to reach people back in New York . . . That's what I remember. Making phone calls . . . Over and over again. Trying to . . .

JANE: Billy remembers the littler kids at school, later, drawing pictures of people with parachutes . . .

(Short pause.)

RICHARD: I read that in the museum that they're building— whenever the hell they finish it.

TIM: Maybe another twenty years if they leave it to the "politicians."

RICHARD: It always ends up about money and real estate.

JANE: Do we really need a museum?

RICHARD: Anyway, there's going to be one, and it's going to have a display just about— *(Looks to Jane and Barbara)* —those of you who lived downtown. Supposedly there's going to be a rack of discount jeans—from Chelsea Jeans—remember Chelsea Jeans?—amazingly preserved in all the dust from that day, from a shop window on Broadway.

And they've got a recording of a teenager talking about how her family in Tribeca just wasn't going to leave. Her dad is saying, "Let's go to the supermarket." But there's no electricity. It's pitch dark. And everything in the refrigerator is melting all over the the floor . . .

TIM: Where were you, Benjamin? Do you remember?

BARBARA: He doesn't. *(To Benjamin)* You were making a movie in Bulgaria. One of those crazy places where they make movies to save money. You called me right away. I'd already made it to Midtown. And by some amazing miracle my cell worked for you. *(To the others)* I didn't know about Jane for almost a day. Richard called me and told me she was okay.

RICHARD: God, I remember.

BARBARA: I lied to Benjamin that whole day. *(To Benjamin)* You were too far away not to lie to. *(Smiles at him)*

JANE *(To Tim)*: Richard lost three people from his office . . .

RICHARD: They're the ones we toast—at our breakfasts—every year . . . This morning.

BARBARA: We're a hundred miles away up here, and this morning at church—it was a surprisingly long list of names . . . *(New thought)* We found some notebooks—appointment books is really what they are.

RICHARD: What are you talking about?

BARBARA: Do you know what I'm talking about, Uncle?

BENJAMIN: What?

BARBARA *(To Richard)*: In a bookshop. In a barn up here. We found them in a drawer with a lot of junk. Someone had— "lost" them I guess. For '99, 2000, 2001 . . . They kind of end on September 10th . . . *(To Uncle)* We've spent hours together looking through them . . . He doesn't remember.

JANE: *What* are they??

RICHARD: I don't understand.

BARBARA *(She starts to get up)*: I can get them if you—I'll show you. They're in the living room. *(She hurries off)*

RICHARD *(Calls)*: What sort of . . . ?

JANE: Notebooks, she said. Appointment books? *(Shrugs)* More mysteries, Uncle . . .

TIM: About eight or ten days after— So maybe like September 20th. I'm back from Boston. Everything was still so— fresh. And the subways, we were still all scared. Well, a couple of friends of mine, writers, and I got together for lunch. *(Then, connecting to the previous conversation)* At Un Deux Trois. Next to the Belasco.

RICHARD: I know where that—

JANE *(To Tim)*: What are you going to say?

TIM: I don't think I've told you this. *(To Richard)* As you said, things keep coming in and out. *(Points to his head. Continues)* The three of us made a rule—for the entire lunch we could only talk about theater or books or films—only about Art. Not a word about . . . what had happened. And—there were some very long pauses . . . *(Smiles)* But . . . One of my friends is really into Yiddish plays. He thinks there are all these great unknown plays out there from years ago, now lost. Anyway, he told us a story at this lunch. A young Yiddish student some years ago, he's having trouble finding books in Yiddish to study. So he puts up signs in neighborhoods like Brighton Beach, the Upper West Side—"Yiddish scholar seeking Yiddish books."

Calls start to come. For one "book pickup"—he borrows a little van, drives to Brooklyn, pulls up in front of an old apartment building, rings a buzzer, goes in, an old man appears at the door, takes him inside and shows him boxes and boxes of Yiddish books.

The young man is obviously pleased, and starts to lift one of the boxes. But the man stops him. "What are you doing?" He asks. "I'm taking the boxes to my van." "Wait," says the old man, "first—I must tell you about each book."

(Jane smiles. She looks at Richard, who is absorbed in the story.)

So now, after many hours, the young man's finally got the books in the van. He goes to shake the man's hand, and the old man says again, "What are you doing?" "I have to get home with the van, this van is borrowed." Then the old man, gesturing to the whole eight- or nine-story apartment building, says, "But I've told my neighbors you were coming, and they all have Yiddish books for you . . ."

(He is moved, tries not to cry.)

The young man thought those books had been lost. But they weren't.

 I don't know why, I still want to cry. Those days right after . . .

JANE: I remember.

(Barbara has entered, with a small pile of little notebooks—appointment diaries. Barbara is confused:)

Tim was telling us about some wonderful books being saved.

TIM: More than just . . .

JANE: Are those the notebooks, Barbara?

(Marian then appears right behind Barbara. This gets everyone's attention.)

BARBARA *(About the notebooks, taking them to the table)*: We've figured out that he's an accountant. The owner of these. *(To Marian)* Didn't we, Marian?

(Everyone looks at Marian, who nods.)

His office is on Park Place.

RICHARD: Where the mosque was going to be.

BARBARA: Was that where it was? *(Showing the notebooks)* You can see what I mean here—in 2001—

(They start to get up to look.)

I'll pass them around. *(Continues)* He writes down his appointments, and his habit is to cross them off when he's had them. Even lunches. Shows. *(To Tim and Benjamin)* He went to the theater a lot. Marian, come and join us.

(Then about the notebooks, as Marian sits:)

They stop being crossed off here . . . September 10th. After that, nothing is crossed off . . . And slowly there are no more appointments. A dentist appointment in December. Which he obviously did not keep.

JANE *(To Marian)*: We've been talking about—

BARBARA: I told her. *(To Marian)* You were already at school, I think. Weren't you? That morning.

(Marian nods.)

I think you told me you tried to keep the news from your kids as long as possible.

MARIAN: I did.

JANE: They're just second graders.

BARBARA *(About a notebook entry)*: Look here, he saw *Phantom of the Opera* on May 22nd. He went with "Joan." Then the next weekend, Memorial Day weekend, he obviously stayed in the city—there's a brunch. This restaurant still exists. I looked it up online. And then Marian discovered . . . Show them. *(She hands Marian one of the notebooks)* Here— tell them . . .

MARIAN *(Hesitates, then explains her discovery)*: In 1998, he had dinner here with "Joan" as well. The only two times in the books we could find. For some reason that seemed interesting. Some place on 23rd Street. He put his name in the back of this one: George Satterlee.

RICHARD *(Repeats)*: "Satterlee." *(He doesn't know a Satterlee)*

BARBARA: Here. This is what I wanted you to see. September 11th. Not crossed out. "Breakfast." "Wow."

RICHARD: "Wow"?

TIM: I'd say "wow" is right . . .

BARBARA: We figured it meant "Windows on the World."

(Short pause.)

JANE: How did these get—?

BARBARA: They just sell whole libraries and . . . Estates do. And they have to take away everything. Maybe. *(To Marian)* We bought these at the Book Barn in Hillsdale? Didn't we?

TIM: Amazing where things end up . . .

JANE *(To Tim)*: Maybe he saw a show you were in. That would be incredible, wouldn't it? That he'd have been in your audience?

(Pause, as they all look, turning pages.)

(Still looking) So interesting. Like you're eavesdropping. Sometimes I like to go to restaurants by myself—you hear so much that way. People act like you're not even there. Just look down at a book, and they'll say anything right in front of you . . . Right next to you.

(As they look at the books:)

RICHARD *(To Marian)*: How's *Harry Potter*?

BARBARA *(To Richard)*: It was Evan's . . . *(To Marian)* She read them all, didn't she?

(Marian nods.)

Marian hadn't read them. So she asked me to get them from—her home. How many do you have left?

MARIAN: I've read all of them now. At least once.

BARBARA: When Evan was— When she was how old? *(Continues, as they all look at the books)* About eleven I think. Marian and I—I don't know how you got me to do this.

MARIAN *(Looking at another book)*: You wanted to. I didn't.

JANE: What?

BARBARA *(To Marian)*: That's not how I remember it. *(Continuing; they continue to look through the books)* Oblong was having one of those midnight parties for the publication of one of the *Harry Potter*s. And Marian got us to dress as witches. *(Smiles)* Marian had taught every kid who was there.

Evan then sat and read the book, I don't think she slept for three days. Did she?

(They look at the notebooks.)

MARIAN *(To Richard)*: What did Adam say?

RICHARD *(Hesitates, looks at his sisters, then)*: He didn't say much. We didn't talk that long.

MARIAN: Is he coming to the concert?

RICHARD: I don't think so.

BARBARA: Marian forgets. Sometimes she's worse than you, Benjamin. *(Pats Benjamin's hand)* Even last Christmas she and Evan—she got Evan to do this together—they sewed things for the Sinterklaas Parade.

TIM *(To Jane)*: What's Sinterklaas—?

JANE: A Rhinebeck thing.

BARBARA: Evan told me what fun that was. And *("To the others")* it wasn't me, it was Marian who insisted on us dressing as witches for the *Harry Potter*. She forgets that. Evan would pretend that she was embarrassed? But you could tell she thought—what a neat mom I've got. And she was right.

And every kid there—you could tell how much Marian had meant to each one.

Just this Christmas Evan gave her mother a CD mix of music she liked. *(To Marian)* How many times did you play that? *(To the others)* Every time we were in the car together, she had to play that. She went online, and got the lyrics to these—"songs"—and she learned them. Didn't you? *(She stares at Marian)* Don't forget that. Don't let yourself forget any of that.

Benjamin, maybe you should get changed.

BENJAMIN: Can I have a cigarette first?

MARIAN: No. No, you can't. You've smoked enough.

BARBARA: Your suit's on your bed. Let us know if you need any help.

BENJAMIN: I don't need help. Why am I changing?

BARBARA: For your performance.

BENJAMIN: I'm doing a performance?

(Benjamin goes. They continue to look at the notebooks.)

TIM: Can I see that notebook, Richard?

JANE *(After watching Benjamin go)*: He's such a mystery, our uncle. What is going on in that head of yours? I think he knows everything and is just keeping it all to himself.

MARIAN: Barbara sometimes calls him "Buddha."

JANE: I like that. Buddha. When he comes back I'll rub his stomach for good luck.

BARBARA: He never gets angry. Why doesn't he just say, "This is terrible"? "I can't function properly." Only once, and that was when he'd just come to live with me. That's the only time I have ever heard him say, "Help me." *(Standing)* What about dessert. Vanilla ice cream and cake? Should I just bring it all out?

(Barbara starts picking up plates.)

JANE *(Getting up)*: Let me help.

TIM *(Standing)*: I can help. I'm not a guest. I don't consider myself a guest.

RICHARD *(Trying to make a joke)*: I think Tim has earned those stripes.

BARBARA: Why don't you help too, Richard. You could use a few more stripes.

(They all pick up things.)

It's store-bought cake; I didn't make it.

(Barbara goes off with plates, etc.
As the others clean up:)

TIM *(To say something)*: What's—a Sinterklaas Parade?

RICHARD: Santa Claus.

TIM: I'd guessed that much.

MARIAN: They have giant puppets, and they have a parade and candles—it's beautiful. Sinterklaas rides a white horse . . . *(She carries dishes off)*

TIM: Sounds great. Like a show . . . *(He follows Marian off)*

JANE *(To Richard)*: Here, take these . . . Do something.

(Richard takes a few bowls and heads off.
In the distance, church bells are playing a tune.)

BARBARA *(Entering, passing Richard, listening to the bells; to herself)*: What are they playing now? *(To Jane, piling plates)* Is that what I think it is?

JANE: What?

BARBARA *(To herself, listening)*: "Onward Christian Soldiers." *(Explaining to Jane)* Those "bells." The church. They started playing that yesterday. I couldn't believe it.

(Jane is heading off.)

Close the back door, would you, Jane? Just close it.

(Jane goes off, carrying dishes, on her way to close the door.)

RICHARD *(Entering with Tim)*: The Sinterklaas Parade is *one* day a year—you don't have to move up here to see it.

TIM: It just doesn't feel like I want to be there anymore. Obviously, I'm not talking about just a parade.

(From off, the bells are now silenced.)

BARBARA *(To herself about the bells)*: Thank god . . . Peace . . .

(Marian returns with the cake.)

TIM *(To Richard)*: Do you know *The Visit*? It's a play.

RICHARD: I'm a lawyer, Tim . . .

MARIAN *(To her sisters)*: We still need the ice cream . . . *(She heads off)*

BARBARA *(To Marian)*: Marian, "Onward Christian Soldiers." Today of all days . . .

(Jane returns with a wine bottle.)

JANE: Richard, your wine.

TIM: Do you need the—?

JANE: It's twist off.

TIM *(Continuing)*: In this play, *The Visit*, a woman, a billionaire comes back to her old town that's going through tough times. She's got a grudge against one of the citizens, a man who years ago dumped her.

(Jane and Barbara serve the cake.)

JANE: Tim—

TIM *(To Jane)*: I'm trying to explain to Richard, what I'm feeling.

RICHARD: I don't even like the theater, Tim.

TIM *(Continues)*: So this billionaire says to the citizens, she'll make them all rich. Pay all their debts, everything. The catch is—she wants them to execute the guy who dumped her. Of course everyone is shocked and says no, no, we couldn't . . . But then, pretty soon they start measuring his neck for a noose.

(Marian has returned with the ice cream and a scoop. She is serving.
Then, his point:)

She's Bloomberg. That's what the city's become. He's bought us.

MARIAN *(Confused, still serving)*: What? I don't understand.

TIM: Fucking Bloomberg.

BARBARA: He hates Bloomberg.

(Marian just shrugs. She keeps serving.)

Aren't you exaggerating a little, Tim? Bloomberg hasn't asked anyone to *kill* anyone.

JANE: Not yet.

RICHARD: I see what you're saying now.

TIM: I used to love the city. And we only have ourselves to blame.

RICHARD: You don't need a play to tell you that.

BARBARA: Maybe if you got out of Manhattan . . .

TIM: That's what I'm saying—

JANE: Tim has too good a deal to do that.

TIM: My lease is now my greatest financial asset. Maybe my only—

BARBARA: What do you mean?

JANE: He's been in Manhattan Plaza for years. The rent's based on his earnings—

TIM *(Smiles)*: I can't leave.

JANE: We *talk* about leaving all the time.

TIM: I look at here, Rhinebeck. I think . . .

BARBARA: Rhinebeck's got its share of problems too.
MARIAN: Evan hated Rhinebeck. I don't know why.

(Short pause. The ice cream and cake is ready.)

BARBARA: Shall we sit down?

(They begin to sit down.)

RICHARD: Evan probably hated—lots of things.
JANE *(To Barbara)*: You think Benjamin's all right—
MARIAN: He's not a child. He knows how to dress himself, Jane.

(They all are seated now. As they begin to eat their ice cream:)

TIM *(Back to talking about New York)*: I wait on rich people every day in the city. There seems to be a whole lot of them now. How did that happen? *(He eats)* They give off this—I don't know what.
JANE: Smell?

(Laughter.)

BARBARA: Jane . . .
TIM: Aura. The sense that they think they've really earned what they've got. There are times when I—I see myself in the mirror behind the bar, waiting for an order, and I'm standing there with two or three other waiters—also actors, brilliant fucking actors . . . I'm forty-three. And start to feel like a fool.
MARIAN: You're only forty-three? Jane, he's—forty-three. *(To Tim)* You know Jane isn't forty-three.
JANE: He knows. *(Back to the city)* It makes me angry, those people. After a while it just eats you up. Turns you in on yourself. Just eats and eats . . . What Tim and I could do with what some of them spend on one fucking bottle of wine.

(Richard reaches to pour his wine.)

RICHARD: I didn't spend that much.
BARBARA: Are we going to have coffee?
JANE *(Standing)*: I'll put it on. Coffee or decaf?

(They want coffee. Jane starts to go, then stops.)

(Continuing) You'd think there would be some—humility.
RICHARD: I don't know why she'd think that?

(Jane goes off to the kitchen.)

BARBARA *(Calls)*: It's all ready, you just have to add the water. *(To Richard)* Jane's asked Uncle for a loan, Richard. A few thousand. I think he can afford it. What do you think?
RICHARD: I think so. I think he can. *(Noticing Tim's discomfort)* Sorry, Tim—
TIM: No, no. It's fine.

(They eat.)

RICHARD *(To Tim, back to New York)*: A lawyer in my firm, he's always saying about New York— *(He tastes the icing on the cake)* Look at the elections. He took me to a website. Shows how people vote—every district, across the country. *(Eats)* In Manhattan, pretty much every race is won by something like—ninety-two percent, ninety, ninety-five percent. Always by the Democrats of course. Only last election, Rangel, he got a little less. Think what we'd say if someone like him, in the South say or way out west, some place we ridicule, if someone who had been accused and full of bullshit, if in the middle of all that, they elected him with eighty-five percent of the vote. And we did.

(Shrugs, then) He was my congressman. Hardly anyone even seems embarrassed. We moved to Brooklyn.

MARIAN: That wasn't the only reason, Pamela wanted—

(Jane returns.)

JANE: Coffee's on.

(Tim looks at her.)

What?

BARBARA *(Eating)*: Is today really a day to talk politics?

RICHARD *(Ignoring her, to Tim)*: Cuomo's not as bad as I thought he'd be. I'm really surprised.

TIM: Me too. But we'll see.

RICHARD: We're just talking about the city, Barbara. *(Continuing, to Tim)* We went through the whole map on this website and the only other place that even comes close to such lopsided elections—northern Texas. *(Eats)* You can swing a dead cat on the corner of Broadway and 72nd and have about the same chance of hitting a Republican as winning the lotto. In lots of ways, New York has to be one of the most parochial places in the country.

MARIAN *(Eating)*: Do you now believe everything your rich Republican friends tell you? Mother, Father, close your ears.

RICHARD: I don't know where I am going politically, Marian. I know I've—jumped. Just jumped. I'm waiting to see where I land. If I land. *(Eats)*

JANE: What difference does it make what we are now? A Wall Street–sponsored Republican or a Wall Street–sponsored Democrat? *(Mocking)* "Oh which side will I be on?"

BARBARA: I thought you were just talking about the city—

JANE: Tell me, am I the only one here who wakes up almost every morning, and as I am trying to convince myself to get out of bed, I'm thinking: "We're fucked."

(Laughter.)

TIM: I feel— *("like that")*

JANE *(Patting his head, as if to a child)*: I know you feel the same way, dear. I know. I see how you look every morning . . . *(To the others)* He's been reading a book. I tell him don't read that book the first thing in the morning. And don't read it right before you're trying to go to sleep.

RICHARD: What book?

JANE: He comes out of the bedroom—every morning now— after reading a chapter, all red in the face, just stands there, puts his finger to his head—like it's a gun and "shoots."

(Laughter.)

BARBARA *(Laughing)*: Good thing it's only his finger.

TIM *(Out of the laughter)*: We tried to sell the Pennsylvania Turnpike to Abu Dhabi.

BARBARA: What??

JANE: It's from that book—

MARIAN: Who was trying to sell the—?

TIM: The State of Pennsylvania.

RICHARD: I heard about this.

BARBARA: Why?

JANE *(It's obvious)*: Because they're broke, Barbara.

TIM *(Eating)*: And Chicago's already sold a fifty-year lease to all of its parking meters—to a Middle East hedge fund. So if you want to have a block party in Chicago now and need to close down a street for a few hours? Like say on the 4th of July to celebrate American Independence Day? So you can have maybe a fucking parade with someone dressed up as—let's say—George fucking Washington? You have to get permission first from an Arab sheik.

MARIAN: Is that really true?

TIM: Sometimes the only voice I hear in my head sounds like— Lewis Black. There is so much we're not talking about.

(Pause. They eat.)

BARBARA: Well—I like Elizabeth Warren . . .

(This gets everyone animated. The others: "Me too." "I do too.")

Who else? Who else do we like?

TIM: Cuomo, sort of. I'm not convinced yet.

RICHARD: We'll see.

JANE: We already said him. Who else? Anyone else?

(No one else.)

RICHARD: I've never seen this country more brutal.

JANE: Is it "brutal"?

RICHARD: Maybe that isn't the word—maybe lost?

TIM: Lost. That's true.

JANE: And how they keep us wound up and divided. At the same time.

RICHARD: I see them every day—even with a bad eye you can see it—big fucking law firms—like my big fucking law firm—"fix" our so-called reforms.

TIM: Maybe— You know how on your income tax there's a little box if you want a few bucks to go to pay for presidential elections—

JANE: Which no one is going to take anymore—not after our guy—

TIM *(Continues)*: That little box you can check—which is completely meaningless, isn't it?

RICHARD: It is.

BARBARA: I check it off every year.

TIM: Does anyone in the government even look at those little check marks? Do we really think someone is counting them up? *(Smiles)*

JANE *(Holding up her hand)*: I'll take that job.

(Laughter.)

Seriously, Billy would take it.

TIM: Just more bullshit. Anyway, maybe all they need to do to make us feel even better—is just add a few more boxes for us to check.

RICHARD: Good idea. Very good idea.

TIM: That would make me feel better.

JANE: Me too!

RICHARD: A box, say, for—do you want two dollars of your tax to go to buy back—the Pennsylvania Turnpike!

(Laughter, they are having fun.)

JANE: "But we own that, don't we?"

(More laughter. Then:)

BARBARA *(It just comes out)*: Why has our government given money to the families of 9/11?

(Everyone except Marian is taken aback by this.)

RICHARD: What?

BARBARA: I'm asking a question. I've been thinking about this.

JANE: Why we've given—?

BARBARA: Yes. *(She looks at Marian)*

MARIAN: We've talked about this.

RICHARD: Where did this come from?

BARBARA: It's been on my mind all day. Watching TV this morning. It's been on my mind. Can I ask the question? Am I permitted to ask the question? It's just us. The door's closed.

RICHARD: Okay . . .

BARBARA: *That's* something I never hear anyone talking about. You were saying people don't talk about things. I don't mean those who—the responders. And I'm not talking about those with medical problems and helping them— after they were told, "It's okay, it's okay," then—well actually it wasn't. *(Then, after a look at Marian)* This is all right?

JANE: Yes.

BARBARA: I mean—just the families of people who died. Why has the government paid *them*?

MARIAN *(Explaining to the others)*: One of Barbara's students asked her that.

BARBARA: She asked in class—and I had to stop a couple of students from yelling at her. I'm sure once they were out of class . . . I told her I'd think about it. And ask around. What do you think? Why arc wc giving them money?

When a plane crashes or there's a car accident or someone is shot in the street by a robber—the government doesn't give their families money. Does it? Do we?

JANE: But insurance companies—

BARBARA: Not the government.

RICHARD: I see. I understand the question. The Gulf Coast—that was insurance companies . . . What this student is asking is: Why was this different, with the 9/11 families? Good question. Oklahoma City. Very good question. I don't know.

(Pause.)

TIM: I've been asked a similar question. A friend of a friend lost her daughter in the attack. I remember being surprised when she said to me—you know my daughter was a victim, why do they call her a hero?

(Then:)

RICHARD: I suppose—"we've" needed to call people "heroes" to justify— *(Then)* With "victims"—well for them, you just hunt down the "criminals." And bring them to "justice." But that's not all we've been doing, is it? We've been at war. A war on terror. What the hell does that mean?

BARBARA: Obama stopped using that—

TIM: So he stopped using the name, Barbara.

RICHARD: He had his chance to denounce all this—crap. And he said he would. And then he didn't. Do we still believe in trials? Do we really think torturers should go unpunished? I'd ask our president that.

Are principles compromised—any longer "principles"?

BARBARA: He got Bin Laden . . .

(Short pause.)

RICHARD: But to shoot him, unarmed, in the head. It sounds like he didn't even resist. Why do that? Because we're scared??

JANE: How did they know he was unarmed?

MARIAN: I'm happy he's dead, Richard.

RICHARD: So am I. But I also think it's sad that we're that scared.

MARIAN: Aren't you scared, Richard?

RICHARD: I had to get out of the city today. The whole run up to this day—others have kept telling us what we need to feel. What I should feel. This morning with my buddies, normally, in past years, we'd take half a day or more, and crawl home. *(Smiles)* But today you felt the difference. The noise. And I don't mean just the crowds. I mean the noise. Suddenly one of my buddies just said, "Haven't we done this long enough? Can't we stop now?!"

(Short pause.)

JANE: I'll get the coffee . . . *(Stands)*

RICHARD *(To Barbara)*: So what are you going to tell your student?

BARBARA: Not that.

Not that, Richard.

(Then) I can't tell these kids that politicians are all corrupt or complicit or just trying to keep their jobs, and elections are pretty much meaningless. Or that real-estate interests control everything in the city. Or—all those other things. I'm not going to tell my kids that.

I asked Benjamin for advice.

JANE: Benjamin?

BARBARA: He's good to talk things through with. And you can say the stupidest thing and you know he'll forget it.

MARIAN: And he's a very good listener.

BARBARA: That morning, I had friends die. I had a neighbor . . . I couldn't even begin now to tell you what I saw, and what I still see . . . Things out of hell.

    I described it all to Benjamin.

    I decided that this was a big and important subject to discuss with students. My best students. Seniors. Going out into the world. And I felt—this question, it was really only one of so many questions. That I could ask them. That I have. So—I started to make a list. I made a list. Marian's heard all this.

(Marian nods.)

I'll tell you.

JANE: Please . . .

(Jane sits back down.)

BARBARA: I know it by heart. The list:

(The list:)

Are they heroes, those people who tragically died? What does that mean?

    Is a memorial for the dead or the living?

    Some questions are pretty . . . *(To Richard)* They're kids . . .

RICHARD: I understand . . .

BARBARA: Marian's heard all this . . . *(Continues the list)* Why would someone—and I'll expand this to include more than 9/11—why would a human being strap a bomb to his waist, his chest or his feet, or stuff it down his crotch and then go out to find the biggest crowd of strangers to blow up?

(*Continues the list*) Has this sort of killing ever occurred before in the history of the human race? "Suicide bombers"—when did we first hear this phrase?

(*Smiles*) Let's spend the hour today, class, talking about—the meaning of this word, "compensation." How do we compensate for the loss of life? The loss of security? The loss of confidence? Or—a new one I thought of today, Richard.

RICHARD: What?

BARBARA: How do we compensate for the loss of sight? Or vision? Does our other eye compensate and get stronger?

RICHARD: Do we just see less?

BARBARA: And—as they've all met Benjamin, he's come to a few classes. I've had most of the students here for one reason or another. In fact it was their idea to get him to read today. So this question: How does one compensate for the loss of memory?

JANE: Are there times when it's better to forget?

(*Short pause.*)

BARBARA: Why do young people kill themselves?

MARIAN: I asked her to ask that.

BARBARA: I'm not saying they'll tell us. Or can. Or even that they know. But we can talk about it. Can't we? We can at least ask the question.

TIM: And so many of these bombers are also young men and women.

BARBARA: We'll take on one of these each day. We'll spend the whole hour on it. Maybe the kids will have some answers . . . (*Continues the list*) Do you ever feel you can't express your feelings, or speak about what you've seen?

What you read and see on TV, does it or does it not reflect the world you live in?

(*The lights fade.*)

Dressing the Wound

A short time later. Benjamin enters, now dressed in a suit, his tie crooked. He holds a book.

BENJAMIN: What am I doing?

(They laugh.)

JANE: Uncle, you look wonderful. He looks fantastic.
BARBARA: His tie's crooked— *(She goes to straighten it)*
RICHARD: Are we dressing up? I didn't bring anything—
MARIAN: It's casual. You look fine. *(To Barbara)* Isn't it?
BARBARA *(Of course)*: It's at the high school. *(To Benjamin)* You found the book. *(To Marian)* I left it on top of his suit.
JANE: He looks so good. Tim, doesn't he look good? You look so handsome!
BENJAMIN: What the hell am I doing?

(They laugh.)

JANE: You're going to act, Uncle. You're going back on stage!
BARBARA *(Fixing his tie)*: You're giving a reading, Benjamin. Remember? We've been rehearsing all week. For 9/11. Today is its tenth anniversary.
RICHARD: What are you going to read, Uncle?
BENJAMIN: I don't know.
BARBARA *(Still fixing the tie)*: You know. We've been practicing.
RICHARD: Is that it in there? In that book?
BENJAMIN *(To Barbara)*: Is it?
BARBARA: I want it to be a surprise for them. Though I think they probably know it . . . *(About the tie)* There, that's better. Did you shave?

BENJAMIN: I shaved this morning.

JANE: He looks good, Barbara.

BENJAMIN *(Opening the book)*: What am I reading?

BARBARA: It's bookmarked—

JANE: Don't you want to read it to us—to practice, Uncle?

BARBARA: Jane, I want it to be—

TIM: A dress rehearsal.

BARBARA: Tim. *(Looking for help)* Marian—

MARIAN: Let him read it, Barbara.

BENJAMIN: Maybe I should . . . *(Looking through the book)* Where's . . . ?

BARBARA: It's marked. Here . . . *(Shows him)* I really wanted it to be a surprise—

JANE *(Over this)*: Come on, he should practice, Barbara—

BARBARA: We've been practicing. You just haven't been here to help him!

(This stops everyone. Barbara composes herself.)

Maybe a little rehearsal would be a good thing. A friendly audience, Uncle.

TIM: The high school audience won't be—

JANE *(To Tim)*: Sh-sh.

BARBARA: What do *you* want to do, Uncle?

BENJAMIN: What am I doing??

MARIAN *(Taking charge)*: You're going to read this— *(Points out)* poem . . . To us. As practice. *(To the others)* Barbara's edited it a little . . .

(He looks at the poem.)

BARBARA *(To Marian)*: It's like he's never seen it before.

MARIAN: Every afternoon this whole week Barbara and Benjamin have been practicing this. The patience this woman has . . .

RICHARD: We know . . .

BARBARA: Come on, I'm sorry I said—

JANE: Of a saint.

BARBARA: I'm not a saint . . .

MARIAN: She was telling me that a student found a DVD of one of Uncle's movies and they showed it after school. They asked Benjamin to come and talk about it . . . Sign autographs. *(Smiles)*

JANE: That must have made you feel good, Uncle.

BENJAMIN *(He's been reading the poem to himself)*: What?

BARBARA: I think it did. I hope so. *(To Benjamin)* Go ahead . . . They're insisting, Uncle. Read it. Do you know where to start? My god, we've been rehearsing this. *(Points)* There . . . *(To the others)* It's Whitman . . . "The Wound-Dresser."

BENJAMIN: I should read?

BARBARA: Yes! Read it.

BENJAMIN *(Reads)*: "An old man—"

BARBARA: Speak up. Come on, you know better.

(Benjamin looks at her.)

BENJAMIN *(Louder)*: "An old man—"

BARBARA: That's right. Go ahead and read.

BENJAMIN *(Reading)*: "An old man bending I come among new faces . . ."

JANE: Sit down. Shouldn't we sit down?

BARBARA: We have to go soon.

TIM *(To the others, over this)*: So we're more like an audience.

(As they move chairs, etc., and sit:)

MARIAN *(To Benjamin)*: Sit here, Uncle. You're going to be sitting on stage tonight.

(Benjamin looks to Barbara.)

BENJAMIN: Barbara?

BARBARA: Go ahead, Benjamin. Go ahead. We can use the practice.

JANE: What's it about? I forget.

RICHARD *(To Jane, over this)*: Whitman working in hospitals. During the Civil War.

(Benjamin sits, then looks up.)

BENJAMIN *(Explaining)*: I haven't memorized it.

(They laugh, he smiles.)

BARBARA *(Smiling at his joke)*: Just read, will you?

BENJAMIN *(Reads)*:

An old man bending I come among new faces,
Years looking backward resuming in answer to children,
Come tell us old man . . .

But in silence, in dreams' projections . . .

Bearing the bandages, water and sponge,
Straight and swift to my wounded I go,
Where they lie on the ground after the battle brought in,
Where their priceless blood reddens the grass the
    ground . . .

(He turns two pages by mistake and is confused. Barbara sees this, and goes to help him.)

BARBARA *(Explaining)*: You turned two pages . . .

(She stands by him as he continues. As he reads, she will walk around the room, sharing looks with everyone.)

BENJAMIN:

> From the stump of the arm, the amputated hand,
> I undo the clotted lint, remove the slough, wash off the
>   matter and the blood,
> Back on his pillow the soldier bends . . .
> His eyes are closed, his face is pale, he dares not look
>   on the bloody stump,
> And has not yet look'd on it.

JANE *(To Barbara)*: Thank you, Barbara.

BENJAMIN:

> I dress a wound in the side, deep, deep . . .
>
> I dress the perforated shoulder, the foot with the bullet-
>   wound,
> Cleanse the one with a gnawing and putrid gangrene . . .

RICHARD *(To Barbara, offering his chair)*: Barbara?

(She shakes her head.)

BENJAMIN:

> I am faithful, I do not give out,
> The fractur'd thigh, the knee, the wound in the
>   abdomen,
> These and more I dress with impassive hand, (yet deep
>   in my breast a fire, a burning flame.)

BARBARA *(To Marian)*: Do you mind?

(Marian scoots over, and Barbara sits with Marian on the floor.)

BENJAMIN:

> Thus in silence in dreams' projections,
> Returning, resuming, I thread my way through the
>   hospitals,

The hurt and wounded I pacify with soothing hand,
I sit by the restless . . .

(Benjamin stops briefly and looks at the others.)

I sit by the restless all the dark night, some are so young,
Some suffer so much . . .

(Marian puts her arm around Barbara, and holds her. The others notice this.)

. . . I recall the experience sweet and sad,
(Many a soldier's loving arms about this neck have
    cross'd and rested,
Many a soldier's kiss dwells on these bearded lips.)

(He closes the book.)

(Seriously, to Barbara) Should I have grown a beard?

(This makes them all laugh.)

BARBARA *(Trying not to cry)*: No, no . . . You're fine as you are,
Uncle . . .
    That was good. Do it like that . . .

(No one knows what to do.)

We should probably straighten up a little bit and go. You
want to get good seats.

(They begin to stand.)

JANE: I left a sweater in Barbara's car . . .
TIM: I'll get it. *(To Barbara)* It's not locked?
BARBARA *("Of course not")*: This is Rhinebeck.

MARIAN: I lock my car.

(He goes.
They begin to pick up things.)

JANE *(To Benjamin)*: When you read, it's like your old self . . .
The performing self comes out. Do you like that? Do you
enjoy that?

BENJAMIN: I do.

BARBARA *(To Jane)*: I'll pull out your couch, Jane.

MARIAN: I can do it. You can't do everything. And I'll get sheets
and pillows.

(Marian goes into the living room.)

BARBARA *(Calling after her)*: And towels.

JANE *(To Barbara)*: This must be very satisfying for you.

BARBARA: I think it is. Especially when he remembers things.
(To Benjamin) You do remember some things, don't you?

BENJAMIN: What things?

(They laugh.)

BARBARA: One morning—always in the morning—you started
talking about Mom.

RICHARD: Mom?

BARBARA *(To Benjamin)*: You said you once bought her a coat.
Remember? *(To Jane)* It might be the one I still have. The
purple one, from the fifties?

JANE: That we kept in the dress-up trunk?

BARBARA: That one.

(Jane turns to Richard.)

JANE: The one your dog chewed half up, Richard.

RICHARD: It wasn't my dog.

BARBARA: You brought him here.

RICHARD: How did I know he was sick?—

(Tim enters with a sweater and a suitcase.)

TIM: I brought in our suitcase. Where do I put this?

BARBARA: You're in the living room. Marian's getting you sheets and towels . . .

JANE *(About the sweater, to Barbara)*: Tim's daughter gave me this for my birthday, Barbara.

TIM: I paid for it.

JANE *(To Tim)*: You said, she picked it out.

BARBARA: It's lovely. You have to bring your daughter—

TIM: Karen.

BARBARA: Karen. Up to Rhinebeck sometime.

TIM: I'll ask her.

(Tim goes off.)

BARBARA: Tim has a daughter??

JANE: She's nine.

(Off, from the living room, the Kyrie from Duruflé's Requiem, as heard in the opening of the play, begins.)

BARBARA *(She hears the music)*: What is she doing? Marian?

JANE: What?

RICHARD: She was playing that when I arrived. I told you. It's from your Christmas concert.

BARBARA: Yes.

RICHARD *(To Jane)*: Barbara's community chorus. A CD of one of their concerts last year.

(Tim returns.)

BARBARA: Tim, did Marian put that music on?

TIM: She was putting it on when I went in. *(To Jane)* What should I do now?

JANE: We're just picking up . . . Just clean up . . .

BARBARA *(Listening)*: I hadn't known what the word "requiem" meant, until we sang this. It means "rest."

TIM *(To Richard)*: I've sung this.

(Barbara listens.)

BARBARA: Evan is in— Evan was in our chorus . . . She's singing in this. She's on that . . .

(This stops everyone.)

Marian would never let me play it . . .

JANE: Evan?

BARBARA: Evan was an alto too. She usually was in the row in front of me . . . *(Listening)*
 (To Benjamin, who is listening) Remember this, Uncle? Remember Evan?

BENJAMIN: Evan???

(Marian comes out.)

MARIAN: We should go.

JANE *(To Marian)*: We're picking up.

(They begin to pick up.)

RICHARD: We want to get good seats.

(As the music plays, they take up the tablecloth, pile plates, clean crumbs, etc.)

MARIAN *(At the table)*: Barbara, there are a few stains. *("on the tablecloth")*

(Barbara moves toward Marian.)

I'll do it.

*(Marian begins to fold up the tablecloth.
    Jane stops on her way to the kitchen.)*

JANE *(To Marian)*: Evan is singing on this?

(Marian looks to Barbara, then:)

MARIAN: She is.

*(Jane goes. Marian folds up the tablecloth. Barbara takes dishes
off to the kitchen. Jane returns.)*

JANE: Let's go, Uncle. We need to go now . . .

*(Jane goes off with Benjamin. They are all aware that they are
letting Marian listen to her daughter.
    As Barbara folds up the card table, she is stopped by:)*

MARIAN *(Pointing out a moment in the music)*: The altos . . .

*(Richard has returned and takes the card table. He and Bar-
bara go off, and for a moment, Marian is left alone.
    She tries not to cry.)*

(To the music, to her daughter) Bye . . .

(And Marian follows the others and goes off. The music ends.)

END OF PLAY

SORRY

———

Conversations on Election Day
Election Day, November 6th
2012

For Sally Murphy, Maryann Plunkett, Laila Robins,
J. Smith-Cameron, Jon DeVries, Shuler Hensley,
Stephen Kunken and Jay O. Sanders

Sorry was commissioned by and first produced at The Public Theater (Oskar Eustis, Artistic Director; Patrick Willingham, Executive Director) in New York on November 6, 2012. The director was Richard Nelson; the set and costume design were by Susan Hilferty, the lighting design was by Jennifer Tipton, the sound design was by Scott Lehrer and Will Pickens; the assistant director was Charlotte Brathwaite, the production stage manager was Pamela Salling, the stage manager was Maggie Swing. The cast was:

RICHARD APPLE	Jay O. Sanders
BARBARA APPLE	Maryann Plunkett
MARIAN APPLE	Laila Robins
JANE APPLE HALLS	J. Smith-Cameron
BENJAMIN APPLE	Jon DeVries

In December 2013, the complete series of *The Apple Family* was presented at The Public Theater in rotating repertory. *Sorry* was revived with Sally Murphy playing Jane.

NOTE

Play One, *That Hopey Changey Thing*, is set on November 2, 2010. Before the play begins, Uncle Benjamin Apple, a well-known actor, has had a heart attack, which sent him into a coma. When he came out, he had serious amnesia. By the beginning of the play, he has retired and moved into his niece Barbara's home in Rhinebeck, New York.

Play Two, *Sweet and Sad*, is set on September 11, 2011. Months before the play begins, Marian's twenty-year-old daughter, Evan, committed suicide, for reasons unknown. Since then, Marian and her husband, Adam, have separated, and Marian now shares Barbara's house with Barbara and Benjamin.

It seems like everyone's asleep.

—Anton Chekhov, *Three Sisters*

A wooden table and four wooden chairs. A few short-stemmed flowers in a small glass vase on the table. Rugs. Regina Spektor's "Fidelity" begins.

Barbara, in her robe and nightgown, enters with a tablecloth, which she begins to lay over the table. The tablecloth has been used and is stained from a Chinese meal some hours before. (She will reset the vase so that it has fallen over and been forgotten.)

Soon, Marian and Jane, both in their nightclothes, enter with the remnants of last night's meal and post-meal—a mostly empty bottle of wine, a bottle of aperitif, a pot of coffee, milk, sugar, a few used cups, a tin of mostly eaten cookies, plates with crumbs, maybe an empty carton of ice cream with a scoop sticking out, a few used ice-cream plates, the peels of a tangerine, a few grapes left on their stems in a bowl and trivets. They have been "grazing" at this table for hours.

Jane places two large books on the floor by the table; she opens them. Then she sets a thin pile of sheet music and other papers on the table.

Barbara returns with a card table, which she sets up. Marian returns with a jigsaw puzzle box. After Barbara sets up the card table, Marian pours the puzzle pieces out and turns over a few of them. Little has been done on this puzzle.

It is five in the morning, November 6, 2012. No one has gone to bed.

The general sense is that the sisters have been hanging out in here all night.

Barbara takes off her robe, drapes it over the back of a chair, and sits at the puzzle. The lights come up.

Shape-Note Singing

Barbara is at the puzzle. Jane and Marian at the table. Jane is looking at the sheet music.

Church bells in the distance toll five.

Jane follows the sheet music (Marian and Barbara know the piece) and is in the middle of singing to herself:

JANE: Fa fa sol fa . . .

BARBARA (*Over the puzzle, to Marian*): I remember when Jane was something like five years old, and we were all doing a puzzle at Thanksgiving. And there was one piece—part of a red scarf. I really wanted to find that piece. Uncle Benjamin said he'd give me a quarter if I found it. I didn't move for hours from that puzzle. But no one could find it. So we finished the whole puzzle, except for that one piece, and it was in the middle, and then Uncle winked at Jane, and Jane you leaned down and lifted up a corner of the rug under the card table, and then smiling you said—"Oh, look, I've found the last piece."

(*Then:*)

JANE (*Looking at the sheet music, "innocently"*): I don't remember that.

(Barbara and Marian exchange a look.)

(Continuing to follow the music) Sol sol fa fa fa.

MARIAN *(To Jane)*: The incredible thing with shape-note singing— *(Turns to Barbara)*

BARBARA: What?

MARIAN *(To Jane about Barbara)*: She doesn't really like this
kind of—

BARBARA: I do. It's just different. I like it. It's hard. But I like it.

MARIAN *(Over the end of this, to Jane)*: The student conductor,
he gave us a talk.

BARBARA *(To Jane)*: They have students conduct at Bard. They
teach that.

JANE: You've told me.

BARBARA *(Over this)*: We're like their "guinea pigs." Marian
said, like their "cadavers."

JANE *(To Marian)*: What sort of talk?

MARIAN: How these songs— They're not meant to be *per-
formed* for anyone.

BARBARA: Marian, I like the longer pieces. I like the Mozart
we're doing. I just like that better. *(Shrugs)*

JANE *(To Marian)*: I don't understand. What do you mean?

MARIAN: He told us— *(To Barbara)* Let's sing one, Barbara.
Show her.

JANE: Told you what?

MARIAN: In shape-note singing, you're supposed to get in a
circle. And everyone just sings. No one can just listen.
You're not allowed to do that. *(To Barbara)* Right?

(Barbara nods.)

You can't just stand on the sidelines. There is no *audience*. It's not *for* anyone. We sing with each other. To each
other. For ourselves. *(To Barbara)* You can't just sit and
watch. Did I explain it right?

(Barbara nods.)

(To Jane) He did say one thing that was very interesting. *(To Barbara)* Didn't he?

JANE: What?

MARIAN *(Over this)*: He said—he imagined these "pioneers," say in the wilderness, in the middle of nowhere, in a storm. They don't know what's going to happen. Anything could happen. What the night will bring. The roof of their cabin feels like it's about to blow off. Or cave in. That's what it feels like. They can imagine the worst. And the family, and whoever else happens to be there—sheltering—so maybe neighbors, or maybe just the family—they all get together in a circle, face each other and sing. That's how he imagines it. The student conductor. And, as loud as they can sing. Loud seems to be a big part of it. The louder the better. As if that would ward off any evil, I suppose. Just the act of the singing together. And that—was all they had left . . . *(Short pause)* Barbara?

BARBARA: Which one?

MARIAN *(Choosing a piece of sheet music)*: "As We Travel . . ." *(She hands Jane the sheet music to follow)*

BARBARA *(Still doing the puzzle, starts to sing)*: "As we travel through the—"

MARIAN *(To Jane)*: And it doesn't matter how well you sing.

BARBARA *(Stops doing the puzzle)*: Marian's been in the chorus three months and she's already one of the favorites. No one still even notices me.

MARIAN: That's not true. That is not true. *(To Jane)* We know that isn't true, Barbara . . .

BARBARA *(Sings)*:
> As we travel through the desert
> Storms beset us by the way.
> But beyond the river Jordon
> Lies a field of endless day.

(Marian joins in for the chorus.)

BARBARA AND MARIAN:
> Farther on, still go farther
> Count the milestones one by one.

MARIAN *(Pointing out to Jane)*: We changed the "Jesus" to "we."
JANE: Why?
MARIAN *(It's obvious)*: It's Bard College.

BARBARA AND MARIAN:
> We will forsake you never.
> It is better farther on.

(Barbara now leaves the puzzle table and joins her sisters at the table. They are getting into this.)

MARIAN *(Pointing to the place)*: Jane.

JANE *(Hesitates, then sings)*:
> Oh, my brother are you weary
> Of the roughness of the way?

(The sisters help her, support her.)

> Does your strength begin to fail you
> And your vigor to decay?

(Marian and Barbara come in with the chorus—very loud and joyous:)

JANE, MARIAN AND BARBARA:
> Farther on, still go farther
> Count the milestones one by one.
> We will forsake you never.
> It is better farther on.

MARIAN *(To Jane, pointing out)*: That's an oval. There. So it's "sol."

(Marian and Barbara sing the melody together, they've obviously practiced this and are having fun. Note they are not singing into the meaning of the lyric, but the opposite, joyous:)

MARIAN AND BARBARA:
> At my grave, oh still be singing
> Though you weep for one that's gone.

(They urge Jane to join, she does hesitantly, then in and out.)

MARIAN, BARBARA AND JANE:
> Sing it as we once did sing it.

(Loud:)

> It is better farther on.

> Farther on, still go farther
> Count the milestones one by one.
> We will forsake you never
> It is better farther on.

(They finish—laughing—having enjoyed that a great deal.)

MARIAN *(As they laugh)*: We rehearse it all the time. *(Listing)* When we do the dishes.
BARBARA *(The list)*: The laundry. We even had Benjamin singing it during the hurricane.

(Then:)

MARIAN: He tried.

(As they settle down:)

JANE: When's the concert?

MARIAN *(To Barbara)*: Three weeks?

BARBARA *(Same time with Marian, feeling the coffee pot)*: About a month. *(Getting up)* Maybe I should put on more coffee. This is cold. We're not going to bed.

JANE: No. *(About the concert)* I should come up and see it.

MARIAN *(Getting up, about the coffee)*: I'll do it. You'd like it I think, Jane. And Tim could sing in the chorus too.

JANE: You know, I think he'd really like to do that. He's almost said as much.

MARIAN: They should be so lucky. *(To Barbara)* You know tonight's chorus night.

BARBARA: I'd forgotten.

MARIAN: That'll be nice. Won't it? It'll be nice to be singing tonight.

(Marian goes into the kitchen.
Barbara sits back down and sighs.)

BARBARA *(To Marian, off)*: I'll need that.

JANE *(Joking)*: Maybe we all will . . .

(Barbara looks at her.)

(Seriously) It's the right thing to do, Barbara. We all know that. There is absolutely nothing to feel guilty about. It's the only thing to do. Give him time. Benjamin will see this— *("too")*

BARBARA *(Hearing a noise, over the end)*: What's that?

MARIAN *(Off, calls)*: Jane! Could you come in here, please! I need your help!

JANE: What does she need my help—? *(She gets up)*

BARBARA: I don't know. I don't know.

JANE *(Hesitates, then)*: Coming . . . I'm coming . . .

(Jane goes. Barbara sits at the table, suddenly lost in her thoughts.
The lights fade.)

Barbara and Benjamin

A short time later. Barbara still sits at the table, her back to the kitchen door.

From the kitchen comes Richard, followed by his sisters. He is gesturing to them not to make a noise. He is "tiptoeing." Jane goes around the table so she will be able to see Barbara's face.

Richard approaches Barbara from behind. As he grabs her shoulder:

RICHARD: I need your vote!!

(Barbara screams.)

BARBARA: What?!! *(She is shaken)*
JANE *(Trying to calm her)*: It's Richard.
MARIAN *(Over this)*: Richard's here early.
BARBARA *(Over this, gasping for breath, to Richard, very upset)*:
    What? Oh, fuck you! Fuck you, Richard! Jesus Christ.
RICHARD: What did I do?
BARBARA: Don't you ever do that to me!
MARIAN: I told him you weren't going to like it.
JANE *(To Barbara)*: I told him too.
RICHARD: I'm sorry. *(To Jane)* You thought it would be—
BARBARA *(To Richard)*: Fuck you. What the hell are you doing?
    You scared the hell out of me.
RICHARD: I didn't mean—
JANE *(To Richard)*: What were you thinking?
RICHARD: I—
BARBARA: For Christ sake! *(Calming a little)* It's five in the morn-
    ing. You're not supposed to be—
RICHARD: I know. I came early. Was that wrong?
BARBARA *(Over the end of this)*: It's not time to take Benjamin
    yet. They're not ready for him—

MARIAN *(Over the end of this)*: I told him not to. *Jane* thought it'd be funny.

RICHARD: I didn't think I'd scare you that much.

BARBARA *(Takes a big deep breath)*: My god . . . Jesus. So—how are you Richard? Welcome home.

RICHARD: I'm fine. Nice to be here. Nice to be welcomed with open arms.

BARBARA: It's like five in the morning.

RICHARD: I know. I'm sorry, Barbara. Get over it. Nice to see you too.

BARBARA: Now you're pissed at me?? *(To their sisters)* That doesn't seem fair. Does it?

(Neither wants to answer that.)

What are you doing here?

RICHARD: You asked me to come as soon as I got back—

BARBARA: I mean right now. At five in the fucking morning.

RICHARD: Language, Barbara.

JANE *(Over this)*: He said he's jet-lagged. *(To Richard)* She's a little on edge.

BARBARA: I'm not—"on edge." Let's start again. Welcome home, Richard. We've been waiting for you.

(They hug.
Then:)

RICHARD: By the way, I haven't had breakfast.

JANE: Who are you saying this to?

MARIAN: There's the kitchen.

RICHARD: Come on, I've been staying in a hotel for two months, I've gotten used to someone making me breakfast.

MARIAN: Is he serious?

JANE: And what does your wife say about that?

RICHARD: I haven't told her yet. *(Then)* I'm joking. It was a joke.

MARIAN: No, you're not. He's not.

JANE: No.

RICHARD: I can get my own breakfast. I assume that's all right? I'll get it. I'm sorry I'm early, Barbara. And I'm sorry I made a joke. I just woke up. Pamela rolled over and took one look at me and said—go to your sisters. *They* can't wait to see you. *(Smiling)* I guess she was wrong.

(He laughs. No response to that.)

MARIAN *(To Jane)*: It wasn't a joke.

RICHARD: I'd thought I'd wait in the car. I wasn't going to wake you. But the lights were on.

BARBARA: Everybody's up.

RICHARD: I can see that. And why is everyone up?

JANE: I don't know why I'm doing this—but I'll get your damn breakfast.

RICHARD: I'm not asking—

BARBARA: There's a stale bagel in the bread box.

RICHARD: That's fine. I'm happy with that! Anything stale is fine.

JANE: You are so spoiled, Richard. He always was.

(She "smacks" him on the stomach, he pretends to smack her back—something they did as kids.)

How do you want your eggs?

MARIAN: He likes them scrambled.

JANE: Why did I know that too? *(To Richard)* Do you know how I like my eggs?

MARIAN *(To Richard)*: Do you?

(No response. Jane starts to go.)

JANE: You still can't drink grapefruit juice?

RICHARD: I can't. I wish I could, but I can't.

(Jane goes off to the kitchen. Awkward pause.)

I am very sorry, Barbara, that I scared you so much.

(He touches the coffee pot.)

MARIAN: It's cold. She'll get you coffee too. Just like a hotel. Sit down.

(Richard sits. Barbara and Marian begin to straighten up the table.)

BARBARA *(Explaining the mess)*: We've been up all night.
MARIAN *(Nodding toward where Jane exited)*: Tim's in Chicago. *(Amazed)* He got a part in a play.
RICHARD: He emailed me—
MARIAN: Someone pulled out at the last second.
RICHARD: He sounded excited.
MARIAN *(Over half of this)*: He already knew the part. Jane said he had to pay his own way out there.
RICHARD: Why would he have to do that?—
BARBARA: How was the flight?
RICHARD: Fine.
BARBARA: And the kids? Pamela said they loved getting out of school last week.
RICHARD: I saw them for like two seconds. You said you needed me here the moment I got back, Barbara—

(Benjamin has appeared in yesterday's clothes, stocking feet; this stops Richard.)

BARBARA: It's Richard.
BENJAMIN: I know it's Richard.
RICHARD: Benjamin.
BENJAMIN: How do you do, son?
BARBARA: He's your nephew.
BENJAMIN: I know.

(Barbara looks at Richard. Benjamin sees this.)

(To Barbara, very insistent) I know it's Richard!

(Richard is surprised by this. He shares a look with Marian.)

MARIAN: He was just in England for months, Uncle.

RICHARD: Two. Two months.

MARIAN: We haven't seen him for two months.

(Benjamin looks at Richard, then:)

BARBARA: You worked a lot in England, Benjamin.

BENJAMIN: Did I?

RICHARD: Good to see you, Uncle. Very good to see you. You're looking well.

(Richard goes to hug Benjamin, but stops, they shake hands, awkward moment. Richard tries to laugh it off.)

MARIAN: Benjamin's been watching his own movies. It's been an all-night marathon. Hasn't it? How many of your movies did you end up watching, Uncle? *(To Richard)* We gave up after three . . .

Who else wants breakfast? Jane's making Richard eggs.

BENJAMIN: What about dinner? I've been waiting forever for dinner.

BARBARA *(A little fed up)*: We had dinner, Benjamin. It's five, almost five-thirty, in the morning.

BENJAMIN: I didn't have any dinner.

(Marian and Richard share a look: "See what it's been like?" Then:)

MARIAN: We had Chinese food. From your favorite place. China Rose? You went with me to pick it up. *(To Richard)* We stood on their patio and looked at the river. *(To Benjamin)* And you had a smoke? *(To Richard)* Barbara had cooked him a whole dinner—

BARBARA: His favorite.

MARIAN: Then he wanted takeout . . .

BARBARA: I don't care.

BENJAMIN: Where's the Chinese food?

MARIAN *(To Barbara)*: Cold?

BARBARA *(Shrugs)*: Cold. *(To Benjamin)* Okay?

BENJAMIN: It's from my favorite place?

MARIAN: You want chopsticks, Uncle?

(Marian goes without waiting for an answer, passing Jane, who is returning from the kitchen.)

BARBARA *(About the mess)*: Maybe I should . . . We've been up all night.

RICHARD: You said.

(Barbara begins to clear things.)

JANE: What do you want with your eggs, Richard?

RICHARD: I don't need anything else.

JANE: Barbara has bagels. They're fresh. And there's cereal.

(Richard is watching Barbara.)

I'll get cereal. Barbara has all kinds of cereal.

BARBARA *(Correcting her)*: Barbara and Marian . . .

RICHARD: I don't care . . .

Shouldn't we sit down at the table, Uncle?

(Benjamin looks to Barbara.
Jane goes back into the kitchen.)

BARBARA *(Touching Benjamin on the shoulder)*: Sit down with Richard.

(Benjamin shakes her hand off him. Richard watches this. He "sees" the puzzle.)

RICHARD: Who's been doing a puzzle?

BARBARA: We keep giving up.

RICHARD: You've hardly done anything. *(Big smile)* You need me!

BARBARA: You were never any good at puzzles, Richard.

RICHARD *(Ignores her, looks at the box, reads)*: "The Luncheon of the Boating Party." I didn't know you liked puzzles, Uncle.

(Short pause.)

BARBARA *(Suddenly, as she goes into the kitchen)*: I'll help bring things in . . .

RICHARD: If eggs are a problem—

BARBARA: What about an egg roll?

(She is gone.
    Richard and Benjamin are alone.)

RICHARD *(To say something)*: You look good.

BENJAMIN: Thank you.

(Then:)

RICHARD: Rhinebeck seems to have dodged the bullet.

BENJAMIN: A bullet?

RICHARD: The hurricane. I think I saw like one tree down.

BENJAMIN: Uh-huh.

(Then:)

RICHARD: I just got home. Last night about five. *(Smiles)* Stupidly I turned on the TV. *(Smiles, then)* All the noise, right? Doesn't it drive you crazy? You must really be sick of it.

BENJAMIN: Of what?

RICHARD: The noise. The election. I'm really happy I've been away for two months.

A lot of lawn signs out in Rhinebeck. I noticed that right away. Even in the dark— There seems to be a guy running up here named "Gibson" with a "B." And another guy running named "Gipson" with a "P." *(Smiles)* I suppose that's a difference . . .

BENJAMIN *(Gestures)*: Could I have some wine?

RICHARD *(Looks toward the kitchen)*: Is that all right?

(Richard changes the subject, Benjamin just looks at him.)

I don't think I could vote for Gillibrand even if my life depended upon it. *(Smiles)* Don't they trust us to have elections in New York anymore? Thank you, Mr. Schumer.

(Barbara and Marian return with glasses, orange juice, plates, etc.)

Benjamin wants some wine.

(Without hesitating, Barbara reaches and takes the bottle and hands it to Richard.)

BARBARA *(As she picks up a glass, to Benjamin)*: I think this is your glass.

(She sets it on the table, Richard pours.)

(To Richard) Good flight?

RICHARD: You already asked that.

BARBARA *(Not listening)*: I'll bet Pamela and the kids were happy to see you.

RICHARD *(Handing Benjamin his wine)*: I brought gifts. *(Smiles)* To make sure.

BARBARA: I'm sure that was the only reason.

RICHARD: That was a joke.

BARBARA: Pamela said on the phone the kids were driving her crazy. What with no school.

(Benjamin has sat down at the table.)

BENJAMIN: Where's the Chinese food?

MARIAN: It's coming.

RICHARD *(Smiles)*: I was eager to see all of you.

BARBARA *(Setting the table)*: You going to sit there? We expected you around ten.

RICHARD: Where do you want me to sit?

BARBARA: I don't care.

RICHARD: I woke up, Barbara . . . You want me to go out, drive around Rhinebeck and come back at ten? I'm sorry.

(Barbara sits down at the card table.
Richard looks at her and at Benjamin. He turns to Marian:)

How's school? *(He watches Benjamin drink his wine)*

MARIAN: I'm teaching third grade this year. So I have a lot of the same kids as last year. That's mostly good.

BARBARA: Marian's talking about quitting teaching.

RICHARD *(To Marian)*: You've talked like that before. What would you do?

(Jane enters with some bagels, cereal, etc.)

JANE: What are we talking about?

(Jane sets out food.)

BARBARA *(To say something)*: Tim's trying to convince Jane to move to Rhinebeck.

JANE: He is.

RICHARD *(To Barbara)*: She mentioned this in an email. I think she has some concerns about this. Jane's a city girl, aren't you?

BARBARA: Tim's trying to get his daughter full-time. That's a lot to ask of Jane.

(Marian moves the milk pitcher to Richard.)

MARIAN: This is skim. It's all we're allowed to have in the house now.

RICHARD *(To Barbara)*: What do you mean?

MARIAN: Karen's been up three, four times. She's a terrific kid. Ten years old. I love that age. All downhill after that. *(Smiles)* I've given her some of Evan's old toys and books and things. *(Smiles)*

JANE: And clothes. You kept everything.

RICHARD: I'm sure Karen liked that.

JANE *("Are you crazy? Of course")*: She's ten years old. *(To Barbara)* You going to have breakfast? It seems like we're having breakfast. I'll get you the cold Chinese food, Uncle.

BENJAMIN: Thank you.

(Jane goes. Richard starts to eat.
Marian and Barbara sit and begin to pick at things as:)

BARBARA: Richard, when Benjamin was filming one of his movies . . . *(To Benjamin)* Right?

BENJAMIN: What—?

BARBARA: We watched it tonight. You told us about this. Sometimes it just comes out of him, Richard. You think he doesn't remember and then . . .

BENJAMIN: What movie?

(Barbara tries to take Benjamin's hand. He won't let her. Richard watches this closely.)

BARBARA: You're in a big water tank—like a swimming pool. Only much bigger. The Columbus movie, Benjamin.

(Jane returns with the Chinese food, still in the little white takeout containers.)

When you were in Malta. *(To the others)* He did that whole movie in Malta. *(To Benjamin)* You were telling us about it tonight. *(To Jane)* Wasn't he? *(To Benjamin)* And . . . ? Come on.

MARIAN: Barbara . . .

BARBARA: He knows it. He does.

BENJAMIN: The director?

BARBARA: That's right! That's right. *(She's very pleased, too pleased; then to Richard)* That's right. It's very funny. He has so many amazing stories.

RICHARD: He always did.

BENJAMIN: The director . . .

BARBARA: And . . . ? And what? *(Prompting him)* He's in a little boat. Remember? With a megaphone. In the big water tank. In Malta!

MARIAN: Barbara—

BARBARA *(To Benjamin)*: And you said he shouts back through his megaphone to all of you actors gathered on the side of the ship. *(To Richard)* The *Santa Maria*. He remembered that earlier tonight. He just remembers. A lot more than you think.

BENJAMIN: He says . . .

BARBARA: Go ahead. You remember.

BENJAMIN: Says . . .

BARBARA *(Jumps in)*: "Okay, body in the water. All very sad. All very sad. All very sad." He's telling them to act very sad. *(She "laughs")*

BENJAMIN: "All very sad."

BARBARA: Then, what? "Shark! Horrible!" And you're all supposed to now act "feel horrible."

(She "laughs." Richard forces a smile.)

RICHARD: That's very funny, Uncle.

(They pass food around.)

JANE *(To Benjamin, pointing)*: Moo shu pork. Egg rolls in there.
I ate all the vegetarian ones. Sorry. *(To Richard)* I'll get your
eggs. *(She goes)*
RICHARD: So that was one of the movies you were just watch-
ing? The Columbus movie?
BENJAMIN *(Checking out the Chinese food)*: I don't know.

(Richard looks to Marian who nods.)

RICHARD: I liked that movie. Didn't we all see that together? At
the Ziegfeld, I think.
MARIAN: I saw it in Kingston at the mall. With Adam.
RICHARD: Maybe it was just Jane and *her* husband.
MARIAN: It wasn't me.
BARBARA *(Another effort to engage Benjamin)*: He likes to watch
them over and over. He seems endlessly fascinated by
himself. *(She is trying to tease him)* Aren't you? Actors . . .

(She smiles. He ignores her.
Barbara starts to serve Benjamin, putting the food on a plate.
Jane enters with the eggs as:)

BENJAMIN *(Pushing Barbara's hand away, and a bit harsh)*: I can
do it.

(This is noticed by all, especially Richard.)

MARIAN *(To Jane)*: He's tired.
BARBARA *(To Benjamin)*: Of course you can.

(As she watches Benjamin serve himself, spilling a little on the
tablecloth:)

Someone in town asked Uncle if he wanted to be in *A*
Christmas Carol this year. Didn't they? *(About the tablecloth)*

It's dirty already. *(She moves a box closer to help him)* To play the Ghost of Christmas Future. That part doesn't have any lines. But it's a good role. Very good. People here in Rhinebeck, they know all he's done. We even went to one rehearsal. *(She is serving him now)* You could tell it was a big thing for them. Benjamin Apple being there. Someone even asked for his autograph. And he was—amazing.

RICHARD: I'll bet.

BARBARA: Incredible. Scared the living daylights out of Scrooge and all of us. Didn't you? Just by the looks he gave. *(Smiles at Benjamin)*

RICHARD: I can picture it.

JANE: I forgot the jelly— *(She starts to go)*

RICHARD: I don't need—

BARBARA: Then—he wouldn't go back.

(Jane stops to listen.)

I told him he can still rehearse every weekend. This doesn't change that. He's going to be here every weekend. I don't think he understands that, Richard. Maybe you can help. Maybe he'll listen to you. I've promised to pick him up every Friday after I finish school.

JANE *(Gently)*: Talk to him, Barbara.

BARBARA: I have!

(This stops everyone. Then:)

Beacon's only forty-five minutes away. Fifty in traffic. And he can spend Friday night, and all day Saturday and most of Sunday. The Rhinebeck theater society was fine with that.

The Ghost of Christmas Future is only in a couple of scenes. *(As a joke)* And he already knows his lines. *(Smiles)*

(Benjamin reaches for his glass of wine.)

(*As she pushes it away*) It's morning, Uncle. You don't really want that, do you?

BENJAMIN (*Explodes*): Will you fucking leave me alone?!!

(*Pause.*)

RICHARD (*Stunned, confused*): Benjamin?!

JANE (*To Richard*): Leave it, Richard.
　　How was London?

(*The lights fade.*)

Ideas for Jane

A short time later, Richard, as he eats, is in the middle of a story. The sisters start to have their own ad hoc breakfasts from what's on the table.
　　Benjamin eats his Chinese dinner out of the takeout containers.

RICHARD: So Pierce knows he's made this promise to his wife— never to run for political office again. She got him to agree to that. To swear an oath. She just couldn't stand being a politician's wife.

JANE: Understandable. Certainly today.

MARIAN (*To Jane*): I know. Once Adam said he was going to run for the Assembly—

JANE: When was this?

BARBARA: Marian, let him tell his story.

RICHARD: It's— (*"fine"*)

JANE: I'll bet if you asked Michelle Obama—

RICHARD (*To Jane*): I don't know about that. I used to think that . . .

JANE: When he decided to run the first time.

RICHARD *(To the table)*: Was she *really* like that?

MARIAN: I told Adam no.

BARBARA: Go on with your story, Richard.

(Richard looks to Marian and Jane.)

JANE: Go ahead. We're listening.

(Then:)

RICHARD: So how was Pierce now going to explain to his wife that—that he'd just been nominated by his party for president?! Of course he'd been hoping for this. He'd maneuvered behind the scenes to get this. And of course behind his wife's back. Because he'd promised her. Now the convention had nominated him, so . . . He has to tell her—something. "What could I do?" he says. "They're forcing me, Jane." *(To Jane)* She was a Jane too. *(Continues)* He says this. She looks at him—and supposedly says something like, "If you're lying to me, Franklin Pierce, may the wrath of God come down upon your head, and God have mercy on your soul . . ." *(Sips his orange juice)* She really didn't want to be a politician's wife.

JANE *(The most obvious thing in the world)*: No.

RICHARD: Anyway, then he wins the presidency.

MARIAN: This is when again? I know nothing about—

JANE *(Over this)*: 1850s?

RICHARD: Fifty-two. *(Continues)* And it's so obvious that he's pleased and that he wanted this. He can't hide that from her. And so by now she knows that he'd lied. Even though he swore to God—he'd lied.

MARIAN: I know nothing absolutely nothing about Franklin Pierce.

JANE: Who does?

RICHARD: That's why I think, for Jane, this could be interesting.

JANE: Keep going. *(To her sisters)* I am looking for what to write next.

(Then:)

RICHARD: So he wins. And then—
MARIAN: What?
RICHARD: His nightmare begins. That's what's so chilling.

(Barbara has been looking at Benjamin.)

BARBARA *(To Richard)*: What were you saying?
RICHARD: Remember what his wife said, ". . . If you break your promise, may the wrath of God . . ." and so forth. Okay. That is just what seems to have happened.
JANE: What do you mean?
MARIAN: Let him tell us, Jane. *(To Barbara)* I love the way Richard tells a story.
BARBARA: You love the way Richard does anything.
MARIAN: That's not true. That is not true.
RICHARD: So before Pierce is even sworn in, before the inauguration and everything, during the transition, Franklin and Jane, they're on a train from Boston to—Andover, Mass. With them is their son, Benji. *(Looks to Benjamin)* Benjamin. *(Continues)* Eight years old, I think. It's a beautiful sunny day in Massachusetts. When all of a sudden—for no apparent reason—maybe it hits something? Anyway, the two-car train just tips over and rolls down an embankment, does a complete somersault, 360 degrees. Right off the tracks. And lands, right-side up. Like nothing had happened. Like a dream. The train now sits in a cornfield. All the passengers were of course shook up, but not one was even scratched—except for young Benji.
MARIAN: What happened?
RICHARD: As the two railroad cars flipped, it seems one chair or seat got loose and thrown into the air, and it hit Benji.

In the head. With incredible force. In front of his mother and father—the now President-elect of the United States, Benji, to their utter horror, was struck, and—decapitated.

MARIAN: Oh my god.

JANE: Jesus.

(Benjamin is listening now, too.)

RICHARD: In front of their eyes. Jane of course was inconsolable, who wouldn't be. Franklin tries to comfort her or maybe himself, but she suddenly gets it into her head that this must be God's wrath, His punishment upon them for Franklin having lied. And sworn.

Jane convinced herself of this. Nothing he or anyone else could say could change her mind. Pretty soon, they have to start to make their way to Washington for the inauguration. Jane Pierce makes it as far as Baltimore, where she just stopped, refused to go any farther, or closer to that evil city—of lying politicians: Washington. Franklin finds friends there with whom she can stay. And she will spend the next two and a half years—the bulk of Pierce's presidency, in Baltimore, trying, she said, to make amends with God, and writing letters to herself, and all of which she signs—"Benji."

(Short pause. They eat.)

MARIAN: Poor woman.

BARBARA *(To Benjamin)*: Interesting, isn't it, Benjamin?

(He ignores her.)

RICHARD: Pierce of course had no choice but to continue on his own to Washington, in full mourning now, not just for his son, but also for his wife. The balls are canceled. There are no parties.

And then one more thing—and because of this, rumors start to fly that maybe this is God's punishment. *(Then)* The newly elected vice president, Franklin is now told—his name was King—is in Havana. And he's not going to make the inauguration. He's in excruciating pain. Various of his appendages have turned black and are falling off. And soon he dies in Cuba. Syphilis.

And so, Franklin Pierce began his presidency.

(Short pause.)

JANE: And we think Obama had a rough beginning.

MARIAN: Joe Biden's fingers and toes weren't falling off.

JANE: I'm not sure it was just the fingers and toes, Marian. *(She looks at Richard and smiles, about Marian)*

MARIAN: What? I don't understand. You mean . . . ?

RICHARD: I knew nothing about this. Nothing. As I said, I just happened across this book—in a stall under Waterloo Bridge. *(To Jane)* So I don't know if it's a biography of Jane Pierce . . . Or about their marriage? Or his first one hundred days. I don't know. You said you're looking for ideas for your next book.

JANE: I am—

(Benjamin has stood up. All look at him.)

All done, Uncle?

BARBARA: Enjoy your Chinese food?

(After a look at Barbara, Benjamin goes off toward his room and the conversation changes.)

MARIAN *(To Barbara)*: Is he going to change? *(To Richard)* He's been wearing that since yesterday. *(To sisters)* We should get dressed too sometime.

RICHARD: What time are we going?

MARIAN *(To Richard)*: We took the day off school.

RICHARD: You told me you were going to do that. Was that a problem?

JANE: I can't stand watching this. It's so unfair to you, Barbara. It really is.

RICHARD: I didn't know this was going on.

MARIAN: I told—

RICHARD: Not like this. *(To Barbara)* He blames you?

MARIAN: When he remembers.

RICHARD: I'm sorry, Barbara.

BARBARA: I thought we said we'd go *late* morning. Isn't that what we said?

MARIAN: They expect us around eleven, I think. I'm sure we can go earlier. I think we were just waiting for Richard, weren't we?

RICHARD *(To Barbara)*: What does he understand?

MARIAN *(After realizing Barbara is not going to answer)*: Sometimes—everything. You'd be amazed. Then he forgets, and—is happy.

BARBARA *(Standing, to pick up Benjamin's plate)*: Why do we have to get there so early?

RICHARD: Sit down, Barbara.

MARIAN: Don't tell her to sit down, Richard. She doesn't like that. Don't you know that by now?

(Then:)

BARBARA: I'm just saying why so early? Richard wasn't supposed to even be here until—

RICHARD: I'm sorry, I could go someplace and come back—

MARIAN *(To Barbara)*: You said when Richard got home! He's home. Here he is. We're all here. And we'll all do this together. That's what we agreed.

BARBARA: He's furious with me.

MARIAN: He doesn't know what he's saying. You're just the one who . . . *(Turns to Richard)* Beacon's the hot community up here now. A lot of artists.

RICHARD: I've heard that.

MARIAN: What with Dia:Beacon.

JANE: And the sculpture park across the river.

MARIAN: There are a couple of restaurants. A nice old-fashioned coffee shop. Like out of the sixties . . . *(Smiles)* And, Barbara, what did we find out? You haven't told Richard yet.

RICHARD: What?

BARBARA: Umm . . . There's someone already there who years ago worked with Benjamin.

RICHARD: You're kidding? That's great.

BARBARA: I met her. I didn't like her.

MARIAN: She's a theater producer I think. Maybe she was something else. Anyway, so he already knows someone there. *(To Barbara)* And what else? Tell Richard.

(Barbara doesn't.)

There are two or three other actors in this home.

BARBARA: It's not a "home." They don't call it that.

MARIAN: And—there's going to be a "talent show" there. In a couple of weeks. Barbara's already got Benjamin rehearsing.

JANE: He rehearsed for us tonight.

MARIAN *(Teasing Barbara)*: She's going to do her damnedest to make sure he wins.

JANE: Do they really have "winners"?

MARIAN: I'm teasing Barbara.

*(Barbara suddenly hurries off to the kitchen.
No one knows what to do.)*

JANE *(To Richard)*: Do something.

RICHARD: What can I do? I can't even get her to sit down.

MARIAN: He told her—that he doesn't want to even bring her photograph with him. He's bringing pictures of all of us . . . Of . . . Just not her, he said. I think he'll forget that.

RICHARD *(To Jane)*: Have you seen this place?

JANE: Marian picked me up at Croton, that's as far as the trains were running. So she drove me by . . . It was on the way. *(To Richard)* You staying the night?

RICHARD: I thought I might.

JANE: Where are you going to sleep?

RICHARD *(Shrugs)*: I thought maybe in Benjamin's room.

MARIAN: She's not going to let you do that.

(Barbara returns, with nothing from the kitchen.)

BARBARA: He needs to be watched. I can't do that anymore.

RICHARD: No.

BARBARA: He nearly set the house on fire, didn't he? Here by himself.

I teach.

RICHARD: You have your own life.

MARIAN: He just lets people into the house. Doesn't he? Gives people things. When one of us isn't here.

(Barbara sits back down.)

BARBARA: I suggested to Jane that she and Tim move up here and we'd pay her to watch Benjamin during the day.

(Then:)

RICHARD: Jane doesn't want to do that, Barbara.

*(Then:
    The lights fade.)*

A History of Private Life

A short time later. All still sitting. Jane has picked up the large books, and she and Marian are looking through them as they eat. All are seriously eating a breakfast now.

JANE: Tim called earlier tonight. "Last" night. It's now last night.

MARIAN *(To Richard, about what Jane is going to say)*: This is interesting. I don't know what it means.

RICHARD: What?

JANE: He's had his first day of rehearsal.

MARIAN: He's doing a musical. *(To Richard, noticing)* You are hungry.

BARBARA: It's like lunchtime for him.

RICHARD: What show is Tim doing? He told me.

JANE: That musical. Based on that Joyce story. He's done it before.

MARIAN: Someone pulled out at the last minute.

RICHARD: He said.

(Richard reaches for something, and moves the wine bottle out of his way.)

BARBARA *(About the wine bottle)*: Marian thinks Benjamin is trying to drink himself to death. We let him do what he wants now. I stopped fighting.

(Then:)

JANE: Anyway, he says the director—

BARBARA *(To Richard)*: On Tuesdays— *(Realizes)* Today's Tuesday. We have chorus. Marian and . . . So we drop him off at Foster's. He sits and drinks and talks there. You didn't know about that.

RICHARD: Makes sense.

JANE *(Continuing)*: The director made a little speech to the actors. The director said—he wanted to be very clear about what they were trying to do.

RICHARD: What did he—? *("mean")*

JANE: He said—our job—that is, the actors' job—is to put people on the stage who are as complicated, confused, lost, ambiguous . . . *(Turns to Marian)* What else?

MARIAN: I didn't talk to him—

JANE *(Continues)*: . . . Frustrated, uncertain—as any one person in the audience.

And then the director said: "And of course we will always fail."

(Then:)

MARIAN: Interesting, isn't it?

JANE: Tim said he loved hearing that. Said it gave him goose bumps. Anyway, that's what made me think of these books I had with me. And I showed Barbara and Marian—

RICHARD *(Making a joke about how big they are, as he lifts one)*: My god, they're huge! *("Trying" to lift one)*

JANE: I found them; actually Tim did. Someone had mentioned these—an actor, of course. Said they were so useful for his research. And I was intrigued by the title.

MARIAN *(Explaining to Richard)*: We were looking through them earlier.

RICHARD *(So heavy)*: You brought these up on the train?

JANE: I know. Crazy. I thought I'd do a little light reading . . . *(Smiles)* Take some notes. What else is there to do in Rhinebeck? And I'm staying a week.

RICHARD *(About his own idea)*: So you already have an idea for your next book.

JANE: I don't know. The story about President Pierce was interesting too.

(Barbara suddenly stands.)

BARBARA: I can make pancakes.
MARIAN: Barbara, we have— *("plenty")*
BARBARA: Then you don't have to have any. Richard?
RICHARD: I have eggs. I have cereal. There's moo shu.

(Barbara sits back down.)

MARIAN *(To Barbara)*: You want to check on him?
RICHARD: You were saying, Jane. About this idea for a book . . .
JANE *(Reads the title)*: *A History of Private Life.*

(She opens one to a marked page. Marian also has one of the books.)

We found some interesting things. This is about the Middle Ages: *(Reads)* "Did people undress when they made love? The length of time that it takes the husbands in various tales to recognize their wife's true nature makes one doubt it . . ." What we don't know. And this— *(She reads from another marked page)* "Even if the historian cannot hope to discover the private thoughts of people who lived long ago, he can identify the places where they thought and the objects on which their thoughts centered." Ordinary things. A comb. *(Shows)* A picture of a comb.
MARIAN *(With her book open to an entry)*: Jane?
JANE: Marian found something very interesting.
MARIAN *(Reads from her book)*: "In the nineteenth century the battle against masturbation was waged by parents, priests and, above all—physicians. Women who rode horseback aroused their suspicions"—and here, Richard, the three of us couldn't figure this out, maybe you can help, you always seem to know things: ". . . who rode horseback aroused their suspicions *as did the sewing machine.*"
RICHARD: Maybe—

MARIAN *(To the sisters)*: I told you he'd have an opinion. I was joking, Richard. Why would I ask you? It's the pedal. *(She demonstrates)* They pumped a pedal.

JANE: And the vibration.

MARIAN: That too. *(To the sisters)* He was going to tell us. Unbelievable.

RICHARD: I thought you were asking—

JANE *(Over this)*: So all those photographs of women in those long rows of sweatshop workers, pumping away? You start to wonder if maybe something else was going on. *(Smiles)*

MARIAN: They're still sweatshops, Jane.

JANE: Please don't take everything seriously. Jesus. It was a joke. *(Reads from a third book)* "Increasingly private toilet facilities encouraged communion with the self. Around 1900 when bathrooms first began to be equipped with locks, it became possible for people to experience their naked bodies without fear of intrusion. The bathroom was transformed into a place for contemplation and taking stock."

RICHARD: This *is* interesting. "Taking stock."

JANE: You see why I think there might be a book here.

MARIAN: And it is sort of a follow-up, in a way, from her American manners book.

JANE: The private life. What no one sees. What we otherwise keep hidden. Ordinary things. How they have meaning. A dinner, a bath. How one looks at oneself when alone. There's a world we don't know. And of course rarely if ever see.

(Marian has her book open to an entry.)

(To Marian) Do you want to read that one, Marian?

MARIAN *(Reads)*: "When suffering became too great, suicide was a possible option. More than half of all male suicides chose to hang themselves. Half of all successful female suicides chose drowning." *(Looks up, then continues)* "Most

nineteenth-century suicides were committed—" Listen to
this. It's not what you think. "—were committed in the
morning or afternoon; nighttime was seldom chosen. The
rate rose from January to June, then declined from July to
December. Long days, sunshine, the spectacle of people
outdoors, and the beauty of nature seem to have provoked
more suicides than did the solitude of evening, the chill of
winter, the tortures of the night . . ."

*(They notice Benjamin, still in the same clothes, still in stocking
feet, has just entered.*

*Benjamin smiles at them. This surprises Richard, who looks
to his sisters.)*

JANE: What have you been doing, Uncle?
BARBARA: Not getting himself dressed. Obviously.
JANE: What have you been doing?
BENJAMIN: Writing.
MARIAN: In your journal?
RICHARD: What—?

(Benjamin nods.)

JANE: Good for you.
BARBARA: It's Richard.
BENJAMIN: I know it's Richard.
BARBARA: You said hello to him twenty minutes ago.
RICHARD: Barbara . . .
    He's keeping a journal? You're keeping a journal, Uncle?
BENJAMIN: Yes.
RICHARD *(To Marian)*: That's a very good idea.
MARIAN: Barbara's idea.
RICHARD: Why am I not surprised. *(To Barbara)* And he writes
    in it? *(To Benjamin)* You write in it?
BENJAMIN: I do. I write in it.

(Then:)

MARIAN: Why don't you get it, Uncle?
BARBARA: Marian—
MARIAN: Richard would like to see it.
BENJAMIN: Richard?
RICHARD: I would—
BARBARA *(Knows what she's up to)*: Marian—!
JANE: Good idea.
BARBARA: Jane—
RICHARD: I'd like that.
MARIAN *(Getting up)*: Let's go and get your journal, Uncle. Come on.
BARBARA: Marian—
RICHARD *(To Barbara)*: What's wrong?

(Marian and Benjamin head off into the living room.)

BARBARA *(Calls)*: Then also bring his shoes! They're by the TV I think! *(To Jane)* Is this necessary?
RICHARD *(Confused)*: What?
BARBARA *(Ignoring the question)*: He's going to want to go out for a cigarette. And then he'll be looking for his shoes . . .
RICHARD *(To Jane)*: He doesn't appear at all upset now . . . Does he know what's happening? Where he's going?
JANE: No. No. *(Shrugs)* He forgets. He's forgotten . . .

(Then:
  The lights fade.)

Missing Pages

A short time later. Jane, Richard and Barbara are still at the table.
    Benjamin and Marian have just returned; he holds his notebook/journal; she carries Benjamin's shoes.
    Barbara stands up and goes to the puzzle table, to keep her distance. Richard watches this.

BENJAMIN: What should I read?
JANE: Give it to Richard, Uncle.
BENJAMIN: I'd rather . . .
MARIAN: Benjamin says he wants to read from it.
JANE: Let Richard see it, Uncle.
MARIAN: He wants to.
JANE: Barbara?
BARBARA: It's his journal.

    (The siblings look at each other.)

RICHARD: Sit down.

    (As Benjamin sits:)

JANE: Do you want anything?
BENJAMIN *(To Richard)*: What do you want me to read?
MARIAN: Richard doesn't know. Let me find a place . . .

    (She tries to hand the shoes to Barbara, who doesn't take them. Marian sets them down.)

    (Not expecting an answer) Barbara, anywhere you'd like to suggest?

(Marian looks through the journal. Barbara says nothing. Richard watches this closely.)

What about . . . here . . . Start here . . . This is a good place. *(Pointing to a place, she hands Benjamin back the journal)*

(Richard looks at Barbara.)

RICHARD *(Concerned)*: Barbara?

MARIAN *(To Benjamin)*: Go ahead . . .

BENJAMIN *(Reads)*: "Saturday. I am brought to an acceptance of the fact that damage has been done to my memory, and my knowledge of this has been strengthened by the realization that it is hard for me to draw conscious memories of previous events. It's important to prepare for the worst, because if you don't, you risk being in a state of denying the problem."

RICHARD *(To Barbara)*: Are you all right? *(To sisters)* What's going on?

MARIAN: Read, Uncle. You stopped there . . . *(Points)*

BENJAMIN *(Reads)*: "I've been reading a book but I've been unable to recall actually what I've read. I need to work with a system which I can trust in the same way that I have always been able to rely on my conscious recollection to confirm that something was true."

RICHARD: When is this?

(Marian shrugs.)

BENJAMIN: "But now I need to find a new system—to find what is true. The system I am learning to rely upon involves my trusting my own writing. I must learn to look in my journal when I want to know if something is true."

JANE: You'll get a sense of what you've missed, Richard.

RICHARD *(Confused)*: What I missed . . . ?

BENJAMIN *(Reads)*: "Saturday."

MARIAN: Another Saturday. Some other Saturday.

BENJAMIN: "I didn't want to get up, feeling depressed. Barbara went to the grocery store and bought fish and flowers. She helped me get up. We went for a walk at the Mills Mansion. Marian suddenly was there too. She had cookies. I told Barbara my silence was an aspect of depression."

(Another entry:)

(Reads) "Wednesday. Barbara says, 'Remember always to mark the date and time . . .'"

BARBARA: I can never get him to put in the dates. *(Shrugs)* So it all runs together . . .

MARIAN *(Over this)*: Let him read, Barbara . . .

BENJAMIN: "Barbara takes me to see a play called the *Death of a Salesman*."

BARBARA: He knew the director.

MARIAN: Last spring.

BENJAMIN: "I must not forget that we went to the theater by subway, the first time I've undertaken such a journey since my illness began." *(Turns page)* "I must recover from the rather blank depressed tone of these pages. What is the matter with me? I don't feel that all the time, it's true, but much too often for comfort."

RICHARD: It's like we're listening to him talk to himself.

(Benjamin hears this and looks at Richard.)

MARIAN *(To Richard)*: Just listen. Uncle . . . ?

BENJAMIN: This page is torn out.

RICHARD: What do you mean?

(Richard looks to Marian, then to Jane.)

BENJAMIN: "Saw a film in Italian at Upstate with Barbara tonight. She says I am now a member. It's Barbara's birthday."

MARIAN *(Stating the obvious, they all know when Barbara's birthday is)*: Four months ago.

BENJAMIN: "I have realized that losing my memory has always been a source of fear, but I must cope with it. And now— look! I'm coping with it."

(He looks up and smiles, even laughs, as he thinks that's funny. Then notices:)

Another page torn out. Another. Another.

RICHARD *(Confused)*: Marian—?

JANE: Sh-sh . . .

(Then:)

BENJAMIN: "Someone came to dinner. We sat on the porch for a while so I could smoke. I felt very tired though because there was a mishap over the medicine. Barbara is driving me mad, continually reminding me to 'write what I feel.'"

(Richard looks at Barbara. Benjamin turns a page.)

"Wednesday. Barbara and I looked at my journal together. We looked at the entry for Saturday and saw I had written: 'Barbara is driving me mad, continually reminding me to write what I feel.' I feel upset. But I could see she was right. I ask her: 'Why are you tearing out pages in my journal?'"

(Benjamin looks at Barbara.
  New entry:)

(Reads) "Watching a video at Lincoln Center. Barbara and I watch together."

BARBARA: I took you to the library there. They have shows on video.

MARIAN *(Over)*: Barbara.

BARBARA *(Continuing)*: They have *The Cherry Orchard* you were in at BAM. Your Gaev.

BENJAMIN *(Reads)*: "I don't recognize myself."

BARBARA *(To Benjamin)*: In the video. *(Without looking at the journal)* You wrote this on the train home.

MARIAN *(Over)*: Barbara, please.

BARBARA: That's why your handwriting's . . . The ride was bumpy.

(He turns a page.)

BENJAMIN *(Reads)*: "Nine fifty-five P.M. Pitch dark outside. That's all I want to write." *(Turns the page)* "I walk back from the bank on my own. And later to the bookshop where I meet Barbara. We had coffee and Barbara was very fetching. I stand among all the books and look at her a long time."

(Next:)

(Reads) "Barbara has just torn a page out of my journal . . ." *(He looks up; to Barbara)* That's what it says. That's what's written.

BARBARA: I know.

BENJAMIN: " . . . has just torn a page out of my journal. I ask Barbara to give the page back to me. She does. I copy it back into my journal. Here it is, I quote: 'Today I stare at Barbara in the shower. She does not see me. I stand in the door and watch her for a long time. She's—so . . .'" *(Looks up, to Barbara)*

BARBARA *(To Benjamin)*: I scratched that word out. I scribbled over it.

(He nods.)

BENJAMIN *(Reads)*: "'She's so—'" something, whatever "'. . . and—beautiful' . . . Barbara won't let me copy down any more of

the page . . . Barbara sits with me on the couch and cries.
I ask Barbara what I was like before . . ."

BARBARA *(Standing)*: That's enough . . .

(She takes the journal and closes it.
Pause.
Benjamin stands.)

Do you want a cigarette, Benjamin? You need to put on
your shoes first.

BENJAMIN *(To Barbara)*: I can put my shoes on.

(Barbara helps him.)

BARBARA: I know you can. It's just a little easier . . . With help.

(Awkward pause, as she gets on his shoes.)

BENJAMIN *(Frustrated)*: I can do it.

BARBARA: Do you have your cigarettes?

(He shows her.)

Stay in the backyard.

(He goes off into the kitchen to go outside.
Short pause.)

RICHARD: What did he write—in the pages you ripped out?

MARIAN *(Answering for Barbara)*: Different things. One night
he came down to the basement where Barbara sleeps, and
just watched her.

For god knows how long. He wrote about that. He
described that. Barbara hid this for months. It's been
going on for months. Since long before you went to England, Richard. Then it just came out.

We talked to his therapist. Barbara showed her some of
the pages. I made her do that. I think she even showed the
therapist pages she won't show me. Is that right?

(No answer.)

There are pages she won't show me. I was scared. What is
going on in that head of his? We have no idea.
BARBARA: We have some idea . . . *(Laughs to herself)*
RICHARD: What did the therapist say? *(Realizing, to Jane, "of
course")* You know all about this . . .

(Jane nods.)

MARIAN *(Defensive)*: You were away.
JANE *(To Barbara)*: Barbara, tell Richard about . . .

(Barbara turns away.)

(To Barbara) He needs to know. He's our brother. *(To
Richard)* One of the younger teachers came over. Had
to talk to Barbara about something. Right? Marian told
me this. Not Barbara. A very attractive young woman.
Teaches chemistry? Barbara walks in and Benjamin's talking to her. He's telling her that she has two very nice firm
lovely breasts. Could he touch them? *(To Barbara)* The
poor woman was beet red? *(Then)* Could he "rub them"?
MARIAN: I asked the therapist if she felt—could he ever do
more than just talk? She said—she didn't know. Maybe.
Maybe. So be on our guard.

(Short pause.)

RICHARD: Has he?
Has he tried to do more than just talk, Barbara?

(Short pause.)

MARIAN: I don't know.

(She looks at Barbara who says nothing.)

RICHARD: I'm sorry, Barbara. This is . . .

(Then:)

BARBARA: I still think I can handle this.
MARIAN: You agreed—
BARBARA *(To Marian)*: I know I agreed! You made me agree! But I think he's gotten better. Richard saw him tonight. What did you think, Richard?
RICHARD: Barbara—
BARBARA: You saw him tell stories. Remember things.

(Richard says nothing.
Barbara stands and heads for the kitchen.)

MARIAN *("Looks" at her watch as she "calmly")*: We'll be leaving in a few hours, Barbara.
BARBARA: Fuck you, Marian!!! *(She hurries off to the kitchen)*
MARIAN *(To Richard, but loud enough for Barbara to hear)*: He's already packed. *(Shouts)* She agreed!
RICHARD: Marian—

(Barbara hurries back, she never made it to the kitchen, this isn't over:)

BARBARA: Richard's here, why can't we ask him?! Why is he here then?!
MARIAN: Ask him.

(Barbara and Marian look to Richard.)

RICHARD: What??

(Spent, Barbara goes off into the kitchen.)

MARIAN: You're just being selfish! And you know that!

RICHARD: Marian—

MARIAN *(Shouts to Barbara)*: Grow up!! *(Then, "smiling" to Richard)* And she's the oldest . . .

(Pause.)

JANE *(To Richard)*: The therapist— *(Looks for the word)* —"thinks" that because of the memory loss, there's also the loss of inhibitions. That's what's going on. And it's just going to get worse.

(Then:)

MARIAN *(To Richard)*: This is hard for her. For all of us, of course, but . . . We have a few hours. The sun's not even up yet. *(Stands)* Are we finished?

RICHARD *(Stopping her)*: I'm not.

(Marian sits back down.)

I'm going to have a drink.

(Jane looks at him.)

It's like almost noon—in England.

(Pours himself a glass of water in his juice glass, swirls it around to clean it, then drinks, then pours wine into the now "clean" glass. Jane watches him do this.)

MARIAN: So how was London? You haven't said anything.

RICHARD: Nothing much to say. I took depositions.

JANE *(About rinsing the glass, etc.)*: Have you cleaned a glass like that before?

RICHARD: In college. But with beer.

(No one knows what to say.)

JANE: I never go anywhere.

MARIAN *(Looking off toward the kitchen)*: You're going to Chicago for Thanksgiving.

JANE: By bus . . .

(Marian gets up and goes to the kitchen. They watch her go. Then:)

RICHARD: Did you know about—?

JANE: They keep secrets those two. You must know that by now. Marian made Barbara tell me when I got here on Friday. They showed me the journal . . .

There's more that she didn't rip out . . .

RICHARD: I think we do what Barbara wants us to do. She's been the one—

JANE: She keeps changing her mind, Richard.

RICHARD *(Sighs, then)*: Has Benjamin really forgotten about today? That he's going? What's happening?

JANE *(Shrugs)*: Seems like it.

RICHARD: And they're not going to remind him?

JANE: I get that impression, don't you?

RICHARD: And we're not going to? Is that right? The right thing for us to do?

JANE: I don't know. I don't know.

You tell him then.

(Marian returns without Barbara. Then:)

RICHARD *(New thought)*: Tim okay?

JANE: He's great.

MARIAN: She's doing dishes. She'll be okay. You know Barbara, now she's embarrassed. *(Goes to the puzzle)*

JANE *(To Richard)*: Can I have a sip?

(Jane sips from Richard's glass.)

MARIAN *(At the puzzle)*: Should we get clean glasses? Why not?
   (Starts to go)
JANE: These are fine. We're family . . .

(The lights fade.)

Firs

A moment later, Richard talking about England, as they all drink, and pick at the food. Perhaps even the Chinese food now.

RICHARD: An old friend was passing through London.

(Barbara has just arrived in the doorway. Richard looks at Barbara.)

Barbara, they were asking me about London. *(Back to Jane and Marian)* An old friend was passing through London. We'd been together at the Attorney General's office. For both Eliot and Cuomo. He's still quite close to Andrew.

(Marian gestures for Barbara to come and sit with her by the puzzle. It will take her some time, but she will go and sit with Marian.)

And they'd had a dinner together, he said, where my name came up two three times. Andrew himself brought it up. He said I was an example of a lawyer who was totally fair. Who didn't carry any—"agenda." By which I think Andrew meant—"I don't believe in anything." *(Smiles. The sisters don't)* And that I was, he said, just the sort they now needed up in Albany. I'm guessing my friend was told to tell me that.

JANE: You hate Andrew Cuomo, Richard. You make fun of him. You don't trust him.

RICHARD: That's true. I don't—

JANE *(Obvious)*: "The Dark Prince."

MARIAN: He's done some good things— Hasn't he?

RICHARD *(Over this)*: Maybe what we need right now is— "ruthless." God knows he's that. Anyway . . . *He* knows how to lead. We'd know who he was.

MARIAN: Richard—

RICHARD: The question of course is—where he'd lead us.

MARIAN: That's what I was going to say—

JANE *(Over the end of this)*: He's in it for himself.

RICHARD: And that's—unique? If you eliminate all politicians who—

JANE: You're not seriously considering . . .

BARBARA *(To Marian)*: He's sitting in the backyard. I left him alone.

(They eat. Jane looks at her sisters.)

RICHARD *(Eating)*: Andrew's pumping money into Buffalo. So he can be the governor who "turned around" a rust-belt city. That plays well in—Ohio. Michigan . . . He's always thinking . . .

JANE: About whom?

(Pause.)

RICHARD: This same friend? We got together three four times. I think we were both just lonely. One night we went to see a show. A character in the play talks about visiting the men's public bathroom in some fancy part of London years and years ago. The walls are all marble. And the urinals have glass tanks full of water. In each tank swam ten, maybe twenty goldfish. And so—you'd flush and suddenly the water level would go down, and he said the fish would huddle together and you could see a real "consternation" on their faces.

But then—the water would start to fill up again, and so would rise, and the fish, he said, they all relaxed—because everything was going to be fine after all. And then— someone would flush again . . . *(Smiles)* My friend leaned over and said, "That's how it is going to be like on election night." "Hope . . . and change . . ."

Glad I'm not in the city tonight . . . God, what that'll be like.

Speaking of England. I got presents for you. They're in the car. *(He gets up)*

JANE: We weren't expecting—

RICHARD: I'll get the gifts. *(He goes)*

JANE: Shouldn't we get dressed?

MARIAN *(To Barbara)*: Are you going to vote before we go to Beacon? Or when we come back? I suppose when we come back, it'll be something for you to do.

BARBARA: I don't need something to do.

MARIAN: To take your mind— *(Stops herself)*

(Then:)

JANE *(To no one)*: I'm not registered here.

MARIAN *(To Barbara)*: I thought I would vote. Polls are open. They open at six.

JANE: Why are we not surprised?

(Jane smiles at Barbara. Barbara, at the puzzle, smiles to herself.)

MARIAN: What? Why are you smiling? I want to vote. It's not what you both think. Jesus.

JANE *(Changing the subject, to Barbara)*: I think Richard wants to quit his job. All that about Cuomo . . . What do you think, Barbara?

BARBARA: Pamela wouldn't be too happy. *(Shrugs)* I don't know. He's got kids. He's just talking. We just talk.

MARIAN: I don't think he's saved anything. He seems to spend what he makes. I'm guessing that he feels ashamed about the work he's doing—so he hasn't really earned it.

JANE *(To no one)*: Or he just likes to spend money . . . *(Sees Benjamin coming)* Benjamin.

BENJAMIN: "Benjamin."

BARBARA *(Getting up)*: Benjamin! Why don't you sit here, work on the puzzle. It's too hard for me. I need your help.

(Richard enters with a shopping bag.)

RICHARD *(To Benjamin)*: There you are. *(To his sisters)* He was sitting on the front steps. I said he should come in.

(Benjamin goes to Barbara's chair. She brings another chair to the table.)

JANE *(About the shopping bag)*: Richard, you really didn't need to— We don't expect gifts.

MARIAN: I do. I'm joking.

JANE: She's not.

BARBARA *(Over this, to Benjamin about the puzzle)*: I was trying to work on the tablecloth—the white there . . .

*(Benjamin looks and smiles at Barbara.
The others notice this.)*

RICHARD *(While watching)*: I wanted to, Jane. It gave me a reason to get out of the hotel room.

MARIAN: Uncle, Richard's bought us presents.

RICHARD *(Realizing)*: I didn't bring anything for— *("Benjamin")* I should have. I don't know why I didn't think—

BARBARA: You should have, Richard. You should have thought of that. What's wrong with you?

(Then:)

RICHARD: Sorry. *(He opens the bag—presents wrapped in Christmas wrapping. Then, handing out the gifts)* Jane. Marian. Pamela only had Christmas wrapping . . . Barbara.

(They are not well wrapped.)

JANE: You wrapped them yourself. *(To her sisters)* That's cute.
RICHARD: How could you tell?

(Jane and Marian share a look.)

MARIAN *(As she and Jane open their gifts)*: Pamela let you wrap these yourself? *(To Jane)* That's very unlike her.
RICHARD: She was asleep.

(Barbara hasn't begun to open hers.
Richard watches as she does the puzzle.)

I didn't get you anything, Uncle. I always think of you as the man who has everything.
BENJAMIN *(In a smiling happy mood now)*: I do!

(Benjamin reaches across the card table and surprises Barbara by taking her hand. He holds it.
The others try not to watch, as he kisses her hand. She lets him, "smiles" at him, then she takes her hand back to "open" the present:)

BARBARA *(To Benjamin, explaining, as she removes her hand)*: I have to open my present.

(Jane changes the subject, having opened her gift—a sweater. She holds it up.)

JANE: It's beautiful, Richard. Is it cashmere? You shouldn't have—

MARIAN *(Her point earlier)*: He likes to spend his money.
RICHARD *(Oblivious)*: I do. That's true. *(Laughs)*

(To Marian and Barbara, who have opened their presents:)

I got both of you the same scarf.
BARBARA: It's very pretty, Richard. Isn't it, Benjamin?
BENJAMIN: Beautiful.
RICHARD *(Explaining the same gift, over this)*: Remember the last time—and you two argued over—I thought this would be easier. The same scarf.

(No one is listening to him.)

MARIAN *(To Barbara)*: They must have cost—
BARBARA: Handmade. *(Looks to the label)* From— *(Decides not to read the label)* Handmade. Thank you, Richard. *(She kisses him on the cheek)*
RICHARD *(A joke)*: I didn't want you two fighting over—
MARIAN *(Thanking him)*: How much did they—?
BARBARA: Marian, don't ask. He can't take them back . . .
RICHARD: You don't like them?
BARBARA *(No enthusiasm)*: We—love them. We love them. Here . . .

(She puts her scarf around Benjamin's shoulders.)

Like an ascot. Didn't he used to wear—?
JANE: I think you did, Benjamin—
BARBARA: I remember. When we were kids. *(She looks at Benjamin, smiles at him)* I have a picture somewhere . . .
MARIAN *(Distracting her)*: We were just saying, we should get dressed. Barbara? *(To Barbara)* Come on. We should get dressed.
BARBARA: We're not going for a few hours.
MARIAN *(Over this)*: We should get dressed.
BENJAMIN *(At the puzzle)*: Are we going somewhere?

(This stops the room.
Jane has put her sweater on over her nightgown.
Then:)

JANE: They're going to vote, Uncle. It's election day. *(As a joke)* Who are you voting for?

BENJAMIN *(At the puzzle)*: I don't know.

BARBARA *(Staring at Benjamin)*: He used to wear the ascot when he took us out to dinner. When Dad wasn't around . . . He'd take Mom and us out to dinner . . . My god . . .

JANE: What?

BARBARA: It's just sparked so many memories.

MARIAN *(To Barbara)*: Come on. Come on.

RICHARD: Barbara. I was thinking when I was outside just now. That— *(He looks at Benjamin, then)* and I need to choose my words carefully—that all of this, what we're doing, what we have to do, I know it's hard. For you especially. Actually I can't imagine how hard it must be.

BENJAMIN: What?

JANE: Nothing, Uncle.

RICHARD: But—I really do think it will help you get on with your life.

BARBARA: Go to hell, Richard.

RICHARD: What?

MARIAN *(As they go)*: He means well . . .

(Barbara goes, Marian right behind her.)

BENJAMIN *(Laughs to Richard)*: I've never heard Barbara say that before to anyone . . .

JANE *(Calls off)*: I'll pick up!

MARIAN *(From off)*: Get Richard to help!

RICHARD: I meant—

JANE: I know what you meant. What did you expect her to say? Thank you? *(She starts to pick up)*

RICHARD: I can help.

JANE: Yes, Richard. You can help.

RICHARD: What did I say?

(No response, then:)

(About Barbara and Benjamin) I had no idea about all she's been going through.

JANE: She thought she could handle it. Barbara always thinks that. She only told Marian when Marian happened to read the book *(Gestures to "Benjamin's journal")* with him and—

RICHARD *(Looking at Benjamin)*: He hasn't done . . . ?

JANE: Barbara would have told us that.

But I'm sure there are "incidents"—like the watching, that she hasn't told us. She's scared.

BENJAMIN: What are you talking about?

JANE *(To make a point to Richard)*: Uncle, I hear that you sometimes call Barbara—"Laura."

RICHARD: Really?

BENJAMIN *(Same time with Richard)*: Do I?

JANE: That was our mother's name. *(To Richard)* Barbara sort of looks like her.

RICHARD: She does. A little.

JANE: So I can see how one could get confused.

BENJAMIN: Did I know your mother?

JANE: Yes, you did, Benjamin. You knew her very very well.

(Then, to Richard) Don't expect Barbara to appreciate that you think she's been wasting her life doing this— *(Gestures to Benjamin)*

RICHARD: Is that what she heard?

JANE: We'll pick up later. We've got time.

(Jane sits at the table.)

You can sometimes be so goddamn thick. I'm hungry . . . *(She looks at the Chinese food)* Sit down . . . Have an egg roll . . .

RICHARD *(About Barbara)*: That's not what I meant.

JANE: I know. And she probably knows it too. Sit down.

We've been waiting for you. *(Looks at him)* Are you thinking of quitting your job? That's what all that sounded like to me.

(No response.)

Tim thinks we should move to Rhinebeck.

RICHARD: I know. It's a nice place.

JANE: Pour me a drink.

(He pours.)

Tim says he wants to raise a pig for the Dutchess County Fair.

RICHARD: You're kidding.

JANE: He says he thinks it must be like doing a play. Because there's a beginning, middle and end . . .

(They smile.)

The strangest things come out of his mouth. Actors . . .

RICHARD: What do you want?

JANE: There are restaurants here. He could get a waiter job I think in a heartbeat. Having experience in New York. *(Then answering his question)* I'm thinking about it too.

RICHARD: Do you know yet when—or if—they'll bring your book out?

(Short pause.)

JANE: I took it away from them. They were taking their time. I'm going to start a new book.

RICHARD: I know. We were just talking about what that could—

JANE *(Changing the subject)*: Tim wants to have his daughter full-time—

RICHARD: I heard.

JANE: Karen's a very sweet girl. Marian falls all over her.

RICHARD: Why does that not surprise me.

JANE: You know Marian now has a Girl Scout troop?

RICHARD: No. I didn't know . . .

(Barbara returns, dressed now.)

Barbara, I'm sorry—

BARBARA: I thought you were picking up—

JANE: Sit down. And join us. Let's live in a mess for a change.

BARBARA: For a change?

JANE: I mean—in terms of dirty dishes.

RICHARD: Have a glass of wine, Barbara.

(Barbara looks at Benjamin.)

He's been working hard on that puzzle. Really concentrating.

(Barbara begins to pick up.)

JANE *(To "Richard")*: Marian was telling me about Barbara and her dish-washing? Marian said no matter how well she did the dishes—how much she cleaned up and scrubbed everything, Barbara always finds one thing more to do. She has to do the last thing.

(Barbara takes some dirty dishes out into the kitchen.)

A glass, a spot on the counter. This drove Marian crazy for a while, then she decided that she'd always leave one thing unfinished. So Barbara can do that. She said she feels like one of the Muslim rug-makers who leave one fault in the rug on purpose as their homage to Allah.

(Barbara has returned with a tray and continues to straighten up.)

(To Richard) Marian has a boyfriend. Barbara told me. *(To Barbara)* When you said that was a secret, you didn't mean from Richard, did you?

BARBARA *(To Jane)*: That sweater will look better when you're not in your nightgown.

JANE: I'm getting dressed. *(Makes a face at Richard about Barbara; to Barbara)* You don't have to tell me to get dressed. *(Then, to Richard)* Marian's new boyfriend is poll-watching now. That's why she can't wait to vote.

BARBARA *(Moving to go)*: What about dessert, Richard?

JANE: He just had breakfast.

BARBARA: He's been eating Chinese food. *I* feel like dessert. *(On her way out)* You all right there, Uncle? *(She goes with the tray of dirty dishes)*

JANE *(To Benjamin)*: You find a piece that fits yet?

BENJAMIN: Not yet.

JANE: You know you can't force them. *(Then, to Richard)* Barbara's a little jealous I think. About Marian's boyfriend.

RICHARD: I doubt that. If she didn't want you to tell me, then— *(To change the subject)* I haven't asked you how Billy is.

JANE: Got a job. Part-time. Which he sort of likes. That's not easy for kids these days.

RICHARD: No. It isn't easy.

(Barbara returns with ice cream, plates, etc.)

BARBARA: What "isn't"?

JANE: Billy.

BARBARA: Oh. Yes. Good for him. Tell Richard about Billy and the intern. Who wants that disgusting fake whip cream that Marian bought? *(Then)* I think I do.

(As Barbara heads off:)

RICHARD: Barbara, is there another bottle of wine?
    What intern?
JANE: At Billy's job— An intern arrives. She arrives *with* another young woman. Who's that, everyone's wondering. Then the intern introduces the woman as "my personal assistant."
RICHARD: You're kidding.

(Marian enters, now dressed.)

JANE *(To Marian)*: The intern.
MARIAN: Oh god.
JANE: She started her day by giving dictation to her assistant. "If you need anything and I'm not around," she told everyone, "just ask my personal assistant." *(To Marian, who stands over Benjamin at the puzzle)* Barbara's getting dessert.
MARIAN: Good. *(Picks up a puzzle piece)* I hope it's chocolate— something.
RICHARD: Was she handicapped in some way? The intern.
JANE: No. Just rich.
MARIAN: How's the puzzle going, Uncle? We bought that for him. *(To Benjamin)* You picked it out, remember? At Stickles. You said you liked it because they all seemed to be having such a nice meal together.

(Barbara is returning with wine bottle, fake whipped cream and chocolate sauce.)

BARBARA *(To Marian)*: You're dressed . . . *(A look at Jane)*
JANE: I'm getting dressed . . .
BARBARA *(Holds up the bottle)*: It's a screw-top, Richard. *(To Marian, knowing she'll ask)* I got the chocolate sauce. *(To Richard)* You going to want more cereal or anything?
RICHARD: I'm switching to chocolate sauce and ice cream.

(The sisters serve themselves ice cream.)

So Marian, I hear you have a boyfriend.

MARIAN *(Turns to Barbara)*: I said that was a secret.

BARBARA: I didn't tell him.

RICHARD: That's—good. That you do.

BARBARA: We don't think it's serious.

MARIAN: How do you know? *(To Richard)* We tell each other it's not serious. He's only been separated from his wife for a few months . . . I only met him after—

BARBARA: You've known him for years. He's lived here for years.

MARIAN: I meant . . . You know what I meant.

BARBARA *(Serving the ice cream)*: He's a Republican.

MARIAN: He's not a Republican. *(To Richard)* He's an Independent. Libertarian. Like a lot of people were in the sixties, seventies.

BARBARA: He had a Ron Paul bumper sticker on his car.

MARIAN *(Over the end of this)*: I made him take that off.

RICHARD: And you used to give me so much shit just for working with Republicans. And now she's—

(Barbara stands to reach for something across the table.)

MARIAN: He's not a Republican.

    Anyway, you see people differently, when you sleep with them. *(She smiles)*

(Richard and Jane laugh, Barbara "laughs," then:)

JANE: That's true. When I first met Tim, I thought—

BARBARA *(Surprised, to Marian)*: You sleep with him??

MARIAN *(To Barbara)*: Sit down. Sit down.

RICHARD: That's not how to get her to—

(Barbara sits.)

BARBARA *(To Marian)*: You've only been dating him for . . .

MARIAN: I don't tell you everything. Because you can't keep a secret.

BARBARA: I can keep a secret.

(Barbara looks to Jane, who looks down at her ice cream.)

They're your brother and sister. They worry about you.

(They eat. Richard checks his watch. Barbara notices this.)

RICHARD: So Jane was telling me Billy's doing fine in Philadelphia.
MARIAN: I visited him there.
RICHARD: Did you? Good for you. You're a good aunt. I feel like a bad uncle.
BARBARA: It's not a competition, Richard.

(Then:)

MARIAN: John wanted to see a show in the museum in Philly.
RICHARD: John?
BARBARA: The boyfriend. He's a painter. Not houses. People. More money in houses. At least up here. This isn't Chelsea. Or Hudson.
MARIAN: So we went and took Billy out to lunch.
RICHARD: He can make a living painting?
MARIAN: Not a great one, but . . . And he has to do some teaching, which he hates. Says the students now are like "consumers."
    I hardly knew him, and then one day out of the blue he asks me to pose for a portrait. *(To Barbara) With* my clothes on. That's the first thing she asked.
BARBARA *(Eating)*: Sounds like they didn't stay on long.
MARIAN: He first asked Barbara. She was scared.
BARBARA: I wasn't "scared." We were—are—taking care of Benjamin. *(To the others)* I thought that's what we were doing.

(They look at Benjamin.)

JANE: I think he's asleep. He's bored listening to us complain. I can only imagine what we sound like sometimes . . .

(Barbara has stood, goes to check on Benjamin.)

MARIAN: Let him sleep.

(Barbara nods.)

He's been up all night.
JANE: So have we . . .
BARBARA *(To Benjamin)*: Do you want to lie down?
BENJAMIN: No.

(Barbara takes a cushion off Benjamin's chair at the table, and goes to Benjamin. She puts the cushion on the card table, and slowly helps Benjamin's head onto the table.)

RICHARD: Shouldn't he go to bed?
MARIAN: He'd just wake up. I think he likes the voices.

(Barbara returns to the table.)

BARBARA: Maybe we should keep our voices down. *(Then, quietly)* I'm glad you have a "boyfriend," Marian. She thinks I'm jealous.
MARIAN *(To Richard)*: Jane's worried about Tim—
JANE: Marian.
MARIAN: She was telling us tonight, right? That maybe Tim has never really forgiven her for—for when she went back to Alfred that time.
JANE *(To Marian)*: That was a secret too.
MARIAN: We told her to talk to you, Richard. How you dealt with—when Pamela—left you. You've forgiven her, right?
RICHARD: I've forgiven her. I haven't forgotten. But I think I've forgiven. But you can't forget . . .

MARIAN: Unless you're Benjamin.

(They eat.)

(Prodding Jane to tell more) And Tim is right now staying—where? With whom? Tell Richard.

JANE: He's in Chicago, staying on a friend's couch. *(To Marian)* To save money. *(To Richard)* To get the job he had to lie and say he was local. She's an old girlfriend. Her couch. He didn't exactly tell me that at first. When he suggested it as a "cheap alternative" to a rented room somewhere. *(She shrugs)*

MARIAN *(To Richard)*: So Jane thinks if she can get Tim to move to Rhinebeck—that'll sort all this out.

RICHARD: I thought it was Tim who wanted to . . .

(Then:)

JANE: Tim told me he went on a "pilgrimage" to Obama's pizzeria.

RICHARD: What? What's that?

JANE: In Chicago. On the South Side. Hyde Park. They had pictures of Obama all over its walls he said.

MARIAN: He went all that way—?

RICHARD: He's in Chicago.

MARIAN: I know.

JANE: The theater's around the corner.

RICHARD: Oh.

JANE: A couple of blocks away.

Tim said he happened to go in. He wanted pizza. He was sitting there and saw all the photos.

I guess it wasn't really a "pilgrimage."

MARIAN *(Then, to Jane)*: Rhinebeck's not all you and Tim might think it is.

JANE: What do you—?

BARBARA: Marian's right, Jane.

MARIAN: Look what Barbara's been going through.

RICHARD *(Eating)*: What, Barbara?

JANE: You told me. *(To Richard)* They told me.

MARIAN: You haven't told Richard. It's all been really silly. You want to tell him?

(Barbara doesn't. She eats.)

There's a writer who lives around the corner on South Street. He writes novels. He wrote a novel about of all people Benedict Arnold. Barbara knows the writer, and now for years she's asked him to come into her class and the students read the book and . . . It's a chance for the kids to hear from a real writer. About—what? Fiction versus history? Opens up a lot of good discussion, right?

BARBARA *(Eating)*: The difference between what a novelist is after, and say a biographer—

RICHARD *(To Barbara)*: I want to take your class. It always sounds so interesting.

MARIAN: In this novel, George Washington is shown to be— *(Looks to Barbara)* frustrated? Even bitter? He's even drinking a bit.

(Richard "toasts" Washington.)

Angry at the politicians.

(Richard toasts again.)

(To Barbara) Tell him.

BARBARA: Last Friday before my friend is to come to our class—the principal wants to see me. He's in his office with the superintendent, and some parent has complained about the way Washington is treated in this novel. And now I'm told my students aren't allowed to read or discuss this book anymore.

I made up some excuse to the writer. I was embarrassed.

MARIAN *(To Jane)*: It's not the liberal haven you think it is, Jane. I keep telling her that. It's more complicated than that. Rhinebeck is not going to solve all your problems.

(Barbara smiles.)

BARBARA *(Eating)*: Marian and I sometimes say we should move back to the city. Or into the city, she's never lived there. "Back" for me.

RICHARD: Are you serious?

BARBARA: Sell this house, quit our jobs and—to New York! To New York! *(Smiles to herself)*

JANE: For what you'd get for this, maybe you could buy a closet in Queens. You never go *back* to New York. Tim and I have talked about that. We know that. You go—you go. You're gone . . .

MARIAN: Still, I'd like to stop teaching.

BARBARA: Marian says that all the time.

MARIAN *(Over this)*: I meant it. More and more. You used to be able to do what you thought was best. If you did good teaching, if you were passionate and energetic, kids would learn, and that would be enough. But the faith—that's the word, the "faith" we once had in ourselves—as professional teachers—it's been ruined. By all the rankings . . . those tests. The . . . At staff meetings, right Barbara, we talk about "brain games," healthy "brain" food. No homework the week before the tests. So they can rest their little brains.

The really sad thing is that you now see young teachers— *(To Barbara)* Correct?

BARBARA: Right.

MARIAN: We comment on this all the time. The young ones— and *this* is all they know. They think—this is what teaching is . . .

(Short pause. Benjamin, his head on the puzzle, coughs. They look at him. Barbara has gotten up and goes to Benjamin.)

JANE: He's going to be all right there, Barbara. It's for the best. It really is.

(Then:)

MARIAN: Are we doing the right thing, Richard? We waited for you to come home to tell us. *(Then, quietly)* Barbara . . .

(Barbara looks at Benjamin.)

BARBARA *(Whispers to the others)*: What it must feel like . . . All the things you feel you're missing . . . The gaps . . . My god . . . *(To Jane)* Talk about a private life . . .

(They watch him. Then:)

MARIAN: I was listening in the car the other day to NPR. They were talking about that feeling—of missing something. The worry of having missed that day of "school" when they talked about something that everyone else now knows—but you.

BARBARA: That's what he must feel about everything. Every day.

MARIAN: They talked about a woman, a friend of one of theirs— a smart woman, maybe thirty years old, with a good job. One day, she's on a committee for a benefit, I think, and it's been decided that there would be a petting zoo, at the benefit. So they go around the table, someone suggests: sheep. Another: a horse. A third: he knows someone who has a llama. And then it's this woman's turn and she says: how about a unicorn?

Everyone thinks she's joking. They laugh. But it's soon clear that she's not. Somehow, in her thirty-some years, which included a very good and expensive education, she's missed the fact that unicorns weren't real. *(Laughs)* She said it made her wonder: what else has she missed? What else doesn't she know that everyone else does?

(Barbara has sat with Benjamin at the puzzle table.)

RICHARD: Or you make "leaps" trying to make sense of things that at first don't make sense. It must be—"wired" into us—this need to try and make sense of things.

BARBARA: What do you mean?

RICHARD: When I got the flu in London?

MARIAN: You got the flu?

JANE: And did he whine about that. In his emails.

MARIAN *(To Barbara)*: Did you know he had the flu?

(Barbara shakes her head.)

How come you tell Jane—?

JANE *(Shushing her)*: Marian—

RICHARD *(Over this)*: I was on the couch in the hotel room watching TV, the news. Half asleep. *(To Jane)* Feeling sorry for myself. Feeling like shit. And I hear this report on TV about a disease infecting British sheep. And how they've just learned that the disease is being transmitted to England from the continent—by midgets.

JANE: What??

RICHARD: By midgets. I'm lying there thinking, this is odd. What a different culture this is, we may speak the same language, but . . . I mean in America, we wouldn't even use that word. Would we? I fall back asleep, wake up, TV is still on, the news again. Same thing. From the continent—by midgets. Wow. I start to use this as a way of really understanding England—its culture, its whatever. And how different they are from . . . I even start theorizing—why "midgets"—and not other people as carriers. I'm thinking this is very very interesting.

In the morning, the newspaper is delivered to my door, and I see the same story about the sheep. And as I read it, I suddenly see that it's not "midgets," it's "midges"—little flies that the wind carries . . .

(The sisters laugh.)

I'd made up this whole complicated theory . . .

(They look at Benjamin.)

BARBARA: This semester, I assigned my students to write a story based on Greek myths. So I decided to write one myself.

RICHARD: You're writing, Barbara . . .

BARBARA: I write when Benjamin is writing in his journal. It helps him, I think, seeing me sitting there doing the same thing.

The story's about a girl who is born blind. Her father's the king and he gets all the kingdom to conspire, so that his daughter will never know that there is such a thing as sight. He does this for the best intentions. She grows up, she's happy, she meets someone; and magically sight is given to her.

In my story, which I keep as a fairy tale, she's now conflicted—thrilled with being able to see; and just as angry that for all this time she'd been told she'd been missing—nothing.

I don't know what it's about. Except—as you say, *that* feeling—that you're missing something. In her case, waking up to the realization that you've missed almost everything.

When I took Benjamin to Lincoln Center to see the tape of his show. His Gaev.

JANE: I'd really like to see that again.

BARBARA: He loved it. Utterly absorbed. Until the end, when the old servant is left behind? And the servant realizes the door is locked from the outside? And he's been forgotten?

Benjamin stopped watching. I asked him why? He said he didn't like that part. What does he know?

(Then:)

JANE *(Looking at Benjamin)*: Will he vote before we take him to Beacon?

BARBARA: I don't know. Is that necessary? Does he have to?

RICHARD: I ask myself the same thing.

MARIAN: Richard . . .

JANE: We'd have to tell him who to vote for.

MARIAN: He'll vote Democrat.

RICHARD *(To himself)*: Glad that's settled . . .

MARIAN: That's what he said last night. We watched a little of Obama's last rally—

BARBARA: Until I made her turn it off—

MARIAN: Obama with Bruce Springsteen? And Uncle said he'd vote for him.

JANE: You sure he didn't mean Springsteen? That's what I thought he meant. *(Then, to Richard)* Did you vote absentee, Richard?

(No response.)

MARIAN: Did you?

(No response.)

(To Richard) Then, Richard, I'll blame you—

JANE *(Over her)*: He's going to win.

MARIAN: Do you really think so?

JANE: He's going to win New York.

RICHARD: I would have voted for Obama. I think I would have. Does that count for something? *(Smiles)*

(Then:)

JANE: I tell myself—and try to convince myself—that voting is like—recycling. I know it doesn't seem to make any difference. What the hell is another Coke can more or less? But—for that second, when you're throwing something in the recycling trash—you can feel like you're part of something—greater than yourself. That's what I tell myself. I'm trying to convince myself.

RICHARD: The way I see it now is that most people seem to just want somebody who can articulate their hatreds.

(Then:)

MARIAN: I think we're arguing about important things, Richard. Medicare, Social Security, Ryan—

RICHARD: Shouting. Scaring people. Demonizing.

MARIAN: There are differences, Richard.

(Richard shrugs.)

Don't just shrug . . .

(Pause.)

RICHARD: Do we know what *we're* rooting for? I think we know what we're rooting against. And is that enough? Why have we become—"not them"? Oh, but today anyone with doubts must shut up. Save the doubts for tomorrow. I'm sorry. Sorry. I should shut up. "Today" we're interested in—who is going to fucking win. *(Then)* Because— "Today, thank god we're not *them*."

(Benjamin makes a noise.)

BARBARA: Just dreaming.

MARIAN *(To Richard)*: I want to be more—than just disappointed.

(Then:)

JANE: I want to be useful.

MARIAN: So do something useful, for god's sake.

BARBARA: Marian . . .

MARIAN *(To Barbara)*: What a stupid thing to say.

JANE: No one's listening. It's just us. Let me say stupid things, okay? *(Then)* I voted. Absentee.

MARIAN: Good.

RICHARD: Was that you saying something stupid?

JANE: Something—useful. Something—good. I know how that sounds. I admire Barbara—all she's done—

BARBARA: Don't patronize me.

JANE: I wasn't—

MARIAN: What are you trying to say, Jane? And don't do that to Barbara, you know she hates that.

JANE: I was just reading in a book Tim gave me about a small village in Switzerland. It'd been chosen to be the site of a nuclear waste dump? It does have to go somewhere right? But the villagers have to vote on it first. The government offers them thousands of Swiss francs each. And—they vote "no." Then someone gets what sounds like a crazy idea—to vote again, but this time, offer them nothing. And so they vote, and it passes. I understand that.

When did sacrifice become something foolish? Or have I just woken up to this, and it's always been this way? It's always been—take what you can get. You are an idiot if you don't. God what I must sound like. Glad no one's listening. "I want to do useful things." People are starving, Jane. Go feed them.

BARBARA: We understand.

(Then:)

JANE: An important man, who was in the Obama administration. He'd been president of Harvard.

RICHARD: Larry Summers. That's Larry Summers.

JANE: He's quoted in this book, the same book—

MARIAN: As the Swiss village?

JANE *(Nods)*: That Tim wanted me to read.

The man says: we have only so much altruism in us. Only so much generosity. So much civic spirit. So we need to think of it as a commodity that gets depleted. And so, he says, you—and I think he means politicians—have to be careful how you ask it to be spent.

I've asked myself this and wanted to ask you. What do you think? Is generosity, is being good, is goodness itself for Christ sake, even love of country—are these all just commodities, goods that can be depleted with use? Or—are they more like muscles that can develop and grow stronger with exercise? And atrophy if not used?

If I could have one minute with our president, I would ask him that.

(Short pause.)

Four years ago, I thought he knew the answer. Now?

MARIAN: After four years of being beaten to a pulp by Republicans—

JANE: I hope that's not all he'd say, Marian. I hope to god he wouldn't just say that.

RICHARD: He might.

JANE: I know.

RICHARD: That's what he seems to say—

JANE: I know.

MARIAN: FOX has been on his back, Richard, since the day he was elected. Even before—

RICHARD: And "our" side's better? "We" put Al Sharpton on TV. "Why the fuck not?"

(Short pause.)

JANE: I remember being on 86th and Broadway getting on the bus and the black driver putting his hand over where you put your MetroCard, and saying—not today, it's free tonight. It was a party.

RICHARD: It won't be like that tonight . . . No matter what, it won't be like that tonight.

What would you ask the president, Marian? If you had a minute with him?

(Then:)

MARIAN: I'd thank him.

JANE: You would.

RICHARD: For what?

MARIAN: I think he's done his best. I haven't agreed with everything, sir.

(Jane makes a face.)

I'm not even looking at you. *(Continues to "the president")* And a lot of things didn't get done that should have, sir.
    My boyfriend, John—

BARBARA: You're going to tell the president about your boyfriend?

MARIAN: Why not? It's not a secret anymore.

BARBARA: I don't think he's interested—

MARIAN *(Continues)*: John says, sir, that even he has admired how hard you've worked. But he isn't voting for you. And we both think you've survived with integrity intact, sir. *(To the others)* That's an accomplishment.

RICHARD: If it's true.
    Is it true? *(Shrugs)*

MARIAN: When John and I were in Philly visiting *(To Jane)* your son—by the way did you know he wants to be called "William" now—

(Jane rolls her eyes.)

John asked if he and his friends felt at all—disappointed. Some do, he said. One of his friends, who was staying with him—I asked her—

JANE: "Her"?

MARIAN: A friend. I think. She said, his friend— *(To Jane)* We both liked her. *(Continues)* —that it wasn't really a feeling of betrayal. Nothing at all like that. More like the everyday disappointments you have in a long-term relationship. *(Smiles)* Of course she wasn't quite old enough to know about long-term relationships. But I get it. She said it was part of what she thought growing up meant.

JANE: Being—"sort of" disappointed?

RICHARD: I don't talk enough to young people. I tried during Occupy—that seems like years ago . . . I remember some kid saying to me, that it was just a natural reaction—anger, angst, scorn at the way things are. The overwhelming sense that things are fucked up—so the only response is to fix it. And so that's what they were trying to do. How? That's what I don't understand. What do they want to do? I couldn't figure that out from being down there then.

BARBARA: My students— My kids of course are younger, but the older ones also come back. And I see them. They come back and seek me out.

RICHARD: Why am I not surprised.

BARBARA: I asked one of my favorites. She was back from college. Like you, Richard, I was curious. So I asked her: what do young people want now?

RICHARD: And?

BARBARA: Damn it, she said, why separate out the "young people"? She got quite angry with me. Which I liked of course. She said it really pisses her off that people keep emphasizing "our youthfulness"—that feels to them infantilizing and dismissive. And, she looked right at me—and, she said, it also lets older people off the hook.

(Then:)

JANE: Billy said—

MARIAN: "William."

JANE *(To Marian)*: I'm his mother. *(Continues)* Billy said something to me. He does talk to me too. Not just to his aunt and her sexy boyfriend.

MARIAN *(To Barbara)*: I'm glad she thinks he's—

BARBARA *(Over this, to Marian)*: She hasn't even seen him, Marian. She's making fun of you.

MARIAN: I don't think so.

JANE *(Continues)*: I was going on about the "millennials" or whatever that generation is now called. All this—what looked to me like—just constant self-absorption? Who the hell cares what you ate for lunch? I said it seemed like they were just wasting their lives. To me.

RICHARD: I agree. That's what it looks like.

JANE: Listen to our music, he said. The belief is out there now that anyone can make his own music. Or video. YouTube. And he said, isn't that a good thing? Why isn't that a good thing? Isn't it—to use a word you, Mom, always liked to use, he said to me—isn't it—democratic?

Then he said, that in maybe two, three years, or my god maybe ten—he said that like he'd never live to see it . . . *(Smiles)* In maybe ten years—what now looks to be an inextricable mess, Mom, or what you call "self-absorption"—it's going to be seen as only something we're going through, and after we've gone through it, it will all make sense.

(Benjamin mumbles in his sleep. Barbara leans over and listens.)

RICHARD: What's he saying?

BARBARA: It sounded like "bullshit."

(They laugh.)

JANE: One night when I was visiting Billy, while I couldn't sleep—Billy was giving me his bed, he slept on the floor. He and I talked.

He said—Mom, let me explain it to you this way. How I see the country.

It's like two divorcing parents, Mom. Like you and Dad. And they hate each other. They're screaming at each other. They're certainly not talking and listening to each other. And they both turn to their son and they say to him—who's right, son? They shout at him: damn it, son, you need to take a side! They scream at him: take a god-damn side!

But the son says, I can't. I won't take a fucking side. Can't you and Dad understand what I'm trying to tell you? I don't want to be like either of you . . .

(Then:)

RICHARD: How did we get talking about our children? It's election day. *(Then, the answer)* Because it's election day.
MARIAN: On Evan's iPod . . . it took me about six months after Evan died . . . After she killed herself . . . That's the first time I think I've been able to say those words. *(Looks to Barbara)*
BARBARA: I never heard you say it.

(Then:)

MARIAN: Six months after—for me to really listen to—the songs on her iPod. To really hear them.
BARBARA *(Smiles, teasing)*: Now it's all she listens to.
MARIAN: That's not true.

Really listen. And hear them. She had good taste. I'm learning her taste. It's so strange to hear some of these young women singers . . . They sound like kids. Little girl voices. They are kids. There's one I keep listening to. I'm sure you don't know her.

I've played it for Barbara. It starts: "They made a statue of us." And this young female, child-like and so-innocent voice, she sounds so proud, "And put it on a mountaintop / Where tourists come and stare at us. / Blow bubbles with their gum, take photographs for fun." Then a swell of strings: "They'll name a city after us!"

"And later say it's all our fault. / Then they'll give us a talking to. / They'll give us a talking to, / Because they have years of experience." The latter is sung with just dripping distain. "Years of experience." Then, "We're living in a den of thieves." Which she repeats over and over. Until, she just sings: "It's contagious. / It's contagious."

(Then:)

JANE: If *I* could have another minute with the president.

(All interested in this.)

I'd tell him what Billy said recently to me. Mom, I think mine is a lost generation. We're doing shit jobs, and not being trained for anything. And when the economy gets better, it's the younger ones they're going to want to train then. He's twenty-two years old. And he and his friends think they've been forgotten.

(Then:)

MARIAN: What about you, Richard? If you had one minute with the president. What would you say to him?

(He thinks, then:)

RICHARD: President Obama or President Romney?
MARIAN: Jesus—
RICHARD: Which one?
MARIAN *(Over this)*: That can't happen. I'd move to Canada.
JANE: No you won't.
RICHARD: Dear President Obama . . .

(They all listen.)

How did you, the voice of our better selves, begin appeal-
ing to our hates? How did that happen? How?
    Do you accept any responsibility for that?
    And are you sorry?
MARIAN: That's not fair, Richard.
JANE: If it's what he feels . . . Anyway who's listening? And
    I doubt if he's the only one who feels like that today.
BARBARA: Romney—Richard. Just in case he wins. Say a fluke.
JANE: I'm not sure he needs a fluke—

(They all wait. Then:)

RICHARD: Dear President Romney:
    Well, Nixon went to China. So there's that sort of
    hope. But if this really is all about helping your rich
    friends; if you are scamming us. If you really see us just as
    the heavy baggage to be tossed overboard to keep the ship
    sailing smooth and fast. If those who are saying this now,
    warning us—turn out to be correct, sir. Then—god have
    mercy on your soul . . .
JANE: And Barbara? What would you like to say, to either one?

(Then:)

BARBARA: I suppose I'd tell them both that I sort of stopped
    paying attention a while back. Sorry.
    And then I think I'd ask them—you both spent how
    much on this election? I think I read—two billion dol-
    lars. Maybe I'm wrong but it seems to me, it was mostly
    spent—scaring people about the other guy. And so now—
    look what you've got—a whole lot of people who are very
    scared . . .

*(Then:
    The lights fade.)*

Sorrow and Its Beauty

A short time later. Benjamin is still asleep at the card table.

JANE: I should get dressed . . .
MARIAN: I need to vote.

(Marian starts to pick up plates, etc.)

BARBARA: Leave it. Leave it. We'll do all that later.
MARIAN: Has some alien taken over our sister's body?
BARBARA: Shut up.
JANE *(Getting up)*: What time are we expected in Beacon?
MARIAN: Anytime after ten.
RICHARD *(To Jane, as she starts to go)*: Where have you been sleeping?
JANE: With Marian. *(She makes a face)*
MARIAN: Why do you make a face? What are you saying?

(Jane goes.)

Barbara, what is she talking about? *(To Richard)* She's the one thrashing around . . .
RICHARD *(To Barbara)*: It's all going to be for the best.
MARIAN *(To Barbara)*: Listen to Richard. *(She kisses Richard on the cheek; quietly)* I'm going to go and vote.
BARBARA: Do that, Marian. Do that.
MARIAN: I'm so glad you're here, Richard. *(Then, to Barbara)* Are you going to vote? *(Then, about Richard)* Don't listen to him. *(She goes)*
BARBARA: "John" is poll-watching.
RICHARD: You said.

BARBARA: That's why she wants to—

RICHARD: I figured.

BARBARA: Marian's put her contacts in.

(Barbara stands and heads to the table to pick up.)

RICHARD: Hey, I thought you said to leave it.

(Barbara sits at the table.)

I realized recently— Something I used to do as a kid. I remembered when I was in England.

BARBARA: What's that?

RICHARD: I don't think I ever told anybody this. I used to— draw lines between things.

BARBARA: What??

RICHARD: In my head, my mind. Between say the edge of the table here to that chair. And then—I'd cross the line. And then draw another. And I'd cross that. And another. I'd forgotten about doing that. Then I found myself doing it again. In London. I suppose, it gives you the illusion that you're moving forward.

It's the right thing to do.

BARBARA: For him or for us, Richard?

I could—can—still take care of him. I'm not scared of what he might do.

RICHARD: I think you are. And I think that's fine. I'm going to stay the night. Is that okay?

BARBARA: Of course. They're saying another storm's coming tomorrow.

RICHARD: I'll risk it. Can I have Benjamin's bed? Think about it.

I'm going to follow Marian to the polls.

BARBARA: You can't vote here.

RICHARD: I want to see what "John" looks like. *(Smiles)*

BARBARA: He's not very handsome. That's not a nice thing to say. Sorry. He's okay.

RICHARD: Marian really needs someone, don't you think? I'm glad she's found someone. You should find someone too.

(Barbara stares at him.)

Now you won't have any excuse . . .
    That came out harsher than I meant. I'm sorry, Barbara.

(Richard quickly goes.
    Pause.
    Barbara looks at Benjamin. She wakes him up.)

BENJAMIN: What time is it?
BARBARA: Seven in the morning. Richard and Marian are coming back. Jane's getting dressed. *(She picks up)* Earlier, Benjamin, you were dreaming. I wonder what you were dreaming about.
BENJAMIN: I don't know.
BARBARA: We often forget our dreams. I know I always do.

(Barbara has picked up some folded pages off the table.)

BENJAMIN: What's that, Barbara?
BARBARA: For your talent show. You read it to us last night.
BENJAMIN: What talent show?

(As she hands him the pages and continues to straighten up:)

BARBARA: I've told you about it. You were excited about it. Jane said how much she loved hearing you read that tonight . . .
BENJAMIN *(As he looks at the papers)*: I don't remember this.
BARBARA *(Explaining)*: He's in prison. He's writing his lover. It's just the end of the letter . . . They told me it couldn't be more than a few minutes long. *(Smiles)*

(Benjamin is reading it to himself.
    She picks up.)

Out loud, Uncle. Read it out loud. It's good practice. It's always good to practice.

(As she straightens up:)

BENJAMIN *(Reads)*: "I am to be released toward the end of May. I tremble with pleasure when I think both laburnum and the lilac will be blooming in the gardens—" *(He looks up)*
BARBARA: Yes. We have lilacs in our garden, Benjamin.

(Barbara sits and listens.)

BENJAMIN *(Continues)*: "—and that I shall see the wind stir into restless beauty the swaying gold of the one, and make the other toss the pale purple of its plumes so that all the air shall be Arabia for me."

(Jane enters, and sits down to listen.)

"It is always twilight in one's cell, where it is always midnight in one's heart.

"I have lain in prison for nearly two years. Out of my nature has come wild despair: an abandonment to grief; terrible and impotent rage; anguish that wept aloud; misery that could find no voice; sorrow that was dumb. I have passed through every possible mood of suffering. But something tells me that nothing in the whole world is meaningless, and suffering least of all. *That* something hidden away in my nature, like a treasure in a field, is Humility. It is the last thing left in me, and the best. And of all things it is the strangest.

"The gods had given me almost everything. I had genius. I made art a philosophy, and philosophy an art. I summed up all systems in a phrase, and all existence in an epigram.

"And as such—you came to me. I think to learn the Pleasure of Life and the Pleasure of Art. Perhaps now—I

am chosen to teach you something much more wonderful: the meaning of Sorrow, and its Beauty.
"Your affectionate friend,
Oscar Wilde."

(Then:)

BARBARA *(To say something; to Jane)*: That sweater looks nice.
I'll wear my scarf later. That'll make Richard happy . . .
JANE: Where is Richard?
BARBARA: He went to see what "John" looked like. *(She goes to Benjamin)* That was very good, Uncle.
JANE: Maybe I'll go see what "John" looks like too. She said he's not very handsome.
BARBARA *(Smiles to herself)*: Did she?
JANE *(Starting to go)*: Are we taking two cars?
BENJAMIN: Are we going somewhere?
JANE: For a drive, Uncle.

(Jane hesitates going.)

BARBARA *(Suddenly)*: Jane, stay with Benjamin for a moment.

*(Barbara hurries off into the living room.
Short pause.)*

JANE: I remember you reading that at the Y, Uncle. The first thing you did in public, after your—heart attack. We were all there. I remember Richard saying it was like you'd never been ill.
I'll bet you win that talent show.

(Barbara hurries back out of breath with a small framed photo and a dog collar.)

I won't be long . . . *(She goes)*

(Barbara and Benjamin look at each other. She shows him what she's brought.)

BARBARA: I wanted to make sure you had these with you. Okay?
BENJAMIN: What??
BARBARA *(Handing the collar to him)*: It's a dog collar. I want to make sure you put this on your nightstand. It was your dog's. His name was Oliver.
BENJAMIN *(Takes the collar, examines it)*: Oliver. I don't remember Oliver.
BARBARA: I know. *(Then she tries to hand him the photo)* And this is a photo of me. You keep it on your bureau. Will you do that? Please. It'll make me happy.
BENJAMIN: I don't understand—
BARBARA: You will. Please. Keep it.

(He takes it. Looks at the photo, then looks at her. He takes her hand; he kisses it. She moves away from him.)

BENJAMIN: What's wrong? Barbara, have I done something wrong?

(She looks at him, then goes to the puzzle.)

BARBARA *(About the puzzle)*: Are we really going to do this puzzle? Let's put it away. I'd rather it wasn't out when we came back . . .

(She starts to put the pieces of the puzzle back in the puzzle box.)

BENJAMIN: Why? I like it.

(He goes to her. She stops picking up the puzzle.)

BARBARA *(About the picture on the box)*: Look at this girl, Uncle. What is *she* thinking?

BENJAMIN: Barbara?

(She moves away from him and goes to the table "to clean up," but sits. Benjamin sits at the puzzle.)

BARBARA: Jane and Tim are going to move to Rhinebeck, Benjamin.

BENJAMIN *(Beginning to do the puzzle)*: That'll be nice for us. *(Smiles, then)* Who's Tim?

BARBARA *(Picking up)*: You've met Tim, many times . . . He's Jane's boyfriend. He's an actor. Like you. You like him.

BENJAMIN *(Doing the puzzle)*: An actor . . .

(Then:)

BARBARA: Marian has a boyfriend. That's very good. I'm so happy for her.

(He nods.)

So Richard's back from England. That's nice. I'm sure Pamela—that's his wife—is happy about that. And their kids. He was gone for a long time. He seems—at loose ends, didn't you think? We all saw that. But didn't say anything about it. *(Smiles at Benjamin)* I've been worried about him. We all were. We know how he can just shut himself away. Without his family around . . .

(Church bells toll seven in the distance. She looks at her watch, then:)

(To Benjamin) I'll vote later . . .

(They sit.)

END OF PLAY

REGULAR
SINGING

Conversations on November 22nd
The Fiftieth Anniversary of
the Assassination of President John F. Kennedy
2013

For Cynthia, Marian, Bill, Jim and Rob

———

Regular Singing was commissioned by and first produced at The Public Theater (Oskar Eustis, Artistic Director; Patrick Willingham, Executive Director) in New York on November 22, 2013. The director was Richard Nelson; the set and costume design were by Susan Hilferty, the lighting design was by Jennifer Tipton, the sound design was by Scott Lehrer and Will Pickens; the assistant director was Tamara Fisch, the production stage manager was Pamela Salling, the stage manager was Maggie Swing. The cast was:

RICHARD APPLE	Jay O. Sanders
BARBARA APPLE	Maryann Plunkett
MARIAN APPLE	Laila Robins
JANE APPLE	Sally Murphy
BENJAMIN APPLE	Jon DeVries
TIM ANDREWS	Stephen Kunken

The Apples:

RICHARD APPLE, a lawyer in the governor's office, lives in Albany.

BARBARA APPLE, his sister, a high school English teacher, lives in Rhinebeck.

MARIAN APPLE, his sister, a third grade teacher, lives in Rhinebeck.

JANE APPLE, his sister, a nonfiction writer, lives in Rhinebeck with her boyfriend, Tim.

BENJAMIN APPLE, his uncle, a retired actor, lives in an assisted living home in Beacon, New York.

TIM ANDREWS, an actor, lives in Rhinebeck with Jane.

TIME

The play takes place between approximately ten P.M. and a little after midnight on Friday, November 22, 2013.

PLACE

Rhinebeck, New York: a small historic village one hundred miles north of New York City; once referred to in an article in the *New York Times* as "The Town That Time Forgot." A room in Barbara Apple's house, which she shares with Marian and, for the last month, with Marian's ex-husband, Adam Platt, on Center Street.

NOTE

Play One, *That Hopey Changey Thing*, is set on November 2, 2010. Before the play begins, Uncle Benjamin Apple, a well-known actor, has had a heart attack, which sent him into a coma. When he came out of the coma, he had serious amnesia. By the beginning of the play, he has retired and moved into his niece Barbara's home in Rhinebeck, New York.

Play Two, *Sweet and Sad*, is set on September 11, 2011. Months before the play begins, Marian's twenty-year-old daughter, Evan, committed suicide, for reasons unknown. Since then, Marian and her husband, Adam, have separated, and Marian now shares Barbara's house with Barbara and Benjamin.

Play Three, *Sorry*, is set on November 6, 2012. Richard has been on a lengthy business trip to England. Barbara and Marian have been waiting for Richard's return before moving Benjamin to an assisted-living home, a move which Barbara has been resisting. Marian continues to share Barbara's house with Barbara and Benjamin.

For a long time I would go to bed early.

—Marcel Proust, opening of *Swann's Way*

A wooden table and four wooden chairs. A few short-stemmed, mostly dead, flowers in a small glass vase on the table. Rugs.

Animal Collective's "My Girls" begins.

Barbara enters with a tablecloth that she begins to put on the table, with a small bouquet of colorful flowers, with which she will replace the mostly dead flowers in the glass vase. The flowers are a burst of color in the room.

Marian soon follows with a tray of various dishes, bowls, casserole dishes covered in foil—the remnants of a potluck supper: chicken salad, pasta, bean salad, homemade fries, green salad, little hot dogs, etc. The bowls, dishes, etc., have taped labels and are totally unmatched, coming as they do from various households.

Jane soon carries in a tray of used paper plates, plastic glasses, used napkins, used silverware, etc.

Marian and Jane will go off and return a few times, bringing in more dishes, and bottles of wine and soda, and a bottle of Irish whiskey.

Barbara will go off and return with a card table, which she sets up, and on which most of the drinks will be set as "the bar."

Richard and Tim enter with chairs. They make a number of trips and bring in numerous chairs—perhaps as many as twelve or fourteen—which they set around the room, against the walls—in small groupings where the recent guests had gathered themselves.

All set the used paper plates, plastic glasses and cups, and the used napkins around the room—on the floor, under chairs, on empty chairs where the guests recently were, so that a picture finally emerges of a just-finished potluck dinner for ten or so guests.

Benjamin joins Tim and Richard, as the women leave, and then sit . . .

It is ten at night on November 22, 2013.

Gentlemen Singing

Tim, Richard and Benjamin. Tim has some xeroxed sheet music. Benjamin sits at a distance, he looks around the room. Tim sings (from the Ainsworth Psalter, Psalm 13) to Richard:

TIM *(Singing)*:
> How long Jehovah, wilt thou me forget for aye:
> How long-while wilt thou hide thy face from me
> away?

(Then:)

Listen to this . . .

(Sings:)

> How long shall in my soul, my counsels set dayly
> Sad sorrow in my heart, how long shall my foe be
> Exalted over me?

(Then:)

Why would he choose that?

RICHARD: I'm surprised. Adam wasn't even religious. Isn't. Isn't religious.

TIM: You don't have to be religious. It is beautiful. And anyway, how do we know? It's what he wanted. He picked them out. He's organized the whole—service . . .

RICHARD *(Reads)*: "How long shall my foe be exalted over me?" Maybe he's thinking—John Boehner? *(Smiles)* So maybe it's just political, Benjamin. That makes sense for Adam.

TIM *(To Benjamin)*: Are you all right? Tired?

BENJAMIN: I'm not tired, Tim. I'm all right.

TIM *(To Richard)*: He said, they're the very first songs ever sung in America.

RICHARD *(Corrects)*: By white people.

TIM: Adam told me this story: a lot of early American Puritan congregations, they only knew how to sing a handful of tunes? And they couldn't even sing those well. A leader had to sing and the rest would copy him. Line by line. *Line by line.* Adam said—some people wanted to change this, they wanted there to be written-down agreed-upon notes—so that everyone could follow at the same time and sing together. But that got other people incensed: "We need a leader. It will be the end of authority." So, Adam said, all hell broke loose. They even called it a "singing war."

RICHARD: A singing war?

TIM: In the 1720s. In America. You hungry, Benjamin?

BENJAMIN: No.

TIM *(To Richard)*: Just to agree to have notes so people could fucking sing together. A war. Then, after telling me this, Adam looks up from his sickbed, and says—"Nothing's changed. America, Tim . . ."

(Jane enters from the kitchen.)

JANE: They're *almost* all gone. Just Adam's "baby" sister . . .
Why does she keep calling herself that?

TIM: I don't know.

RICHARD *(Standing)*: I have to go, Jane.

JANE *(To Tim)*: She's— ("big")

(Then:)

The sister's on the porch still talking to Barbara. Barbara
got her that far. The mother's upstairs?

TIM: At the bedside. With Marian.

JANE: Marian okay?

(No response.)

I'm going to the apartment and change. Get out of these
. . . *(She starts to go)*

TIM: We're staying?

JANE: I think we should, don't you? I haven't eaten. Have any
of us eaten? There's a ton of food left . . . There's even
more in the kitchen.

(Tim "looks" at his watch.)

TIM: Jane . . .

JANE *(About staying, her reasons)*: Karen's at Tina's. I've been in
Albany all week. I've hardly spent any time with Marian . . .
It's the right thing.

(Jane goes back out through the kitchen.)

TIM *(As she leaves)*: They could just call . . . If we're needed . . .
(To Richard) We're just down the street.

(Richard sits back down.)

RICHARD: I haven't seen your apartment. Nice place?

TIM *(Continues to look through the music)*: Okay. Two bedrooms. Karen likes her room. Thank you god. For an eleven year old I suppose that's everything.

(Benjamin picks up the bottle of whiskey.)

Not the whiskey, Benjamin. Please. You know that's not good for you.

(Benjamin pours a glass of whiskey. Tim just shakes his head.)

Your sisters will blame me . . .
RICHARD: Why would they blame you?
TIM *(Another Psalm)*: Adam wants us all to sing this one . . .
BENJAMIN: Who were all these people, Tim?
TIM: They came to see Adam. Marian's ex-husband. He's upstairs.
BENJAMIN: Some of them were laughing. And some of them were crying . . .

(Then:)

TIM: You're going to sing with us too. Adam wants that.
BENJAMIN: Am I?
RICHARD *(Same time, with Benjamin)*: He is?
TIM *(To Benjamin)*: Let's show Richard. Sing with me now, Benjamin. Show him what we've been practicing . . . Come on. You seem very restless . . .
BENJAMIN: Do I? I don't feel restless.

(Benjamin joins the men.)

TIM: Here. Here's one we've practiced.
RICHARD: You remember the songs?
BENJAMIN: I remember the songs . . .
TIM: The music. This one makes sense for Adam . . . *(Psalm 23:)*

Yea though in valley of death's shade I walk—

(After a glance at Benjamin, Tim continues with Benjamin:)

BENJAMIN AND TIM:
>   —none ill I'll fear,
>   Because thou art with me, thy rod,
>   And staff my comfort are.

(The lights fade.)

Richard Stays for Potluck

The same, a short while later.

RICHARD *(Sees her coming in)*: Barbara . . . *(He stands)*
BARBARA *(Entering)*: I'm going to get out of these *("her shoes")* . . . Put on some slippers . . . *(To Richard)* I'm glad you're still here, Richard. Marian thought you'd leave right away.
RICHARD: I've been waiting. I should get back.
BARBARA: She thought you'd "creep away into the night."
RICHARD *(To Tim)*: Why would I "creep"—?
BARBARA *(Over this, to Benjamin)*: Have you eaten anything, Benjamin? You should.
BENJAMIN: I'm not hungry.
BARBARA *(To Benjamin)*: I haven't eaten. I don't think I've seen you eat anything all day.
TIM: Jane wants to have supper . . .
BARBARA: Richard—?
RICHARD: It's after ten. I have to go.
BARBARA: I just want to change my shoes . . .
RICHARD: I do have to go soon, Barbara. I was just waiting . . . I'm sorry . . .
BARBARA: You're not staying for supper?
RICHARD *(Smiling)*: I think I just said that. No.

BARBARA: He's not going to stay, Benjamin.

RICHARD *(Stopping her)*: Barbara, it's after ten o'clock at night. I'm not hungry. And if I'm going to come back tomorrow—

BARBARA: "If"?! Oh forget it, Richard. Just forget it— *(Turns to go)*

RICHARD: I'm coming back.

(She stops.)

Barbara. I just meant— *("Looks" at his watch)* It's late. *(To Tim)* Isn't it?

(Tim looks away.)

Tim doesn't want to stay either.

TIM: I didn't say that.

BARBARA *(Over this)*: Go ahead, run away. You're always now running away from us. What are you so scared of? What do you think we'll do to you?

RICHARD: What are you talking about?

BARBARA *(To "Benjamin")*: Or hiding from us now. Like a— little scamp.

RICHARD: I don't know what that means.

BARBARA: Or worse. That's Richard, your nephew, Uncle. Do you even remember him?

BENJAMIN: Richard . . .

RICHARD *(Over this)*: He knows who I am.

BARBARA *(To Benjamin)*: He hasn't seen you for a very long time. He's been hiding from us. *(Pointed)* I thought maybe he'd forgotten you.

BENJAMIN *(To Richard)*: I know who you are.

BARBARA *(Over this)*: I'm going to change. Benjamin, are you all right? Do you need anything? *(To Tim)* Is Marian still upstairs?

(Tim nods.)

TIM: And his mother . . .

(Then notices:)

BARBARA *(To Benjamin)*: Is that whiskey? Come on now, Tim . . .

TIM *(To Barbara)*: Some jackass brought whiskey . . .

BARBARA *(To Benjamin)*: Benjamin, you know better . . . *(To Tim)* You both know better. *(To Richard)* Why don't you stay the night? We'll make room.

RICHARD: There's no room, Barbara—

BARBARA *(Over this)*: We'll make room.

RICHARD: I can't.

BARBARA: Then at least stay for supper.

RICHARD: Barbara, I said—

BARBARA: It's a simple question. Requiring a simple answer. Or do we have to beg you now, Richard?

RICHARD: You don't have to "beg" me.

I'll stay for supper. If it means that much to—

BARBARA: Good. Marian will appreciate that. *(She starts to go, stops)* Are you sure? I don't want you to feel pressured. Like you—have to. *(As she goes, gestures at the table)* It's just potluck . . .

TIM *(Beginning to stand)*: Maybe we should pick up some of this?

RICHARD: Let my sisters do that.

They live—to pick up stuff.

(Tim doesn't know what to do, he sits back down.
Then:)

Benjamin, don't tell my sisters I said that.

(The lights fade.)

Albany

A short time later. Richard, Tim and Benjamin.
Jane has just returned, in comfortable clothes now.

JANE: I better pick up.

RICHARD *(To Tim)*: What did I tell you?

JANE: What are you two talking about?

TIM: Albany.

JANE: You look guilty.

TIM: I'm not— *(To Richard)* I've never even been to Albany.

JANE *(As she picks up)*: Karen and Tina are watching some movie on my computer.

TIM: They're in our apartment? What movie?

JANE: I don't know. Tina's dad, they said, was hogging theirs, so . . .

They're fine, Tim. Tina's mom keeps coming upstairs and "dropping by," they said. She's driving them crazy.

TIM *(To Jane)*: Good. Good for her. *(To Richard)* They're eleven years old.

RICHARD: I'm now going to stay for supper.

JANE: So she guilted you, Richard.

RICHARD: That's not the reason.

JANE *(To Tim)*: Karen's cold is a lot better than it was a week ago.

TIM: She missed school on Monday.

JANE: You told me on the phone. And it's like she grew another inch in a week. *(Smiles)* I've only been gone a week—

TIM: It's the lipstick.

JANE: I'm surprised you've allowed that. *(To Richard)* How long can you stay? Or should I ask Barbara? *(Smiles)*

RICHARD: She didn't "guilt" me, Jane.

JANE *(Proving her point)*: You're now staying for supper. *(Noticing)* Someone left her scarf . . . *(Picks it up and sets it on a chair)* You need anything, Benjamin? You hungry?

BENJAMIN: I'm not hungry.

TIM *(To Richard)*: You had started to say something about your office.

RICHARD: About?

TIM: A young lawyer visiting . . . ?

RICHARD *(Remembers)*: From D.C. He's visiting us.

TIM *(To Jane)*: I asked Richard about "life in Albany."

RICHARD: And a few of us in Andrew's office, we get together and tell the young man—make sure when you meet him, ask Andrew where *he* went to law school. *(Smiles)*

TIM: What?

RICHARD: We want the kid to think this would only be polite. This kid went to Harvard. But we all know where Andrew went.

TIM: Where?

JANE: He told me this.

RICHARD: *Albany. Albany Law.* Not exactly Harvard. Or— *("his alma mater")* Columbia. *(Smiles)* The kid doesn't know this. So we're hoping he'll innocently ask. And we'll get to see—"it."

TIM: What's—"it"?

RICHARD: The—"expression" Andrew Cuomo gets when you know he's about to reach down someone's throat with his bare hands and pull out a beating heart. *(Laughs)* That expression. We hardly see it anymore. He really keeps it hidden now. He really wants to be president.

(As Jane heads into the kitchen with the garbage:)

JANE: You should eat something, Uncle. *I'm* hungry . . .

TIM: What happened when this kid—?

RICHARD: He didn't. The kid didn't. He chickened out. He's smarter than we thought.

(First Barbara and then Marian enter from upstairs. Barbara is in slippers and a sweater now. Marian hasn't changed.)

TIM: Jane's back. She's in the kitchen.

BARBARA *(Going to the table)*: Let's see what our choices are, Marian . . .

RICHARD *(To Marian)*: Everything all right upstairs?

MARIAN *(That was a dumb thing to say)*: No.

RICHARD: I meant, Marian . . .

MARIAN: Adam's sort of sleeping.

(Then:)

(To Richard) He's dying.

RICHARD: I know.

MARIAN: I told Adam's mom I'd bring her up some food. And Nadine . . . Let's see—what do we think a Jamaican will like of this . . . ? His mother seems to eat anything . . .

(They watch her.)

That was nice . . . I don't think he recognized anyone, but they got to see him. Look at all this food . . .

(Barbara nods, then:)

BARBARA: Chicken. Chicken's always good.

(Marian starts to fill a paper plate.)

(Over the various bowls, to Marian) On some of these, they didn't write their names, Marian . . .

MARIAN: I think I know who brought what.

TIM *(To say something)*: I've been asking Richard about "life in Albany."

BARBARA: I'd like to hear all about his "Albany life" . . .

RICHARD *(To Tim)*: Andrew's giving himself a birthday party in a couple weeks. Fifty thousand dollars a ticket.

TIM: Jesus.

RICHARD: Maybe Sandra Lee is cooking and so it'll be worth it . . . *(Another thought)* Do we really need more casinos?

BARBARA *(Still looking at the bowls, etc.)*: Marian, look at this— they're hoping we scrub that off for them . . .

MARIAN *(After a quick glance)*: I know who that is.

(Jane enters with plates.)

JANE: I thought we deserved real plates. Is that okay, Barbara? *(Nodding to the scarf)* Someone left a scarf . . .

(Barbara goes to look at it.)

BARBARA: And real glasses too. I hate these plastic things. *(About the scarf)* I think it's the mom's. I'll take it upstairs . . . *(She sets it aside)* I'll get glasses . . .

JANE *(Calls)*: And napkins. Real silverware!

MARIAN *(To Jane, about the plate)*: For Helen. And Nadine. We hope she eats chicken.

JANE: Nadine? You should give her a real plate.

MARIAN: I've already . . .

JANE: Here I'll hold this . . .

(They begin to transfer the food onto a real plate.)

I thought you said Nadine brought her own food?

What if she came down and saw *us* with real plates? She'd get the totally wrong idea about us.

What else? You said the mom eats anything . . .

MARIAN: So, tell us all about Albany, Richard . . .

RICHARD: Marian, I hadn't realized how much Andrew and Albany are like this . . . *(Holds his fingers together—they are very tight)* I hadn't realized that before I moved there.

Before living there. That penny just hadn't dropped. You have to live there . . .

MARIAN: You going to sit there, Uncle?

BENJAMIN: Where do you want me to sit?

MARIAN: It's fine.

JANE: Should we put some of these chairs back in the other rooms?

MARIAN: Quite a few people said they wanted to come back tomorrow . . .

JANE: I thought you were against that.

MARIAN: His "baby sister" liked the idea. *(To Tim)* She says the Beekman Arms is—"so cute," Tim.

RICHARD *(Continues)*: Marian, I'm betting that Andrew first met Gillibrand there—in Albany . . . They both pretty much grew up there . . .

(Barbara returns with a tray of glasses, silverware and napkins.)

Now Gillibrand and Albany, that's really . . . *(Same gesture with the fingers)* They're like . . .

MARIAN: Are they?

RICHARD: Big time.

BARBARA *(To Marian)*: That can't still be warm.

MARIAN: I think it's fine, Barbara. *(The plates)* I'll take these upstairs.

BARBARA: Tell them both that they can join us . . .

MARIAN: I'll tell them . . . His mom's not going to want to . . .

BARBARA *(To Jane)*: I put the salad in the refrigerator. *(To Richard)* What are you talking about?

MARIAN: "Albany."

(Marian goes with the plates.)

BARBARA: She makes it sound like it's Sodom and Gomorrah.

RICHARD *(Smiles)*: Not far from the truth. I tell my friends, Tim, I have jumped into the muck, I just hope I can float. *(Smiles)*

BENJAMIN: What does that mean?

BARBARA: I don't know, Benjamin. *(To Richard)* So why live there?

RICHARD: I work there. *(Then continues to Tim)* Gillibrand. Her grandmother . . . Big time Albany. I never really "got" Gillibrand—the idea, the concept of "Gillibrand"—but then you go to Albany. I really get it now.

BARBARA: I'm glad . . . *(To Benjamin)* Do you know who Gillibrand is, Uncle?

BENJAMIN: No.

RICHARD: That's my point—people don't know who the hell she really is.

TIM: I should come up to Albany and let you show me around.

RICHARD: You should. Everybody should. *(Looks to Barbara, then)* Jane had a good time, didn't you?

JANE: I did.

RICHARD: You weren't bored.

BARBARA: I've been to Albany. *(To Jane)* The mall. *(Fixing up the casseroles, etc.)* So you had a good time with Richard, Jane? In Albany?

JANE: I did.

RICHARD *(Over this)*: Jane . . .

JANE: What??

RICHARD: Tell them about that statue in the museum. It's a good story.

JANE: It's not really a story—

RICHARD: Tell them.

JANE: More of an—observation . . . *(To Barbara)* I was in the Albany museum— *(To Tim)* Doing my research. I was not slacking off. I think Tuesday? And there's a medieval statue there of a naked girl. Upstairs, right as you go in. She is looking down at her hand, holding something. I just stared at her for the longest time. There was something so familiar about her. I couldn't figure out what.

BARBARA: Did she look like someone—?

JANE: No. No. Then I realized: she was in the exact pose of someone scrolling through their iPhone.
Same look. Exact same look.

(Jane puts down her plate and demonstrates. Richard laughs. He shows Benjamin how the statue was standing.)

But she was holding a cross.
BENJAMIN: I don't understand.
JANE *(Over this)*: It was just an observation . . .
RICHARD: I'm not sure one week in Albany is really enough—
JANE: It's enough.

(Barbara laughs.)

We'll do it as a buffet, don't you think? And just sit where we want . . .
BARBARA *(To Richard and Tim)*: Gentlemen, come and serve yourselves.

(The men move to the table.)

I'll get you yours, Benjamin.

(They begin to serve themselves.)

RICHARD *(To say something)*: How's the "inn," Uncle? I hadn't asked.
BENJAMIN: I don't know. Fine. *(To Barbara)* Isn't it?
TIM *(Another thought)*: Benjamin's in a singing group now.
RICHARD: Really? Uncle, I'm not surprised.
BENJAMIN: Am I?
RICHARD *(Over this, to Jane)*: They were just singing—
TIM *(Over this)*: "Gentlemen Singing." That's on the schedule. He and four other "gentlemen," they perform once a month. We all go down to see him . . .

RICHARD: Do you . . .

BARBARA *(To Richard)*: You should come too, Richard . . . A minister visited Benjamin last week when I was there.

JANE *(To Richard)*: You won't believe this.

BARBARA: She—the minister is a she—spoke to him— *(To Benjamin)* like you were five years old. Didn't she?

BENJAMIN: Did she?

RICHARD: That's terrible.

BARBARA *(Over this)*: She said—"You know what song *I* love to sing?" I don't think you said anything, did you?

(No response.)

Sometimes he remembers. Just when you think he's not going to . . . *(Continues)* So the minister says, "I love to sing—" and she starts singing to *Benjamin*, this very accomplished, respected artist, to this man here—she begins singing, *(Sings in a high voice)* "It's a small world after all . . ."

(The others groan, "Oh god, no!" Laughter.)

What you have to put up with—just getting old. Right, Benjamin.

BENJAMIN: Right. I have to put up with a lot.

BARBARA: See what we all have to look forward to.

(And that quiets everyone down. Pause as they serve themselves.)

TIM: The fries look good. A little cold . . .

BARBARA: Look at what Heidi wrote on them.

RICHARD *(Reads a label)*: "Look Adam—'Freedom Fries.'"

JANE: He liked that . . . I could tell.

BARBARA: Could you really?

JANE: It's something he would like.

(Then:)

(The obvious) He'll hate Bush to his last breath . . .

RICHARD *(To Jane)*: I could tell them the coconut story.

TIM: What's that?

JANE: Another Albany—

RICHARD: Should I?

JANE: I don't know, Richard.

RICHARD *(As he continues to serve himself)*: Mario Cuomo, the dad, he tells a funny story about a man named—Dan O'Connell—O'Connell was the behind-the-scenes political boss of bosses of Albany for years and years. In Mario Cuomo's story, Dan and another guy get marooned—on a desert island.

BARBARA *(To Jane)*: Is this true?

JANE: It's a story, Barbara.

RICHARD: And there is only one coconut. Dan suggests—

BARBARA: On the whole island? *(To Benjamin, giving him his plate)* I'll get you more if you want more . . .

RICHARD: One. They take a vote on who should eat the one coconut. The other guy says, but that doesn't make sense—

BARBARA: That's what I was going to say.

RICHARD *(Over this)*: —we'll only each vote for ourselves.

BARBARA: Right.

RICHARD *(Continues)*: No, no let's try, let's vote, says Dan. So— they vote and when the vote is counted, Dan has won— 110 to 1.

(They politely laugh.)

BARBARA: Albany sounds like a really interesting place . . .

(They are sitting down now.)

How long have you lived in Albany now? I forget.

RICHARD: No you haven't.

(He pours drinks for everyone.)

BARBARA: And it's how far away? *(Then)* Not that far . . .

RICHARD *(To Tim)*: "The Albany Mayor for Life"? That's what they called him. Corning. He's dead now. He kept in a closet in his office—glass containers—

JANE: Richard, please. He told me this.

RICHARD: You're right. I'll tell you, Tim, later.

JANE *(Over this)*: We're eating.

BARBARA: What? Now I'm curious.

JANE: You don't want to—

BARBARA: Tell us, Richard. If it is *so* interesting. I want to know all about "life in Albany." We should know more. It's our capital . . .

(He hesitates, then:)

RICHARD: Glass containers filled with preserving liquid—and in each one was a different . . .

TIM: What?

BARBARA: What???

RICHARD: A different animal's—penis.

I'm told, the mayor would bring these penises out when he wanted to make a point to someone . . . To convince them to—I suppose, be on his side.

(No one knows what to say.)

Like trophies . . . Andrew likes to tell that story . . . *(To Tim, as if this explains everything)* Albany . . .

(Short pause. Marian returns.)

MARIAN: Nadine was fine with chicken . . . The mother eats anything.

BARBARA: I made you a plate . . .

(They begin to eat.)

MARIAN: Thank you. *(Sitting)* What did I miss?

(The lights fade.)

A Shared History

A short time later. Barbara is standing, the others sit and eat.

BENJAMIN: What did I do? I don't remember.
RICHARD: I should bring you up to Albany, Uncle. No one
    remembers anything up there, from one day to the next.
BENJAMIN: Then I'd fit right in.

(Laughter.)

JANE: You would . . .
TIM: You visited Barbara's class today, Benjamin.
MARIAN: Get it, Barbara. Show Richard.
BARBARA *(Stops; to Marian)*: Should I look in upstairs?
MARIAN *(Shaking her head)*: It's quiet.

(Barbara goes off.)

(Then, to anyone) Nadine says he's not in pain now . . . I
meant to tell all of you that.

(They eat. Then:)

RICHARD: I always say I want to take Barbara's class. *(To Benjamin)* Did you enjoy visiting her class, Benjamin? Was it fun?

BENJAMIN: I think so.

TIM *(To Benjamin)*: Do you know what today is?

BENJAMIN: No. What's today?

MARIAN: Jane, did you tell Richard about . . . ?

RICHARD: About what?

MARIAN: Today—and Adam.

JANE: I forgot. You should tell him. *(To Tim)* You know.

(Tim nods.
Barbara enters with a pile of papers and some newspapers.
She listens as she sits and organizes them.)

MARIAN *(Explaining)*: When Adam learned he had the cancer . . .

BENJAMIN: What's today?

JANE *(To Benjamin, pats his hand)*: Sh-sh . . .

MARIAN *(Continues)*: You know he had started smoking again.

RICHARD: No.

BARBARA: After Evan died.

MARIAN: He tried to hide it—

BARBARA *(As she goes through the papers)*: He started again. Just like Peter Jennings—after 9/11 . . .

MARIAN *(Continues)*: He told me later . . . I wasn't with him then. We still weren't speaking. He asked his doctor—so how long? Oh, about a few months, the doctor said. Adam—you know Adam—says: could you be more specific, Doctor? So the doctor tells him: two months. *(Then)* Adam immediately does a quick calculation— *(To Barbara)* it's what he told us . . .

(Barbara nods.)

And said—oh, he'd make it longer than that. He planned on making it well into November. At least as far as the twenty-second. He wanted to be around for this. He didn't want to miss this.

(Then:)

(Proving Adam's point) He's made it to today . . .

JANE *(Quietly to Benjamin)*: Today's November 22nd, Uncle . . .

RICHARD: What do you think he was afraid of missing? Today doesn't seem to be about anything . . .

BARBARA *(Shuffling through the papers, about the papers)*: I asked them at the beginning of the week to talk to their parents—or grandparents—it's been that long—

RICHARD: Your students?

BARBARA *(Nodding)*: It doesn't seem that long ago—and see what today means to them. And then I asked them: "What does today mean to you?" If anything. If nothing, come back with that. Which—is what most did come back with. That surprised me. I guess it shouldn't. *(Smiles)* One senior she said—she's very smart—she said for her it was a "mythological time"—"when heroes died."

TIM *(Smiles)*: I like that . . .

RICHARD: Fifty years ago is now "a mythological time"—?

BARBARA: Another said—his grandmother—she is always worrying, still—and especially, he said, during the last election—about an *Obama* assassination. Because of the tensions? . . . He didn't say why. His grandma just told him there was a "Kennedy-aura thing" surrounding Obama.

JANE: Is that still true?

RICHARD: "Hope and change . . ."

MARIAN: Richard . . .

TIM *(To Richard)*: "If you like your health insurance plan, you can—"

MARIAN: They're fixing that, Tim.

RICHARD: I think Obama's dilemma is he wants to look in the mirror in the morning and see someone who is still good. But for a politician isn't that useless, even corrosive? He's going to end up a very bitter man. You sort of see that already happening . . .

JANE *(To Marian)*: Billy doesn't have health insurance. His job is quote-unquote part-time.

MARIAN: So is he trying to sign up?—

RICHARD: "Trying." That is the operative word.

JANE *(Over this)*: He says he's healthy. Why the hell should he pay for sick old people?

MARIAN: Because he's going to be a sick old person one day.

JANE: Oh I'll tell him *that*, Marian. *That* will convince him. He says, they've taken his whole generation and are just screwing with them.

(Then:)

BARBARA: Should I . . . ?

TIM: Jane and I were in the city a few weeks ago. Down on East 4th. To see a friend's show. We got out of the subway and there were all these young people sitting on the sidewalk.

JANE: I told you this, Richard. *(To Marian and Barbara)* They were filthy. Hands just caked in dirt. And they all had dogs with them. And backpacks. Like some lost society. *(To Tim)* That's what you said. *(To the others)* What are we losing? What have we given up on?

MARIAN: De Blasio's going to try and fix that. Isn't he? At least in the city. Isn't he?

(No response.)

BARBARA *(Continues)*: Anyway, one student brought up the sex . . . Marilyn Monroe. It was all over the map . . .

MARIAN: Barbara told me, that her point was to try and make it—present. For the kids.

BARBARA: That's why . . . *(Hands a scrapbook clipping to Benjamin)* Benjamin. They love it when Benjamin comes to class.

BENJAMIN: Do they? Who?

BARBARA: My students . . .

JANE: You're an actor.

BENJAMIN: I am. I'm an actor.

BARBARA: Do you have your glasses?

JANE *(Continues)*: They've seen him in movies on TV.

BARBARA: Anyway, Benjamin gets their attention.

TIM: I'll bet.

BARBARA *(Pointing out)*: There. Remember, only what's marked. Like you did today.

BENJAMIN: From here?

BARBARA: Yes. Right there.

BENJAMIN *(Reads)*: "Dallas. November 22nd. President John Fitzgerald Kennedy was shot and killed by an assassin today." *(He looks up)*

BARBARA: Not today, Benjamin. A long time ago.

TIM *(To Benjamin)*: Fifty years ago . . .

BARBARA: Tom Wicker. Remember him? It's such simple prose. Little details, strung together—it's like a poem.

BENJAMIN *(Reads)*: "Vice President Lyndon Baines Johnson, who was riding in the third car behind Mr. Kennedy's, was sworn in as the thirty-sixth President of the United States ninety-nine minutes after Mr. Kennedy's death."

BARBARA: You can see the writer—as he grasps for facts—like someone drowning, grabbing at the floating wreckage of his ship. He's trying to make it real—"ninety-nine minutes" in this case—in order to try and make sense of something. Real for us or real for him?

BENJAMIN *(Reads)*: "Mr. Johnson is fifty-five years old; Mr. Kennedy was forty-six."

BARBARA: The "is" and the "was." I am always so taken aback when I see that he was only forty-six. My kids didn't understand at all.

JANE: No, no.

MARIAN: How could they?

BENJAMIN *(Reads)*: "Mrs. Kennedy looked steadily at the floor. She still wore the raspberry-colored suit in which she had greeted welcoming crowds. But she had taken off the matching pillbox hat she wore earlier in the day."

BARBARA: Some kids laughed at that. The mentioning of a "pillbox hat." Absurdity is as much a part of death and tragedy, as it is a part of life . . .

JANE: Did they understand that?

BARBARA *(Obviously)*: No.

BENJAMIN *(Continues)*: "The ceremony, delayed about five minutes for Mrs. Kennedy's arrival, took place in the private presidential cabin in the rear of the plane. No accurate listing of those present could be obtained. Mrs. Kennedy stood at the left of Mr. Johnson, her eyes and face showing signs of weeping that had apparently shaken her since she left the hospital not long before."

BARBARA: "Apparently shaken." "Apparently." That's—the very first speculation the writer has made.

JANE: He just snuck it in.

(Barbara nods.)

BENJAMIN *(Reads)*: "As Judge Hughes read the brief oath, her eyes, too, were red from weeping."

BARBARA: There's a comma before and after the "too." So—not just "her eyes too." But "her eyes—too." It's a small thing. But I wonder if that was a subtle way, maybe I'm wrong, a subtle way of the writer's to emphasize that all were weeping. Maybe even Mr. Wicker. "Her eyes—too."

TIM *(To Jane)*: That's interesting.

JANE: I don't think you're wrong, Barbara. *(To Tim)* He is a poet.

BENJAMIN *(Continues)*: "'I do solemnly swear that I will perform the duties of the President of the United States to the best of my ability and defend, protect and preserve the Constitution of the United States.' Those thirty-four words made Lyndon Baines Johnson, one-time farmboy and schoolteacher, the president."

TIM: "Thirty-four words."

BENJAMIN: "At 2:46, seven minutes after he had become president, one hundred and six minutes after Mr. Kennedy had become the fourth American president to succumb to an assassin's wounds, the white-and-red jet took off for Washington."

BARBARA: The utter simplicity. We're reading *King Lear* now. It's the same with Shakespeare—there are times when language gets stripped down to almost nothing.

When Lear says about the dead Cordelia: "No, no, no, no."

One more thing . . .

BENJAMIN *(Reads)*: "The doctors said it was impossible to determine immediately whether the wounds had been caused by *on* bullet or two."

BARBARA: Right. That's just how it's written. It's a typo.

(He hands her back the clipping and she begins to pass it around.)

The *Times* back then, it prided itself on not making typos. They were actually very rare back then. So even this shows . . . Doesn't it? Even the proofreaders were struggling. Even a typo tells a story. "*On* bullet or two . . ."

(Pause. They look at the "typo." Then:)

TIM: What else did you show them, Barbara?

BARBARA: I showed them this, Tim.

(Barbara hands out the things she's collected: other newspapers, period magazines, etc.)

JANE *(Opening up a big Dallas newspaper with the headline; reads)*: "PRESIDENT DEAD, CONNALLY SHOT."

RICHARD: Where'd you get this—?

BARBARA: Tim—

TIM: When I visited my father in the summer. I had some time in Dallas. I'd always wanted to go to that museum there. They sell those. It's a reprint . . . But of the whole paper.

And that's what is really interesting. The ads and everything . . .

BARBARA: The kids loved that, Tim.

JANE *(Seeing an ad)*: "$2.99 comfort bra."

BARBARA: They liked that.

(Laughter.)

TIM *(To Jane)*: Show Benjamin.

JANE *(As she shows Benjamin)*: "Pre-Christmas sale." That's right, it was before Christmas.

TIM: Like now.

JANE: Right.

BARBARA *(Standing)*: Who wants more of something?

RICHARD *(Engrossed in the stuff)*: We can serve ourselves, Barbara. Sit down.

(As they look through the newspapers, etc.:)

BARBARA: I also asked my kids—this was their assignment for earlier in the week, besides just talking to their parents. I said, could you somehow try and connect the Kennedys to us. To yourselves. To our county, Dutchess. To Rhinebeck.

TIM: One kid—

JANE: How do you know?

TIM: They had Karen and me over to dinner the other night. I told you this. *(Continues)* One kid said, well Bill Clinton went to Gigi's during Chelsea's wedding weekend.

(Laughter.)

The connection was that they were both presidents—

RICHARD *(To Barbara)*: Did that count?

BARBARA *(Shrugs)*: My favorite was that same senior I mentioned; she learned that one of John Kennedy's sisters, Rosemary . . .

RICHARD: The one who had the lobotomy.

BARBARA: After the lobotomy—this was in the forties—guess where she was sent? Where the home was? Guess. Guess. *(Then)* She lived there for years. Beacon. Beacon, Uncle. *(To everyone, amazed)* Beacon . . .

BENJAMIN: Why is that—?

JANE: Your "inn" is in Beacon, Uncle.

TIM: Called Craig House. The building's still there. Zelda Fitzgerald also was put there.

BARBARA: And Jackie Kennedy went to Vassar. Five or six of them got that. They liked knowing that.

MARIAN: Robert Kennedy Jr. runs River Keeper.

BARBARA: Someone had that too. Tim, you found one—

TIM: It may not count. It's not about Kennedy, but it's about a presidential assassination and—Rhinebeck.

BARBARA *(To Tim)*: I told them about this this morning. They were really fascinated. I could tell. They all know the Rhinecliff station.

TIM *(His story)*: April, 1865.

RICHARD: So you mean Lincoln—

TIM: The train station in Rhinecliff—Amtrak wasn't there yet—

MARIAN: Oh the good ol' days.

BARBARA: So the trains still ran on time!

(Laughter.)

TIM: It's all draped in flags and the black of mourning. Men, women, children stand on both sides of the track. It's night. Moon on the water. They hold torches. And the funeral train is heading north to— *(Looks at Richard)* Albany where the body will lie in state for a while in the capital. But the train, instead of just chugging through, mysteriously stops. In Rhinecliff.

(Benjamin is now listening.)

According to legend, a William Carroll, from Rhinebeck, is summoned to the train. Carroll is the Rhinebeck mortician. As soon as he arrives he is led up onto the flag-draped train; the steam engine moaning as it just sits there, waiting; and he's taken into a small candlelit room, where—there lies the body of the president. The hole in the president's head—made by the assassin's bullet—has opened. Perhaps maybe the movement of the train, maybe some other reason—but it has opened and it needs to be sewn up.

About twenty minutes later, Carroll, Rhinebeck's own William Carroll, black bag in tow, is helped back down onto the station platform, mission accomplished. He refuses any money and remains just standing there, as the train now again on its way, fades slowly into the night, while everyone, including now William Carroll, waves good-bye to the president . . .

A little Rhinebeck history, Benjamin.

JANE *(To Richard)*: Tim has become consumed—

TIM: If I'm going to live here.

JANE: What about me?

TIM: If *we* are, then . . . We should know about where we live. All that's here . . .

RICHARD: You mean Rhinebeck.

JANE *(To Tim)*: I'm not criticizing. I think it's good. He still worries that he's going to be trapped . . .

BARBARA *(To Tim)*: It takes time . . .

(They eat.)

You're not eating, Benjamin.

BENJAMIN: I'm not hungry.

TIM *(Changing back to the Kennedy subject)*: I started reading a book about Kennedy's dad? The dad had already had his stroke, when Kennedy was killed. When they told him—and obviously, Barbara, what you said made me think of this. About the Shakespeare.

When the father was told about his son, the only words
he could say, because of the stroke, were—"No, no, no,
no . . ."

(The lights fade.)

Speech Acts

---

*A short time later. Barbara has opened a small journal that she
brought in earlier with the newspapers and papers.*
   Benjamin is in the middle of reading. The others eat.

BENJAMIN *(Reads)*: "An older actor tells me that the spells in
   Macbeth by the witches are based upon real magic. And
   therefore you conjure evil every night, as actors we conjure whatever it is we're supposed to conjure—and that
   was this actor's explanation why most productions of *Macbeth* have accidents." We conjure . . .
TIM: I've never heard that explanation . . .
BENJAMIN: We conjure . . .

(As Benjamin turns pages in the journal:)

BARBARA: I thought you would be interested in this, Tim.
TIM: I am.
RICHARD: How did you get—?
MARIAN: She just said—
JANE *(For the second time)*: When Barbara visited Chicago last
   month—
RICHARD: I know Barbara visited— But who—?
BARBARA: Uncle Fred's wife had it. She had it with Mom's old
   stuff. When I was looking for Mom's scrapbook for the

Kennedy things, I found that. Benjamin must have been visiting them at some time and left it there in Chicago.

MARIAN: Most of it's about theater.

BARBARA: I think it's *all* about theater.

RICHARD *(To Jane)*: I remembered about Barbara's trip to Chicago.

MARIAN *(To Benjamin, about the notebook)*: I'm sure you don't remember that notebook.

BENJAMIN *(Looking through the notebook)*: How do you know?

(The others smile.)

BARBARA *(To Benjamin)*: Does it look familiar?

BENJAMIN: The handwriting . . .

BARBARA: Besides that.

Years ago, I remember you saying you wanted to write a book about the theater, Uncle. I think that's what . . . Your notes. *(To the others)* His notes. For his theater book.

BENJAMIN *(Reading)*: "It should be the most unnatural place to be. Talking as if in a normal voice so perhaps a big audience can hear or feel or see or whatever. You're doing it again and again night after night. You're doing it at a funny time of night, when most people are going home or are home. There's nothing normal or natural about it, you'd think. But it can be the place where you feel most at home."

JANE *(To Tim)*: You've said things like that . . .

BENJAMIN *(Another page, reads)*: "Barbara tells me a story about how she'd run backstage . . ."

BARBARA: When I was a kid.

BENJAMIN: ". . . in the hope that if she got to me fast enough in my dressing room she'd find—the character I'd just been playing. But no matter how fast she'd run she never got there in time. But she never found *me* either at first."

BARBARA: I think Mom told me I once even cried.

BENJAMIN: "The person there wasn't yet 'Uncle Benjamin' and it wasn't still the character either, something halfway in between, she said." "Halfway."

BARBARA: I think I just wanted you to pay more attention to me. *(Takes his arm)* I still do . . . *(Smiles, he smiles)*

JANE: You are so handsome, Uncle.

(Benjamin gets up.)

BENJAMIN: Can I read this outside?

BARBARA: It's stopped raining, Marian.

MARIAN: You want a cigarette?

BENJAMIN: I want a cigarette.

BARBARA: He wants a cigarette. Stay in the backyard.

(Benjamin goes.)

He has packs hidden all around the kitchen . . .

TIM: How does he remember where they're hidden?

JANE: You remember what you want to remember.

MARIAN: They're not really "hidden."

BARBARA: "He was something halfway in between." He must feel like that all the time . . .

MARIAN: Richard, Barbara found a photograph stuck in that notebook. Mom and Benjamin in swimsuits. Some place with palm trees. Uncle keeps it at his "inn . . ."

BARBARA *(To Richard)*: You haven't seen Uncle for a while, Richard.

RICHARD: He seems okay.

BARBARA: Does he? Marian thought it was the medicine. The "inn" makes him take all this medicine.

MARIAN: But then we found all these pills stuffed between the cushions of our couch. He comes home every weekend, and stuffs his pills into the couch . . .

BARBARA: So it's not the medicine . . .

RICHARD: Is that safe to just . . . ?

(Then:)

JANE *(To the others)*: Tim and this teacher at Bard— *(To Richard)* Tim's teaching a class there. *(To Tim)* You're not just a waiter.

TIM: Just a workshop. Voice. For a few weeks.

RICHARD *(To Jane)*: You told me. *(To Tim)* She's very proud.

BARBARA: There's nothing wrong with being a waiter.

JANE *(Over this)*: And they've been talking, Tim and this teacher—

TIM: We know each other from Boston—

JANE *(Over this)*: —about writing a book together—or an essay? For a theater magazine. *(To Tim)* It sort of relates to what Benjamin was reading to us. His—notes. *(To Barbara)* He's still having auditions all the time.

RICHARD *(To Tim)*: What's the essay . . . ?

TIM: Comes from a British philosopher. Our idea. We're going to write it together. He's a good writer.

JANE: So are you—

TIM: This philosopher developed a theory—of what he called "speech acts"? Those moments in life when by saying something we are also doing something.

MARIAN: What does that mean?

JANE: Tell them. Explain it. It's interesting.

TIM: When I say, "I promise," I'm in fact—making a promise. *Doing* a promise. Speaking becomes then also an *act*. A speech act. In a marriage ceremony, for example, the saying of "I do"—given the right circumstances—means you're now married.

JANE: And Tim's always felt that that somehow relates to theater. Speech acts.

TIM: Maybe it's nothing. I'm not sure how to explain it exactly.

JANE *(To Tim over the end of this)*: Tim's friend, the teacher, thinks it could make an interesting article or book.

It could be good.

You get it published, and your name gets exposed in this magazine. Theater people read it—it helps, gets you noticed. Helps your acting.

TIM: That's not why—

JANE: That's what you said. *(To the others)* Tim is so worried that he's going to be forgotten, here in Rhinebeck.

TIM: You've told them that.

MARIAN: John was telling me . . .

(This has gotten their interest.)

. . . this was *when* we were still seeing each other—

RICHARD: Maybe now . . . After . . .

MARIAN: Adam's not dead *yet*, Richard.

RICHARD: I didn't mean—

BARBARA *(Explaining to Richard)*: John's moved on.

MARIAN: I knew he would. Why shouldn't he? *(Shrugs)*

BARBARA: John and Marian are no longer together.

MARIAN *(To Barbara)*: I saw them in the CVS, she was just staring at him. *(Shrugs)* He told me about a famous painter— he was painting a portrait. A nude. And one day, he is painting her breasts, his model's breasts, and he suddenly has the feeling—that they are empty. The model's chest is empty. Then two days later, she commits suicide. That was interesting. "Art—" *(To Tim)* "whatever sort of art," John said, "maybe it shows us things that otherwise we can't see with our own eyes."

(To Barbara, explaining) He *("Tim")* was talking about art *doing* things . . .

(Then:)

JANE: Growing up around Uncle—around an actor, it was always difficult for me to know what was true and what wasn't true.

BARBARA: Was that just because he was an actor?

(Laughter.)

JANE: Maybe. But, still, all the "acting." Was I the only one who felt this way?
MARIAN *(Over this, to Barbara)*: We've talked about this too . . .

(Barbara nods.)

JANE: Benjamin being an actor—how strange or odd was that for us? Richard?
RICHARD: I have never thought about it.
JANE *(Continues)*: Didn't you ever wonder—what's acting and what's real? I think there are times when the acting can be more real—more emotionally raw and real . . .
BARBARA *(A joke)*: Tim's an actor too.

(Laughter.)

TIM: I'm never real. *(He laughs)*
JANE: He has an actress friend— *(Turns to Tim)* Kathy . . . Old girlfriend.
TIM: That was a long—
MARIAN: The one whose couch you slept on in Chicago?
JANE: Another one. *(She "rolls her eyes")*
TIM: You told them about—?
JANE *(To Marian)*: You don't forget anything.
RICHARD *(Helping him out)*: I'm listening.
JANE: She had the part of Shakespeare's Rosalind. You know that play?—
TIM: They know it—
RICHARD: Do we?
JANE: Tell them. This is funny. Even if it's a bit—chauvinistic.
RICHARD: Now I'm interested.
TIM: Rosalind literally runs the Forest of Arden. She has complete control. Doing this, doing that. Incredibly orga-

nized. And my friend, she was, shall we say, not the most organized "person"—

JANE: He means "woman." Just say it.

TIM: "Female"—on this planet. But she suddenly—at home, during the run of the play—became super organized and efficient—in her private life, in her home life. Washes everything. Cleans the floors. No more dishes piled up in the sink. Her husband— *(Turns to Jane)* She's been married now for like . . . I don't know. *(Continues)* Her husband says to her after the run of the play is over, and their apartment's a mess again—he says, in a hopeful, even desperate voice: "Kath, couldn't you play a few more parts like Rosalind?"

(Laughter.)

MARIAN: Are we making too much noise?

BARBARA: Adam can't hear—

MARIAN: I meant his mother—hearing us . . . Laughing.

(Then:)

BARBARA *(To Tim)*: Benjamin can put that in his book about the theater.

MARIAN *(To Tim)*: Or like a prayer . . .

RICHARD: What? What is?

MARIAN: Tim's—what did you call it? Speech what?

TIM: Speech acts.

MARIAN: Prayer. Praying. To speak a prayer is an act of faith, isn't it? It's *doing* your faith. By speaking . . .

TIM: I think he even talks about prayer too. The philosopher. In a way like that . . .

(No one knows what to say. Then:)

I have another one for Benjamin's book.

BARBARA: What is that?

(Marian looks toward the living room.)

She can't hear, Marian. They're on the other side of the house.

JANE *(To Tim)*: Go ahead.

TIM: The great playwright—Beckett?

(They know who he is.)

A friend of a friend of mine was actually doing one of Beckett's plays and Beckett himself is directing him. This is obviously years and years ago. In Europe. The play's a monologue, and he has to talk into a tape recorder and shuffle around this little room. In slippers.

Each day the designer brings in another pair of slippers for him to try. And each day Beckett says, "No, no, not right!" This goes on and on, days pass. They've tried twenty pairs of different slippers. Until finally the completely exasperated Beckett leaves rehearsal, goes to his nearby apartment, and comes back with—a pair of old, beaten-up bedroom slippers. The actor puts them on.

They sort of fit. He shuffles around. Beckett "listens." And Beckett then says, "Now that's what I was looking for."

BARBARA: They were *his* slippers.

(Tim nods.)

MARIAN: So he wanted just to hear his own footsteps on the stage?

TIM: I suppose to him what he'd written was—personal . . .

MARIAN: But how would the audience know they were *his* slippers?

TIM: Maybe it didn't matter to him. Maybe, he thought, they would just somehow know that it was—true.

(The lights fade.)

By the Wayside

A short time later. Jane reads from a small notebook.

JANE *(Reads)*: "The travelers should have a notebook always at hand . . ." I wrote this down to give to Benjamin. Richard's idea.

BARBARA: Do you always keep that—? *("notebook")*

JANE: A notebook? I do. I'm a writer, Barbara.

MARIAN *(Getting up)*: I think I heard something . . .

(Marian stands to listen. They all listen. Then:)

BARBARA *(As a joke)*: Marian, I'll bet she writes down what we say . . . *(No reaction, suddenly)* You don't, do you?

JANE: Barbara . . .

BARBARA *(To Marian)*: I was just joking.

JANE: Actually, sometimes I do.

RICHARD: Keep reading. This is interesting.

MARIAN *(To Jane)*: What is that from?

JANE: *How to Observe Morals and Manners.* Written in 1838. I came across it in Albany during my research.

MARIAN: I thought you were done with manners.

JANE: I'm not "done with—" I just happened across this.

BARBARA *(About the manners)*: You said if they're not going to publish your book—

JANE *(Over this)*: We thought Benjamin might be interested, Barbara . . . To put it in his journal. As inspiration to keep writing in his journal.

(Marian goes off to check upstairs.)

BARBARA *(After her)*: I didn't hear anything, Marian . . .

(Then:)

RICHARD *(To Jane)*: Read . . .

JANE *(Continues to read)*: "In all the countries of the world, groups of people by the wayside are the most eloquent pictures. The traveler who lets himself be whirled past them, unobservant or unrecording, loses more than any devices of inquiry at his inn can repair . . . Groups and scenes—because they reveal the thoughts of men—" *(Adds, to herself)* and women— *(Continues)* "should be as earnestly observed and should be noted on the instant."

(Then:)

(Closing the notebook) How to Observe Morals and Manners. 1838 . . .

RICHARD: I'm so glad Uncle's still keeping his journal. Good for him.

JANE: Good for Barbara.

BARBARA: He forgets sometimes . . .

RICHARD: I should start doing that. Keeping a journal . . .

BARBARA: Are there things, Richard, you feel you need to work out? With a journal?

RICHARD: To remember things, Barbara.

(Jane has been thumbing through her notebook. She comes upon another entry:)

JANE: I wrote something else down. In Albany I saw a small show at the museum—the history of the book *1001 Nights*? Very fascinating. I didn't know anything . . . Richard thinks they're trying to reach out to the Arab community—

RICHARD: It's the state museum . . .

BARBARA: Is there a big Arab community—? *("in Albany")*

RICHARD: For the whole state. And there is—in the whole state. Albany is our capital. We seem to forget that.

BARBARA: Do we? I think sometimes we'd like to.

RICHARD: There are interesting things to do in Albany. Ask
   Jane—

JANE: You wouldn't even go with me—

RICHARD: I have a job—

JANE *(To Barbara)*: He never really goes out anywhere—

RICHARD: That is so not true—

JANE: You told me you'd never been to the state museum. He
   just shuts himself away in his little apartment. *(Then back to
   the notebook)* Anyway, you know the story—Scheherazade,
   she has to keep telling stories to keep from being killed.

TIM: By her husband. He's already killed—

RICHARD: I don't shut myself away . . .

BARBARA *(To Jane)*: I know the story.

JANE *(As she looks in her notebook)*: There was a quote on the
   wall, from some famous author. This is what I wrote
   down: *(Reads)* "Every writer is Scheherazade."

BARBARA: Why . . . ?

JANE: Telling stories—to keep from dying.

(Marian returns.)

MARIAN: We've told Nadine that she can go. We can look after
   Adam tonight.

BARBARA: Are you sure—? Is she all right with—?

MARIAN: His mother's wishes.

   Nadine understood. She even said to me, that's not
   uncommon on nights like these. For the family . . .

   She hasn't yet figured out we're not his family. His
   mother's going to stretch out on the cot. It's fine.

BARBARA: And what could you say?

MARIAN: And what could I say. Nadine's getting her stuff
   together. Her car's on the street; I'll take her through the
   front. *(Starts to go)*

BARBARA *(Getting up)*: Should we say good-bye—?

MARIAN *(Stopping her)*: She's exhausted. And she'll come back
   tomorrow . . .

(Marian goes off.)

RICHARD: Where does Nadine live?

TIM *(Shrugs)*: Poughkeepsie? Newburgh?

JANE *(To Barbara)*: You think that's the right thing to do?

BARBARA: She's not a real nurse, she's an aide, so . . . If it's what
his mother wants . . .

You started to tell us about your book. The reason for
spending all week in Albany . . .

JANE: It's not really a book. It's at best a . . . *(Shrugs)*

TIM: You always say that.

JANE *(Ignoring this, continues)*: I spoke to the *Chronogram* about it.

TIM *(To Richard)*: Local thing. Very arty. Very "new" Rhinebeck.

RICHARD: Is that good?

JANE: I didn't find out as much as I had hoped to. They had
some good books, things on microfilm. I started out—just
diving into the Hudson River painters. But then I came
across—

TIM: What?

JANE *(Over this)*: And this was what I ended up mostly research-
ing. I don't know why they had this stuff in Albany.
Anyway—you obviously all know the painting—*George
Washington Crossing the Delaware*.

TIM: Sure.

(They obviously do. They eat.)

JANE: So—who painted this iconic American painting?

(Richard almost says something.)

I know you know. I told you. They don't know. Leutze.

TIM *(Joking: "of course")*: Leutze!

JANE: You don't know! Emanuel Leutze. A German, not an
American, a German. Who at the age of nine, came to
America, his parents fleeing political persecution in Ger-

many. He had some early success as a painter. But the
moment he had money in his pocket, he hurried back to
Düsseldorf, and carrying on his parents' political beliefs,
he sides with those radicals who are hoping to create a
united Germany.

TIM: When—?

JANE: Middle of nineteenth century. And he began looking
for a topic that would inspire—Germans. Something to
symbolize the turning tide of some revolution. And he
stumbles upon: General Washington crossing the Delaware River . . . *(She eats)*

So in his Düsseldorf studio, in the middle of Germany,
he procures authentic American costumes. And I suppose
for authenticity's sake—he decides, in fact insists, on only
real Americans posing for the guys in the boat, and for
General Washington. He starts sending friends out onto
the streets of Düsseldorf to find every real American they
can get their hands on. Any American. They're just drag-
ging them off the streets. Then—once in his studio, he plies
them with liquor and god knows what else. So soon he's got
a studio full of drunken Americans—on vacation . . . And
then—he paints. And that is what he painted. That's what
generations of Americans have found so deeply American
and "patriotic." *(Eats)*

RICHARD *(Eating)*: That's what schoolteachers have dragged
thousands of schoolkids to see . . .

JANE: My question is—what I'm asking in this essay, whenever
I get around to it—is: is that something we really want to
know? I mean, do I really want to look at that painting
and think—they were drunk? They're having a good time
in Düsseldorf and they're sauced?

Sometimes—and I was about to say this when we were
talking about the Kennedys and your class, Barbara. I wonder if sometimes—and Tim, you have kept saying this as
this anniversary approached—if sometimes it's best *not* to
see . . . Not to pick up the rock and look underneath . . .

(Short pause.)

(Eating) An essay about that.

(Then:)

BARBARA: If Marian were here, I know what she'd say.
JANE: What?
BARBARA: *That*—should be on NPR.

(They all laugh—that is so true.)

We were arguing about something the other day. I don't remember what. A recipe. A book. And she just held her hand like a traffic cop and said, "Stop it, Barbara, I heard it on NPR."

(Laughter.)

"It must be true!"

(Marian returns.)

MARIAN: What?
BARBARA: We're laughing at you.
MARIAN: What's new?
    Nadine gave him a kiss on his cheek.
    He's still not responding . . . She'll call in the morning, and come if we need her.
BARBARA: I thought you said—
MARIAN: *If* we need her. *(She sits)* So what about me were you laughing at?
RICHARD: That list is long. Where to begin?
BARBARA: NPR . . .
MARIAN: Why is that funny? Why does she think that's so funny? If it's on NPR . . . They know what they're doing . . .

(Stops herself; then) She said again, that noise he's making—
it's common. And Nadine thinks, he won't make it through
the night. I said we know that . . .

(No one knows what to do or say.
  The lights fade.)

Rhinebeck

A short time later. They hardly eat anymore.

JANE: I called Billy last night and told him about Adam.
  I keep thinking he'll react like a kid, but he's a grown-up.
  (To Marian) He sent his love to you. Unprompted.
MARIAN: And mine back.
JANE: He wanted to know if he should come—
MARIAN: No, no—
BARBARA *(Same time)*: He doesn't have to—
JANE *(Over this)*: I told him that . . . And that you two were
  divorced and . . . So—he's not going to come.
MARIAN: Good.
JANE: Not even to the funeral.
    Are you really sure that's okay?

(Marian nods.)

Billy asked if his dad were dying, would you all come.
Because *we're* divorced. *(She eats)* I told him of course
you'd come. That that's different.

(Then:)

(To Marian) Maybe, he said, you and John will come down
and see him some time this winter. There's some show at
the museum . . .

MARIAN: I liked going to Philadelphia.

JANE: I didn't tell him about you and John . . .

TIM *(To Jane)*: Billy okay?

JANE: We talked for a while. I don't know how we got started—
except of course Adam— Billy said a friend of his died.
Someone from Haverford. And he said there's no easy way
to destroy your Facebook page. No way to just update—
"Jane is dead." You just sit frozen in time until Facebook
can somehow verify with a death certificate, a notarized
letter from the parents, something like that—that you're
dead. So his friend's page is still up, and someone somehow
has gained access to it and is posting photos and videos via
her name. Billy said, it is as if she is still living online.

TIM: Someone dies, you want to do something. That's human.
This is just human.

(Then:)

MARIAN: You're very quiet, Richard. So unlike you.

RICHARD: Is it?

BARBARA: I'm sorry it's such a trial hanging around with your
sisters . . .

RICHARD: I never said—

MARIAN: We'll let you go soon . . .

(Then:)

TIM *(To say something)*: I was surprised that Adam chose Dapson's and not Burnett and White. They're right around
the corner.

BARBARA: Dapson's is just—

TIM: And wasn't Adam good friends with the Burnett and White
people?—

BARBARA: It's complicated. Adam's business has landscaped Dapson's for . . . *(To Marian)* He couldn't decide, could he? He didn't want to hurt either. I don't know how we ended up choosing funeral homes. I think it usually just happens . . .

JANE *(About the funeral homes)*: Tim's now interested in all the Rhinebeck gossip.

TIM: That's not gossip.

JANE *(To Richard)*: He's even thinking of joining the volunteer fire department.

RICHARD: You told me. *(To Tim)* That's—ambitious.

TIM: I'm almost too old.

RICHARD: I've seen guys sitting outside the station who—

TIM: To start. To take on.

JANE *(Over the end of this)*: We live so close to the station, Tim told them he can just put the siren on his head and run there . . . *(She smiles; to Tim)* They didn't find that funny, did they?

RICHARD *(Trying to say something; to Tim)*: I've always thought that the Beekman Arms must be a nice place to work.

TIM *(Shrugs)*: It's a restaurant.

BARBARA: Years ago they used to make the waiters wear costumes. Like from colonial times? I just remembered this. I had a friend— He worked the bar—he had a funny three-cornered hat. He really hated wearing that hat.

TIM: They don't do that anymore.

BARBARA *(To Marian)*: Tim waited on Adam's mother and the "baby sister" at breakfast today.

JANE: You didn't tell me—

TIM: I've hardly seen you.

BARBARA: They didn't know who he was. They've met a lot of people over the past two days.

TIM: I didn't say who I was. I just waited on them.

(Barbara notices Richard checking his watch.)

BARBARA *(To Marian)*: He's checking his watch.

RICHARD: It *is* late, Barbara.

(Phone rings in the kitchen. Marian jumps.)

BARBARA *(To Marian)*: I unplugged the phone upstairs.

MARIAN: It's probably the "baby sister" . . . She was worried about the noise on Route 9 . . . *(Mimics)* "Oh how am I going to sleep?" *(As she goes out)* I don't know what the hell she thinks I can do about it . . .

(Marian is gone.)

BARBARA: The sister's upset. She wanted to stay too, but the mom . . .

(The phone has stopped ringing in the kitchen.)

TIM: Best to stay out of that.

BARBARA: Should we make some coffee?

*(No response.
Marian returns.)*

MARIAN *(To Richard)*: It's Pamela . . .

(Richard gets up.)

She sends her condolences—to all of us.

RICHARD *(As he goes, as a "joke")*: She's tracked me down.

(He is gone.)

BARBARA: Jane? Tell us how Albany was. How's he doing?

(Marian sits to listen.)

JANE: He works. *(Shrugs)*

BARBARA: What's his apartment like?

JANE: Small. Tiny. But very clean.

MARIAN: Really?

TIM: Why is that—?

BARBARA: Does he have a cleaning lady?

JANE: No.

BARBARA *(To Marian)*: Good for him.

JANE: I was there the whole week. He did the dishes. The grocery shopping.

MARIAN: Does he cook?

JANE: He tries. He got a book. And he follows the directions. I wouldn't have believed that, if I hadn't seen it. He doesn't just make it up.

TIM: Why is that—?

BARBARA: Does he have any friends there?

JANE: I don't think so. I didn't meet any.

(Barbara and Marian share a look.)

(Again) He works. And spends almost nothing. There's nothing on the walls. Not even a calendar. Like a monk.

MARIAN: Why is he punishing himself? He didn't do anything.

JANE: He's so angry.

BARBARA *(To Marian)*: He tries to hide it.

JANE: He keeps telling himself: Pamela is going to want more money. "Nothing is ever enough." His words. "She'll never be satisfied. She never is." He told me he "thinks" she's going to sue him . . . Once he gets started on that, he doesn't stop.

(The sisters share a look.)

BARBARA: Sh-sh . . .

(They listen.)

I thought he was coming. *(Concerned)* I don't hear him talking . . .

JANE: Tim, would you stand there and warn us if he's coming?

TIM: No.

JANE: He spoke to Pamela last night.

MARIAN: To Pamela? He called her?

BARBARA *(To Marian)*: Pamela told me this morning.

JANE *(To Barbara)*: After you called about Adam getting worse. To tell her he had to come here. It's Richard's weekend with the kids. He said they fought.

BARBARA *(To Marian)*: She said—he just yelled at her. *(Getting up)* I don't hear him . . . *(Listens)* Is he off the phone? I'm going to go see.

(Barbara goes into the kitchen.)

MARIAN *(Sighs)*: Jesus . . . *(She looks off toward the living room)*

JANE: Adam seems quiet, Marian . . .

MARIAN *(Getting up)*: I'm going upstairs. I'll be right back. *(She goes)*

(Jane is alone with Tim.)

JANE *(Sighs)*: What a night . . . Thank you for staying. I know you don't want to.

TIM: It's fine. I'm family. Aren't I?

(Jane smiles at him.)

JANE: Now I want a drink . . .

(As he goes and pours:)

You know you are a wonderful actor, Tim. And you *should* still audition . . . Even from here. The train's just . . .

TIM: I know . . .

(Then:)

JANE: And Karen's going to get over this—whatever she's going through. I was like this too at her age. It's a good place for kids.

BARBARA *(Returning)*: Richard's out in the yard with Benjamin. They're—smoking cigarettes together.

JANE: Richard hasn't smoked since college . . .

(As Barbara looks around:)

She went upstairs. *(To Tim)* You don't smoke. You'd better not.

TIM: No, I don't. I don't.

(Barbara looks around the room.)

BARBARA: A woman who used to live here . . .

TIM: This is interesting.

BARBARA: She just appeared at the back door last Sunday. She said she'd lived here, in this house, first as a child, then, to take care of her mother. Her mother, she said, died here—in this very room.

They'd brought down a bed. They'd brought down a bed from upstairs. It was pretty much where this table is . . .

JANE: We thought of doing that for Adam . . .

(Then:)

(About the dinner) I think we're done.

(Richard returns.)

RICHARD: Uncle's out in the yard, looking—lost. I should go. Where's Marian?

BARBARA: Don't go yet.

RICHARD: Barbara—
JANE: Marian's upstairs. She's coming right back.

(As they wait for Marian:)

(To Richard) Are you smoking?
BARBARA *(To Richard)*: How's Pamela?
RICHARD: I'll live. My cross: Pamela . . .
JANE *(To say something)*: Barbara had a guest this week, some-
one who used to live in this house.
RICHARD: Did they just knock on the door?

(Barbara nods.)

I've done that. Our house on the South Side. Years ago.
They wouldn't let me in.
BARBARA: She said that when they had the chimney removed—
you know how you can still see the base of it in the basement? They found a bill from a store. Dated 1863. She
said she'd send it to me. That it belonged here.
RICHARD: A bill for what?
BARBARA: She didn't say. And here . . . Here . . . *(She points to
a place on the floor)* I'll show you . . . *(She gets on her hands
and knees and pulls back a corner of the rug)* Here, look here.
I covered this with the rug on purpose. She showed this
to me. Over here . . . Look, she said, see these little cuts?
See?

(The others go and look.)

They were made, she said, by one of her sons, showing
off his new hunting knife. The knife slipped and the boy
cut his foot and had to go to the hospital. The father gave
him hell, she said.

*(Marian enters, seeing Barbara on her knees and the others
around her. Marian has a small baby monitor.)*

TIM: Barbara's visitor . . .

(Marian nods.)

RICHARD *(Getting off his knees)*: How long was she—?
BARBARA: Not long. Marian was out. I wanted her to meet her.
(To Marian) Things okay?

(Marian sets the monitor on a chair.)

(About the monitor) Good idea.
MARIAN *(Explaining to Barbara)*: I thought— His mother falling asleep . . .

*(She turns the monitor on—a little static and the ticking of a
clock upstairs.)*

RICHARD *(In a whisper to Marian)*: I was just waiting for you to
come back down.
MARIAN *(Smiles)*: They can't hear you, we can only hear them.
RICHARD: I wasn't. I've had children . . .
MARIAN: He thinks they can hear us.
BARBARA: I was telling Richard about the woman who visited . . .
MARIAN: Did you tell him that they'd brought a bed down
here? For the mother?
BARBARA: I told him. *(To Richard)* Sit, sit.
MARIAN: So she died, right here . . . We think pretty much
where the table is—
RICHARD: She said.
MARIAN: She left. I never did meet her . . . We almost did that
for Adam . . .
BARBARA: Such an interesting way of looking at your own
house. Through—her eyes . . . For her everything was
just different. Everything changed.
    Who wants more to eat? Richard? Salad?
RICHARD: I'm done.

(On the monitor: "Marian, thank Barbara for the dinner.")

MARIAN: "Thank Barbara for the dinner." His mother. *(Turns the monitor down)* She didn't thank me . . .

BARBARA: This is a mess.

JANE *(Getting up)*: I'll take some things in. And get the trays.

RICHARD *(Standing)*: I should go now.

BARBARA: Sit, Richard. Just for a few more minutes. Please. And visit with Marian. She's hardly even seen you . . .

(He hesitates and looks at his watch.)

Don't look at your watch.

*(He sits.
Jane picks up a few things and goes off.)*

MARIAN *(To Richard)*: I sat with Adam one night a few weeks ago and we talked about all that had changed in this village. He was already here . . . He wasn't going back to his apartment. *(To Barbara)* He never should have sold our house.
  Barbara was so generous . . .

BARBARA: You live here too. It's your house too. You were generous too.

MARIAN *(Continues)*: We—in our imaginations, because he couldn't even be moved by then—we "walked" down Market Street; first one side, then the other. And we told each other—what we remembered being there.

TIM: What do you mean? Jane might write a history of Rhinebeck.

MARIAN: There have been at least two already—

BARBARA: She always has so many ideas—

TIM: She just has to write one, Barbara.

MARIAN *(Answering Tim's earlier question)*: What's no longer there or changed, Tim. The CVS—that *was* the grocery store. The A&P.

(Jane returns with trays; the sisters begin to pick up.)

The honey store was the hardware store . . . Moving the statue of that sexy soldier from the fire station to the parking lot.

Adam remembered the day a house, a whole one-hundred-fifty-year-old house on Mill Street, *(To Richard)* Route 9, they lifted it up, put it on wheels and rolled it down about a block and a half— That's where it is now.

BARBARA *(To Tim)*: Part of the Beekman's expansion. That house in the back.

MARIAN *(Continues)*: There was the pizza church. Adam remembers it being a sort of hippy art center in the sixties—that's even before me . . . He did a performance there once— against the war . . . With a bunch of people he was living with at Rokeby.

JANE: I can't imagine Adam as a hippie.

MARIAN *(Smiles)*: I'll show you pictures. As long as I can cover up me. Tim, Adam reminded me—do you know what Mill Street, Route 9, becomes if you go south far enough? It becomes—Broadway. *The* Broadway in Manhattan. Route 9, our Mill Street . . .

TIM *(Sort of a joke)*: So I guess I'm not *that* far from Broadway.

(Jane smiles and pats him.)

MARIAN: Barbara said her visitor was very happy that school-teachers were living in her house. And not goddamn rich lawyers from New York City who crowd everything out on weekends. *(She has looked at Richard)*

RICHARD: I live in Albany.

JANE: Tim told me the other day—

TIM: What?

JANE *(Over this)*: Above the pizza place? He heard this at Bard. The woman who heads the trust for the composer—John Cage? Do you know who that is?

RICHARD: I don't.

JANE *(Over this)*: Well she—the head of the trust—lives in Rhinebeck above the pizza place. I don't know why, but that seems so fascinating . . .

(Then:)

RICHARD: Benjamin and I noticed that they've been building some sort of stage—behind your house, Barbara.

BARBARA: The back of the town parking lot.

TIM: For Sinterklaas . . .

BARBARA *(Over this)*: The parade.

JANE: Tim's been working on this year's. With Karen. They're making stars.

BARBARA *(To Richard)*: They do a little show on that stage, Richard. St. George and the Dragon . . . *(To Marian)* Adam was St. George once or twice, wasn't he?

MARIAN: Two years in a row. *(To Tim)* Evan and I did stars. For about three years, until we just had fights. I'm sure you're having a better time.

JANE *(To Marian)*: Karen and Tim have fights. *(Turns to Tim)* I can tell them that. We live here.

BARBARA *(To Marian)*: You had some very good times together. You two. Come on.

(Short pause. They listen to the ticking from the monitor. No one knows what to say.)

(Reaches and takes Marian's hand) This woman, Richard— you should know this about your sister—what she has been doing for her ex-husband. These past few months. I can't even begin to describe . . .

   She stopped everything to take care of Adam. Gave up everything . . .

RICHARD: I know.

MARIAN: What did I give up?

BARBARA: She pretty much moved back in with him into his apartment. How much do you know?

RICHARD: I think we're all proud of Marian for all she's done.

BARBARA: How much do you know? You haven't been here—

RICHARD: Jane's told me.

MARIAN: His apartment was—not a place to die in. *(To Barbara)* That's what you said.

I've learned I can do the "bedside thing." I hadn't thought before I could. Could I have a drink? Not that I'm going to feel it.

(Tim goes to pour Marian a drink. A small yawn from the monitor.)

The mother—yawning. *(Continues)* It finally dawned on me—he must really be dying from a broken heart. Evan, she broke his heart. When she killed herself. She broke my heart. *(Looks up at Barbara)*

BARBARA: We're family. It's just us. You're safe . . .

MARIAN *(Smiles, then)*: For some reason, it hasn't killed me yet. I sometimes wonder why.

Just three months ago—I don't think I could even have imagined spending five minutes with Adam. He'd hurt me so much. But, at Barbara's urging—

BARBARA: You didn't need me.

MARIAN *(Over this)*: Her insistence—we all know what that can be like . . .

BARBARA *(A joke)*: What does she mean?

(Laughter, maybe too much laughter.)

Hey, hey . . .

MARIAN: What would we do without Barbara? We heard about Adam being sick, and she took me literally by the hand to visit him. And so I saw so clearly . . . what I just said. Once I saw that, and saw that him blaming me—*that* I could now forgive—because it is so obvious that he blames himself so much more. And in the past month, I've come to see that he is the last person on earth I have left to share—to share Evan with.

(Before Barbara can say anything:)

I know, you too. But . . . it's different. So doing the bedside thing was easy. Even selfish. *(She suddenly gets up)* I should do some dishes.

JANE: They can wait.

BARBARA: She wants to do dishes . . .

(Marian starts to head off. She stops. Then:)

MARIAN *(Trying not to cry)*: Adam and I sat up one night a few weeks ago. "Sat up." He couldn't sleep anyway. He was on his drugs. And together we counted up how many places in Rhinebeck Village there now were where you can eat. When we moved here, there were three. We counted—and came up with twenty-eight. Now there's twenty-eight places to eat here . . .

(She picks up the monitor and heads into the kitchen with it. Benjamin passes her as he enters.)

BENJAMIN: Why is Marian crying?

BARBARA: She's losing Adam, Uncle. They'd been married for thirty years.

BENJAMIN: That's a long time. I'm sorry.

BARBARA: The grass must still be wet. Are your shoes wet?

BENJAMIN: A little.

BARBARA: Did you get cold outside?

BENJAMIN: I did get cold.

BARBARA: Please wear your coat.

RICHARD: I'm sorry it's been so hard on her. I hadn't completely . . .

BARBARA: No. You hadn't . . .

JANE *(Noticing Benjamin watching)*: You know Adam, Uncle?

TIM *(To Benjamin)*: You and I talked a lot about Adam today.

BENJAMIN: Adam's upstairs. He's dying.

JANE: That's right. *(To Tim)* That is right.

RICHARD: I should head back.

BARBARA: Do you have to?

RICHARD *(Standing up, ignoring her)*: Benjamin, always good to see you.

BARBARA: You know who he is, Benjamin?

BENJAMIN: Richard.

RICHARD *(To Barbara, making a point)*: He knows who I am. *(To Benjamin)* I'm so glad you're safe at that "inn." I'm so happy all that worked out . . . For everyone. And now maybe Barbara's getting out more too . . . And doing things for herself . . . *(Turns to Jane)* Jane, thank you for visiting me in Albany. I had a really nice time with you. Tim . . . Thank you for loaning her out. *(Turns to Barbara)* I'll say good-bye to Marian in the kitchen. Barbara . . .

(He goes to kiss her good-bye.)

BARBARA: Can we talk for a minute, Richard?

RICHARD: About what? I have to go . . .

BARBARA: About that. About going.

RICHARD: Barbara—

JANE: Tim . . .

TIM: Benjamin, I'm going to check out that stage in the parking lot. You want to come?

BENJAMIN: No.

TIM: I'll take some of these into the kitchen.

(As Tim heads off with a tray:)

RICHARD *(To Tim)*: What do you know that I don't know?

JANE: Maybe he just wants to have a smoke, Richard.

RICHARD: Tim's smoking?

JANE: No. *He* isn't.

(Then:)

RICHARD: Barbara, what do you want?

BARBARA: How are the kids? Still angry at you?

RICHARD: I'm trying to buy them off. Tickets to shows, ball games. I'm trying . . .

BARBARA: It takes time. So I'm told. Kids . . . So Samantha's the toughest on you?

(He nods.
Marian returns with the monitor.)

I guess girls usually are with their fathers. And Baby Mike is . . . okay?

RICHARD: I guess. And he's not a baby, Barbara. He's now a teenager.

BARBARA: Sorry, an aunt thing.

MARIAN: We all do it.

JANE: We do.

BARBARA: I've never said it to his face.

MARIAN: No . . .

RICHARD: Don't. Please . . .

BARBARA: Are you all right, Richard?

(He looks at her and his sisters.)

Maybe this isn't the right time to ask. Tonight. But when have we had the chance to ask? We haven't seen you in months. I call—and we talk for a couple of minutes—and then you're busy, or you have another call— Or you're outside and your hands are cold.

RICHARD: I'm busy. I have a new job.

BARBARA: Why have you been avoiding us?

RICHARD: I just spent a whole week with Jane. Jane?

(No response.)

What is this?

I'll try and call more often. You're not going to make me feel guilty, Barbara. You've done that enough for one night. So just stop.

MARIAN: Richard, we're worried about you in this "Albany."

RICHARD: Is that what you're worried about? Jane? You just visited me. Tell them. I'm fine. Tell your sisters I'm fine.

(No response.)

(Smiles) "Albany"? Marian, trust me, I know what I've gotten myself into. My eyes are wide open. I'm ready to be terribly disappointed by Andrew Cuomo. We all better be prepared for that. *(Smiles)* I'll be fine. I'm fine. I appreciate the concern. Thanks for the talk . . . *(Stands)* Now my dear sisters I really need to go.

JANE *(Stopping him)*: Richard . . .

MARIAN: You're hurt. And you're just doing what you've always done, Richard, when you get hurt.

RICHARD: Which is—?

BARBARA: You run away. And you hide . . .

And bury yourself in something . . .

MARIAN: We're worried, Richard, that you've buried yourself in Albany.

RICHARD: I have a job. I'm trying to do something good. What am I supposed to do? What do you want me to do?

BARBARA: We'd like you to move here.

RICHARD: You're joking. *(He smiles)*

MARIAN: No . . .

BARBARA: Go and work there. Try and do some good. Maybe you can. Who knows? And it's less than an hour away. So

then every night, come home here . . . Please don't smile.
We hate that smile. What?

RICHARD *(Smiling)*: Pamela warned me—probably the only
true thing she ever said to me—the only *honest* thing—
Your sisters, she said, will never be happy, Richard, until
you're living in fucking Rhinebeck. Well, I guess she was
right. Unbelievable.

BARBARA: Pamela's worried about you too.

RICHARD: What? What are you talking about?—

MARIAN: She's called us. Calls us.

JANE: A lot.

(Then:)

RICHARD: You can't understand.

BARBARA: Try us, Richard. We want to understand.

RICHARD: The three of you have done nothing but criticize her
since the day you met, and now—

MARIAN: And now we're not defending her, except to say she's
not the monster, Richard, that you need her to be.

BARBARA: Marian—

RICHARD: Jane?

JANE: I agree with them, Richard.

BARBARA: But Pamela's sorry. And she's worried about you too
. . . Like us. Your sisters . . .

MARIAN: She's not going to "sue" like you told Jane. And you
know that, Richard.

RICHARD *(Over this)*: What?

BARBARA *(Over this)*: She's not trying to keep you from the kids.
And you know that too. She knows she's hurt you. And
she's very sorry, Richard.

RICHARD *(Over the end of this)*: If Pamela could hear this . . .
She must have said to me a hundred times—watch out,
Richard, your sisters don't have lives of their own up there
in Rhinebeck, and once Benjamin . . .

(Jane looks at Benjamin.)

They're not going to rest until they find someone else's life to run.

MARIAN: Meaning yours?

BARBARA *(Same time)*: I don't think that's true.

RICHARD: "I don't know why can't they just live their own fucking lives."

BARBARA: We have lives.

RICHARD: The three of you have done nothing but make fun of her.

JANE: That is not true.

RICHARD *(Over this)*: Nothing she has ever done has been good enough. You think she didn't know that? You think that didn't hurt her? That didn't hurt me? I guess it's no wonder she left me . . .

JANE *(Over this)*: No. No, Richard.

BARBARA *(Same time)*: No. Richard . . . Pamela left you— because she fell in love with someone else.

(Short pause.)

And we're sorry . . .

Please, think about what we've said. But now, stay the night. It's late. You're upset. You shouldn't be driving back upset.

JANE: How about a drink, if you're not driving now . . . ? You've been making yourself drink seltzer all night.

(Then:)

BARBARA: If you want, until you find something better, you could stay here. There's a full bath downstairs. Even has its own entrance. It's blocked now, but we can open it up. I can move into Benjamin's room.

BENJAMIN: My room? . . .

MARIAN: Only when you're not here, Benjamin. And Jane and
Tim are just down the street . . .

(Short pause.)

JANE: Everyone ready for dessert?

*(On the baby monitor there is a static noise of the monitor being
picked up, and a woman's voice whispering: "Marian . . .")*

MARIAN: I thought this might be a mistake. She always tried to
get me to wait on her . . .

(And Marian goes out into the living room and upstairs.)

JANE: You having dessert, Richard?

(Richard doesn't say anything.)

(To Barbara) Richard never says no to ice cream.

BARBARA: The church ladies brought pies.

JANE: What church ladies?

BARBARA: At Marian's church.

JANE: That's who those ladies were . . . Any ice cream? Richard
likes ice cream.

BARBARA: I don't know. Marian buys the ice cream.

JANE: Let's look.

BARBARA: I know Marian has chocolate sauce . . .

*(Jane and Barbara go to the kitchen.
    Then:)*

BENJAMIN: It will be all right, son. That's what I always try and
tell myself . . .

(The lights fade.)

Evan's Baby Monitor

The same. Richard and Benjamin; Tim has just entered.

TIM: The rumor is—you're staying for dessert. Good.
  Adam told me a story about meeting a girl at the bar at Foster's years ago. That's your old hangout, Benjamin.
BENJAMIN: Is it?
TIM: This is when Adam could still tell stories. And this girl at Foster's is an actress. She's just graduated from acting school. And she's in Rhinebeck because she has just gotten her first professional acting job.
RICHARD: In Rhinebeck?
TIM: That's what Adam said he asked. I think he meant this as a cautionary tale . . .
RICHARD: Where in Rhinebeck? And this was years ago? That pizza church that Marian was—?
TIM: No, no—the Aerodrome. You okay?

(Richard shrugs.)

(Continues) Adam said at that time he'd never been to the "famous" Aerodrome—it wasn't a very cool thing to do and it cost money. And you could see the planes fly over the village for free, so . . . But the girl was cute, and he was curious . . .
RICHARD *(Back to the story)*: This was before he'd met Marian . . .
TIM: Before they'd . . . *(The story)* So one Saturday morning Adam goes to the Aerodrome to watch this cute girl do her first show; he sits in the bleachers in front of a big open field. *(Continues)* Two World War I planes—those biplanes—the evil Red Baron's and the other's, the hero's, they are in a quote unquote "dogfight" overhead.

343

The owner comes out of a tent, with his megaphone and with the young actress, now in a short white skirt, on his arm and he leads her to a stake in the middle of the field, and ties her up there. And the crowd goes wild.

RICHARD: You're kidding.

(Jane returns with the bowls for ice cream, etc.)

TIM: And through his megaphone the owner explains that this is Truly Truegood, the hero's girlfriend, who has been captured by the evil Red Baron. She looks up. And the Red Baron—being evil I suppose—wants to harm her. The owner runs off the field. And the dogfight continues above, but now the Red Baron from his plane, begins to— little white sacks, and they sort of explode when they hit ground. Bombs. Aiming at this tied-up young girl.

(Richard shakes his head.)

She squirms—I suppose that was her acting. And she shouts things that are drowned out by the airplanes' engines. Those were her lines. And all the time the Red Baron's bombs—they get closer, closer to the young wiggling innocent actress . . .

Adam, then just looked at me, smiling, and said: "Maybe there's a job out at the old Aerodrome that's right for you. Rhinebeck, Tim."

(Barbara returns with ice cream, chocolate sauce, etc.)

JANE: I think he was just trying to scare Tim—being an actor. He was trying to mess with you.

BARBARA: He *could* be mean. Adam. Really mean. Ask Marian.

(Marian enters, holding a book.)

MARIAN: Yes he could. (*As she turns on the baby monitor*) I told the mother to lie in my bed, in my room. She's exhausted. I said we had the monitor. I'd wake her . . .

(*The ice cream is served.*)

BARBARA (*Ignoring this*): And his mother agreed?
MARIAN: Not at first.
BARBARA (*Serving*): Was she crying?

(*Marian nods.*)

It can just sneak up on you . . . Of course it can.
MARIAN: She said—for someone who couldn't help Evan, I've been real nice to her son . . . (*Handing the book back to Barbara*) She said she didn't like this.

(*They take that in. Then:*)

BARBARA: She's tired . . . Marian, there's chocolate sauce.

(*Marian takes the chocolate sauce.*)

(*About the book*) Did she even look at it?
MARIAN: I don't know.
TIM (*Reads the title*): *Jane Austen's Letters.*
MARIAN: It's Barbara's.
RICHARD (*Over this*): Who writes letters anymore?
JANE: Who's going to know how we lived? I've read that. ("*the book*") Beautiful thoughts about very trivial things. What will be left for others to know about *our* everyday life?
MARIAN (*To Tim*): You want to borrow it?

(*He shakes his head.*)

(*To Jane, about Tim and the book*) Too girlie for him.

(Benjamin stands.)

BARBARA: You don't want your ice cream, Benjamin?

BENJAMIN: I'm not hungry . . .

BARBARA: What are you going to do?

BENJAMIN: Lie down . . .

BARBARA: He wants to lie down.

BENJAMIN: I just said that. Why do you repeat everything I say? I'm tired. *(He goes)*

BARBARA: He's tired. *(To Marian)* He didn't take a nap . . .

RICHARD: He seems older . . . Benjamin.

MARIAN: "Benjamin."

JANE *(Watching where Benjamin just left, musing)*: Are you my father, "Benjamin"?

(Short pause.)

RICHARD *(To Jane)*: We could just find out. It's easy enough now to find out. We've all talked about this. Do we want to know now?

(As they eat:)

JANE *(Picking up the Jane Austen)*: I love reading people's letters. The "little things" in life. I'm thinking of pitching something like that as a book.

BARBARA *(Eating)*: Jane always has so many ideas.

JANE *(Continues)*: Family Bibles, keepsakes, journals . . . Like that bill discovered in your chimney, Barbara. Small things that might have meanings larger than . . . Than you think they would.

MARIAN: She'd seen a ghost . . .

JANE: What??

MARIAN: Adam's mom. That's what she was crying about, she said. A ghost hovering over Adam in his bed.

(Then:)

A girl . . .

(Then:)

(About the baby monitor) She was calling me to come and
see her. To see "it."

BARBARA: Did you? Did you see—"it"?

MARIAN: No.

RICHARD: She's tired.

(As they eat:)

MARIAN: A couple of days ago. I heard that squeak the school
bus makes when it stops? Probably from Market Street.
And I could see Evan, with her My Little Pony backpack.
The way she stood, all sassy, proud. Years and years ago?
Hand on hip . . . *(Demonstrates)*

(Benjamin returns.)

JANE: Can't you sleep, Benjamin?

BENJAMIN: I'm hungry.

BARBARA: He's hungry. *(To Benjamin)* You're very restless,
aren't you?

BENJAMIN: I feel restless.

BARBARA: He's restless.

TIM: Let's get Benjamin some ice cream. Would you like ice
cream?

BENJAMIN: I would, Tim. I like ice cream.

TIM: I certainly know you do. Sit with us, Benjamin. Every
time we walk into town, we have to stop at "our" new
fancy gelato place.

RICHARD: Rhinebeck has a fancy gelato place?

BENJAMIN: It's expensive isn't it?

TIM: That's what we say every time. "It's really expensive . . ."

BARBARA *(To Richard)*: It's not for us.

(As they eat and serve Benjamin:)

JANE: A couple of weeks ago. *(To Richard)* I don't think I told you this.

TIM: What?

JANE: You know. Barbara's embarrassed by this.

RICHARD: Now I'm interested. What? What embarrasses Barbara?

JANE *(To Barbara)*: Forgetting— *("Benjamin")*

BARBARA: Oh that. Don't listen, Benjamin.

BENJAMIN: What?

BARBARA: Cover your ears. *(As she eats)* A couple of weeks ago, we all go to the mall. Jane and Tim in their car. Marian and Benjamin—it's the weekend so Benjamin's here—in my car. I'm looking at H&M, they're in the music store . . . I think he's with them. They think he's with . . . We get home, take off our coats, put on the kettle—and someone says—

MARIAN: I said:

BARBARA: "Where's Benjamin?"

(Barbara reaches and takes Benjamin's hand.)

We'd forgotten you . . . Do you remember that?

(He shakes his head.)

He actually enjoyed just wandering around the mall by himself. You weren't scared at all . . .

You like being alone sometimes, don't you?

BENJAMIN: I do.

(As they eat:)

JANE: At the "ceremony" today in Dallas . . . They kept away anyone who might—

TIM: "The crackpots."

JANE: They just wanted it to be . . . What? I don't know. What is it? What are we supposed to be remembering?

BARBARA: We watched a bit in class today. Those poor people looked like they were freezing. I kept thinking, why couldn't it have been that cold and raining back then.

MARIAN: I don't understand.

TIM: Because they'd have had the car roof *up*, Marian.

BARBARA: That historian spoke well. I loved his book on the Brooklyn Bridge. The Navy Glee Club—that must not have been fun in that weather. The reading of the speeches . . . "Where power corrupts, poetry cleanses." I made my kids write that down.

JANE: I'm sure you did, Barbara.

BARBARA: The tolling of all the city's bells . . . The moment of silence—at the exact time he was shot.

(Pause.)

JANE: Adam still gets angry when anyone calls him a "progressive."

BENJAMIN: Why?

JANE AND MARIAN *(As Adam)*: "Because, we're fucking *liberals*! Suck it up, Apples!"

(Laughter.)

BENJAMIN: Why is that funny?

MARIAN: He thinks we've given up. Or we've forgotten what we are. He thinks we're lost, Benjamin.

(Short pause.)

BARBARA: One of my kids, in the middle of our discussion today—he asks me: so what do you remember, Miss Apple? About all that. That—day.

The first thing that came to mind was— *(Smiles)* that it was only a few months later—after Kennedy's death—that the Beatles came to America and were on Ed Sullivan. I told the kids, I think our excitement—our squealing—it was our way of—releasing. We hadn't been able to do that for a while, and so it had just built up.

TIM: You hold things in, they just come out . . .

BARBARA: I then said something that surprised even me. I wonder if it's true. It just came out. Tell me if you think it's true. I said—I wonder if there are two kinds of fears in the world. One kind, you learn from your parents. Like spiders and traffic or "Nazis." I certainly was scared of them.

JANE *(As a "joke")*: I still am.

BARBARA: Then there's this second kind of fear. The fear we learn on our own, from your own experience of the world. For me, the assassination was that kind of fear. Maybe the first of that kind of fear for me. For an eleven-year-old girl. I was an eleven-year-old girl, whose father had just left.

MARIAN: Father was still there later.

BARBARA: The first time. When he left that first time, Marian. You don't remember that. Only Richard and I remember that.

How we learn that at any moment the world can change. And there's no one to protect us. A fear like that.

(Then:)

RICHARD *(It just comes out)*: The first person I saw die—was Lee Harvey Oswald . . .

MARIAN: I think that's true for a lot of people our age.

TIM: The first time I saw someone die?

JANE *(To Tim)*: Who did you see die?

TIM: My sociology teacher in college. Collapsed in our class. They tried to . . . For weeks I kept "seeing" him walking around the campus. I'd see other people but think it was him. I think my brain was just trying to work things out . . .

JANE: That's what we do . . . We work things out . . .

MARIAN *(The same point)*: I dreamed of Adam last night.

JANE: There you go. Working things.

BARBARA: A nightmare?

MARIAN: Not really. Maybe.

BENJAMIN: I don't remember my dreams . . . I wish I did . . .

BARBARA: He doesn't remember his dreams.

RICHARD: He said that, Barbara.

TIM *(Over the end of this)*: Know where the word "nightmare" comes from?

RICHARD: Where does it come from?

TIM: The "mare" refers to demonic women—who suffocate sleepers by lying on their chests.

My recurring nightmare—

JANE: Talk about working things out. Listen to this.

RICHARD: What?

TIM: I mean, what used to be my recurring nightmare. It came off a movie. Years ago. A couple have a child, a little girl— the child dies. They're devastated. They visit Venice. He's something to do with restoring art. And there have been all these terrible murders in Venice. No one knows who is doing them. Then the man sees a little girl in a red cape—his daughter wore a red cape. He follows her, along the canals to a church. She runs up the stairs, higher and higher and he runs after. He reaches the top, opens the door—she's not there, then he turns and hiding behind the door is a dwarf, with a beard, in a red cape—with a knife raised . . .

That's what I would dream. All the time. I'd walk into a room, no one there, then behind the door—someone with a knife. And as it plunges into my skull, I scream and wake up.

One day, I thought enough is enough. I decided to do something about this. I found the movie on DVD, this was still years ago, and then even the screenplay, published. In a used bookshop. I chose an afternoon—so it would be light. And I started the movie and followed along in the screenplay, stopping to read ahead, so I couldn't be surprised. And that did it. I beat it. I stopped having the nightmares. I healed.

RICHARD: Good for you.

JANE: He's not done.

TIM: I was so proud of myself. After I was confident that the nightmares were gone, I told my then wife about this. She asked if she could see the movie. Then I couldn't find it. I couldn't find the screenplay either. I went to a store— I think Virgin, and learned that—the movie hadn't come out on DVD. And the screenplay had never been published.

 So I hadn't read and watched it again. Not in real life. We're working all the time I think—healing ourselves. Trying to.

MARIAN: One day about four weeks ago, we'd just moved Adam here, to take care of him. I return from school, Adam I know is asleep. The aide, the one we had before Nadine, she comes downstairs, I pay her. It's a gray day. I don't turn the light on in here. I hear a voice, "Hi Mom," come from the kitchen. "You're back. Hi!" I heard it. And then I saw her. I saw her expression and her face, as she came out of the kitchen. And walked right past me. Right here.

 I swear to god—I could smell her. *(Suddenly realizes the monitor is off, she grabs it and turns it on and off)* Where's . . . ? Shit! . . . Shit! . . .

JANE: What's wrong?—

MARIAN *(Hurrying off upstairs)*: It's off.

TIM: It's . . . off. Probably just the batteries. Barbara, where do you keep your batteries?

JANE: In the kitchen—

BARBARA: In the drawer next to the silverware—

RICHARD: Are you sure it's the—? *(He picks up the monitor)*

TIM *(As he hurries off into the kitchen)*: I don't know . . .

RICHARD *(To Barbara)*: We would have heard something. The mother's in the room.

BARBARA *(Shakes her head)*: The other bedroom.

JANE: Should we go up . . . ?

BARBARA: Wait. Wait . . .

(Then, as they wait:)

JANE *(To Barbara)*: She saw Evan?

BARBARA: I've read that pretty much a majority of people who suddenly lose a loved one—especially mothers with children—they see them or smell them or feel their touch.

(Tim returns with batteries. He and Richard put them in the monitor. The sisters and Benjamin watch as:)

They think it's like how when you lose an arm or a leg, suddenly. And then you still feel it. It's the memory that is real. One feels the memory physically. It is more real than anything. There but it isn't there. I know that feeling.

(The monitor comes on. The clock is heard ticking from the bedroom.)

RICHARD: Sounds like it's okay.

JANE: Or like children and their imaginary friends who can seem totally real . . . There to fill a need. Something missing . . . I had an imaginary friend, Trousers. Remember?

(Barbara nods.
Marian returns.)

MARIAN: Everything's fine . . . Thanks. The mother's back in the room. She can't sleep either.

(They listen to the monitor for a moment. Then:)

BARBARA *(To Marian)*: God knows how long those batteries had been in there . . . *(To Jane)* We just started using . . . *("the monitor")* Marian found it in a box. It'd been for Evan. When she was a baby.

RICHARD: I've been asked to be on the board of a school for the blind.

BARBARA: What? How are *your* eyes, Richard?

RICHARD: My left eye—

BARBARA: Still?

JANE: It's always going to be blurred, Barbara. He's told us that.

RICHARD: Someone in Andrew's office is involved. He thought . . . He thinks I'd be a good fundraiser. It's upstate. Near Utica. I visited . . .

BARBARA: You visited? When?

RICHARD: I don't tell my sisters everything. And I do get out. *(To Jane)* I didn't go out at all this week because I wanted to visit with my sister. I have friends.

One of the kids surprised me, she said, "You know, mister, blindness is a way of life that's not entirely unfortunate." That's a quote from a blind South American writer. They have it on a wall there, in braille.

She said, this kid—really smart kid, as she gave me a tour, she said, people born blind—like herself—"We don't just hear sounds, we can hear objects. We can hear objects as we approach them. Objects at head height, they slightly affect the air currents reaching the face . . ."

We were talking about healing. But I wonder if it's not about trying to heal ourselves. But embracing how we cope. We find ways. People do.

(An example) Congenitally blind children, I'm told, usually have superior memories . . .

(They look at Benjamin. Then:)

BARBARA: You're so handsome. Jane was saying that earlier. I agree . . .

BENJAMIN: Thank you.

RICHARD: The girl said as I left, "Too often people with sight don't see anything . . ."

MARIAN: Nadine was telling Adam's mom and me—she's been through this. It's her job.

JANE: I couldn't do that job. Every day—

MARIAN: I see the rewards.

TIM: What was she saying?—

MARIAN: That, often when someone is very close to dying— they begin having what you could call "fantasies." Their way of coping I guess, Richard.

JANE: Remember when Mom—

RICHARD: She was delirious.

MARIAN: That's an interpretation.

BARBARA: What did Nadine say about these "fantasies"?

MARIAN: That she listens carefully to them. Sometimes even notes them down.

JANE: I'd like to see that notebook.

MARIAN: A dying person working things out. Or so she at first thought. But then she wondered if they weren't something these people needed to say, to convey to us—

TIM: To us?

MARIAN: —something they'd now seen which we haven't.

RICHARD: I don't believe that.

MARIAN: But now—she says she doesn't know. And so she just writes them down in this notebook. She said, maybe some day someone will read it and figure it out.

(Then:)

JANE: Remember when Mom lost her hearing, and she started to hear songs? Songs she said she didn't even know. What was *that*?

(Barbara reads from a pile of papers held together with a clasp. She brought these in earlier with the other papers.)

355

BARBARA *(Reads)*: "I'm good with death."

JANE: What?

MARIAN: You have that. Good. Richard should hear these. Read them.

RICHARD: What's—?

MARIAN: Her students.

(Barbara looks up.)

BARBARA *(To Marian)*: Maybe he doesn't want to . . .

RICHARD: I don't know what they are, Barbara.

MARIAN: She asked her students—this week—about death. Write about what you think when you think about "dying."

BARBARA: Not exactly. The idea was "The Kennedys and Death." I figured some of their parents would be thinking about that—this week. Today. But I said they could just write about death too. A lot did.

(Then:)

(Reads) "I'm good with death."

RICHARD: What does that mean?

BARBARA *(Reads)*: "I'm good with death. And it's important to accept oneself in the now, in case you die at any moment, because you won't always be able to die old and have the chance to be 'at peace' with your life."

RICHARD: How old?

BARBARA: Luke's sixteen.

RICHARD: Good luck, Luke.

JANE *(To Tim)*: "I'm good with death."

BARBARA *(Reads)*: Another one: "Death gives meaning and structure to life." Jamie.

TIM: Sure. Why not?

BARBARA: One of the great perks of being a teacher—is that you have people who will try and answer your questions. *(Smiles, reads)* "Death is not a negative thing."

MARIAN *(Smiling)*: Speak for yourself, young person.

BARBARA *(Reads)*: "Because death forces us to take responsibility for the shape of our lives."

MARIAN: I read them to Adam. God knows what he heard.

BARBARA *(Reads)*: "Because there is death, people feel more accountable."

JANE: Do they? *(To Tim)* Do we?

BARBARA: "People are shaped by experiences and environments but unpredictability gives life shape."

TIM: Can I see?

(She hands him the clasped papers.)

BARBARA: I agree with that . . .

TIM *(Reads)*: "Unpredictability gives life shape . . ." Is he saying—

BARBARA *(Over this)*: She.

TIM: That life then has no shape? *She already* thinks that?

BARBARA: I wrote some older students that I'm still in touch with. They're mixed in.

TIM: So up to college age?—

BARBARA: And they're all mixed together. No order.

JANE *(To Tim)*: Read out loud.

TIM *(Reads)*: "We are all slowly, day by day, piece by piece, creating our own deaths." What does that mean?

RICHARD: She's bullshiting . . .

TIM: I don't know.

RICHARD: I talked like that when I was that age. I know BS.

TIM: I talked like that too. I think sometimes I still do. *(Smiles)*

JANE: I don't think it's BS. They're reaching . . . Don't just dismiss it. I think she is saying like that other boy: it's something we learn to live with . . . Part of what we are. And I agree with that.

TIM: Another. *(Reads)* "When my grandmother died, I remember hearing Mom saying to Dad, "When anyone dies, Henry, we find ourselves asking—what we are doing with our lives. That's only natural."

Another one. *(Reads)* "I go into Special Collections in the library—"

BARBARA: She's in college.

TIM: "—into a vault with the oldest books. When I get down there, it feels so trippy because you completely lose yourself in this other place in the fabric of time. That person's reality that you are reading feels so alive and vibrant, so I'm skeptical about any delineation made between people who are living and people who are—then." "Then."

(Jane takes the book.)

JANE: "People who are then . . ." For her they're just "then." I love that. I love that. Why do I love that? *(Reads)* "We think very much of time being linear—"

BARBARA: I like this one. I like her.

JANE *(Over this)*: "—but recently I've been feeling like time is more like an ice rink, circling around, sometimes connecting with those from an earlier time period who have a similar path to yours, and feel similar emotions." She's a poet, this girl.

(Benjamin has picked up the Jane Austen letters book and is reading it.)

Listen to this: *(Reads)* "Death—is very rarely on my mind."

(Laughter.)

RICHARD: Good for her.

MARIAN: How long will that last?

JANE *(To Benjamin)*: You're reading the Jane Austen . . .

BENJAMIN: I am.

BARBARA: He's read it before.

MARIAN: Not too girlie?

BENJAMIN: No.

JANE: "My life is so contingent on getting shit done that I don't think about death."

(Laughter and a few, "True. That's me, too.")

Another—"Death, it takes care of itself!"

(Bigger laughter.
Church bells off, it is midnight.
Jane hands Richard the notebook, and looks at her watch.)

Adam made it, Marian. Through the whole goddamn day. And why did that mean so much to him?

MARIAN: I did ask him that.

JANE: You did?

TIM: What did he say?

MARIAN: That it was one of the very few times, fifty years ago, maybe the only time in his life, when he felt our whole country was connected.

JANE: So then it wasn't the assassination—it was the coming together.

MARIAN: He said, "Let's at least remember that."

(Then:)

TIM: Some state government recently— This is what we've come to. They hired a guy to actually measure the worth of life in their state.

RICHARD: What??

TIM: To put a dollar value on a life in their state. They wanted to raise the speed limit and knew that was going to cause more deaths. But it was also going to give people more time—because they'd get to places faster. So he counted the hours saved by people getting to work earlier, at so many dollars an hour—and then divided that by the number of deaths that would increase because of people driving faster. So he came up with a dollar figure for the value—of a life in that state.

JANE: That's just stupid.

TIM: Some psychologist, for a study, began asking people how much they would need to be paid to give up something.

JANE: You told me this.

RICHARD (Over this): What do you mean? Give up what?

TIM: Likc how much for a good tooth. How much for your— little toe? And he got prices . . .

RICHARD: How much for a little toe?

TIM: I don't remember. Less than you'd think. He got prices.

MARIAN: Who were these people?

JANE: A "scientific" survey of normal people—like us.

TIM: Like a restaurant menu. Toes. Ears. Whole feet . . . It's one way to look at ourselves. I suppose.

RICHARD: I don't know about anyone else but I was really surprised when I heard that Adam was now going to church. Adam . . . Of all people . . .

MARIAN: I go to church. Sometimes I take Benjamin.

RICHARD: Adam always made such a point about those "religious people."

MARIAN: He meant—

RICHARD: I know what he meant. He had beliefs. I admired those beliefs. They just weren't "religious beliefs."

MARIAN: Richard, maybe he—

RICHARD: I don't want to talk about it.

MARIAN: What is so wrong about talking about religion?

RICHARD: I didn't say it was wrong.

MARIAN: That's what I heard.

RICHARD: As long as it's not just, "Oh my god, I'm going to die. Help me."

MARIAN: Oh come on, why can't we be stupid or sentimental or scared or hypocritical—if that's what you have to call it. But if we don't talk about what we're scared of . . . ? What scares us . . . No one can hear us. I'm scared.

BARBARA: There's more than just us, I think, Richard. And to answer something you implied about us a half hour or so ago, I don't think it is a waste of a life to live for other people. I don't think that diminishes one. Makes your life less valuable . . .

(They listen to the ticking on the monitor.)

Adam asked me to recite something. He wanted— *(Corrects herself)* wants us all to do something. He told me he thought this was very fitting . . .

RICHARD: Is it religious?

MARIAN: Go into the kitchen if it embarrasses you.

RICHARD: I would like to hear, Barbara. *(To Marian)* I'll behave . . .

MARIAN: Good.

RICHARD *(Then)*: Is it religious?

MARIAN: When will you grow up?! Richard!

JANE: Barbara, I'm listening. Go ahead.

BARBARA: It's from a Greek play. Spoken at someone's funeral. I've already memorized it. I thought I should be ready . . . *(Recites:)*

> First let the year of mourning begin.
> Let every head be shaved.
> Let every garment be black.
> Let the cavalry
> Crop the manes and tails of the horses.
> Throughout the city
> Let every stringed instrument be unstrung.
> Let every flute lie breathless.
>
> But then, after, we must sing
> In defiance of this loathsome god
> Who collects our bodies
> Like a debt collector.

(Then:)

That's how Adam wants his service to begin . . .

(The lights fade.)

Rehearsing

The same, a short time later. Tim has a piece of paper with the instructions for Adam's funeral service. Jane sings Psalm 13:

JANE *(Sings)*:
> How long Jehovah, wilt thou me forget for aye:
> How long-while wilt thou hide thy face from me
> away?
> How long shall in my soul, my counsels set dayly
> Sad sorrow in my heart, how long shall my foe be
> Exalted over me?

(Short pause.)

TIM *(To Richard)*: Adam liked her voice. Likes. *(Reading from notes)* Then—next for his service, Adam wants . . . *(Looks up to Benjamin)* Benjamin?
BENJAMIN: What?
MARIAN: Barbara?
BARBARA *(She gets up)*: If we're practicing. *(To all)* We are practicing. Is that what we're doing?
JANE: No one's going to bed.

(Barbara heads into the living room.)

MARIAN *(Calls after her)*: I think I saw it on the top of the piano, Barbara . . .

JANE *(Handing them out)*: The first songs ever sung in America, Richard.

RICHARD: Tim said.

MARIAN: By white people.

TIM: I was showing Richard earlier. Then his mother is going to say something.

MARIAN: She'll talk about Evan. Evan hated her . . .

TIM *(To Benjamin)*: And then you're next, Benjamin.

BARBARA *(Returning with a small book)*: He wanted this. *(Corrects herself)* Damn it, *wants* this . . .

BENJAMIN: What is it?

BARBARA: For Adam's funeral, Benjamin. He wants everyone to do something at his funeral. He wants you to read this.

BENJAMIN: For his funeral?

MARIAN: After he dies. Adam's dying.

TIM: We're practicing. Will you read it?

MARIAN: Adam saw you perform this at BAM, Uncle.

JANE: We all did.

BARBARA: Your Gaev . . . *(She hands Benjamin the book)* The bookcase speech . . .

(He looks at the book.)

From *The Cherry Orchard*, Uncle. A play you were in. Long ago . . . A different time.

BENJAMIN: Adam's still upstairs? . . .

(She nods.)

(Speaks toward the baby monitor) Hello, Adam . . .

RICHARD: Benjamin, he can't—

MARIAN: Richard, sh-sh.

BENJAMIN: I've read this before?

MARIAN: You have, Uncle. Many, many times. You've just forgotten . . .

TIM *(To Benjamin)*: Gaev is looking at an old bookcase—in a child's room. This child has died . . . —and the household has never recovered from this death. Adam and I talked about this. He told me—some deaths you just never get over . . .

(Then:)

BENJAMIN *(Reads)*: "Do you know, Lyuba, how old this bookcase is?" *(Looks up)* Why is he talking to a bookcase?

BARBARA *(Hesitates, then)*: Uncle, why don't you just say it to the table. Talk to the table . . . It's there . . . *(To the others)* Why not?

(Benjamin looks at the table. Then:)

BENJAMIN: Then why don't I just call it a table?

(Laughter.)

BARBARA: Sure, Benjamin. You can do that . . .

BENJAMIN *(Reads)*: "Do you know, Lybua, how old this—table is? Last week I looked underneath and read what was burnt there. This table was made exactly one hundred years ago. Now what do you think of that? Huh? We could celebrate its centennial jubilee. It may not have a soul, but I don't care what you say—it's a hardworking table." *(Looks up, smiles)* "Yes, this thing." *(Touches it)* "My dear friend and honored table! I congratulate you on your existence. Which for one hundred years has supported only the highest ideals of virtue and justice. Your silent summons to profitable labor has never wavered these hundred years. During such time you have upheld virtue, faith, hopes for a better future for a new generation of our race . . ."

RICHARD: What's next?

TIM: Number thirty-nine.

BARBARA: We've practiced this.

TIM: This is just the women.

BARBARA: Or—just "the girls." He always had to call us "the girls."

MARIAN: He thought it was funny. Sometimes Adam was a son of a bitch.

MARIAN, BARBARA AND JANE *(Sing)*:

    I said I will look to my ways, lest I sin with my tongue;
    I'll keep my mouth with bit while I the wicked am
        among . . .

BENJAMIN *(Into the baby monitor)*: That was for you, Adam. Should we all tell him that . . . ?

(The sisters hesitate, then they say toward the monitor: "That was for you, Adam . . ." "Hi, Adam . . ." "For Adam . . ." etc.)

RICHARD *(To Jane)*: It sounds religious. I think he got religious.

JANE: Think of it as music, Richard.

TIM: Then his sister releases the ashes into Crystal Lake . . .

JANE *(To Richard)*: I'll show you later . . . Just behind South Street.

TIM: She is not to say anything . . . He even wrote that down. *(Shows them)* "My sister is to say nothing."

BARBARA: What's next?

TIM: Twenty-three. And that's last.

RICHARD: Short and sweet.

MARIAN: It's late November, he was worried it might be too cold. So he wanted to keep it short.

BARBARA *(To Marian)*: He could be thoughtful.

MARIAN: He could.

JANE *(To Richard)*: We all sing this.

TIM *(To Richard)*: Everyone. He's even underlined: <u>everyone.</u>

(Marian passes out music.)

BARBARA: This is a famous one, Uncle.

MARIAN *(To Richard)*: We've been practicing. Try and follow along . . . Adam jumped over a lot of the "God stuff" in this one, Richard.

RICHARD: So it's not religious.

MARIAN: And here—he changed "in the Lord's House" to "in Barbara's House." Doesn't really scan. But that's what he wants. There— *(Reads)* "in Barbara's House—"

BARBARA: I told him—Barbara and Marian's House.

MARIAN: That doesn't fit, Barbara. You can't sing that.

BARBARA: That's what I told him. That's what it is.

MARIAN *(Reads)*: "And in Barbara's House I shall dwell for long as days shall be . . ." Ready?

ALL *(Sing)*:

> Yea though in valley of death's shade
> I walk none ill I'll fear,
> Because thou art with me, thy rod,
> And staff my comfort are.
>
> For me a table thou hast spread
> In presence of my foes;
> Thou dost anoint my head with oil
> My cup it over-flows . . .
>
> Goodness and mercy surely shall
> All my dayes follow me:
> And in Barbara's House I shall dwell
> For long as days shall be.

(Short pause.)

TIM: That's it. That's the end . . .

(And the "play" is over. A pause as first "Barbara" and then the others look out into the audience.

And then "Barbara" speaks to the audience:)

"BARBARA": And so we live. Sometimes we come together. Something brings us together. And some days we are alone. But it's those days together, that remind us, why we live. Or, maybe it is—how. How—we live . . .

(The lights fade.)

END OF PLAY

AUTHOR'S NOTES

At the time of their respective premieres, I wrote and published an author's note for each of the four *Apple Family* plays. The following are edited versions of these four notes. Together, I think, they reflect some of my process and my thinking while writing this series.

THAT HOPEY CHANGEY THING
(Written for the Opening on November 2, 2010)

I suppose this is what might be called a "disposable" play. That is one so completely tied to a very specific time, that its references and even concerns are certain to be soon out of date. I accept that.

Hopefully this in no way diminishes the ambition of the play or implies that I have taken less care over it than any other. What it hopefully reflects is this ambition: to directly engage as a playwright, that is, as a writer who expresses himself via live people in front of live people, with the politics of my country in the present time.

We have become used to viewing our politics and our political landscape through the lens of journalists or commentators or, now, comedians. Their observations are certainly invaluable to us and the very best of them struggle valiantly to be a check on vanity, arrogance, ignorance and stupidity. However, what has been missing from our public political forum is the individual's voice. There always seems to be someone or something ready to speak for us: organizations, lobbyists, politicians, talk-show hosts and the like; but the voice I hear in my own living room, or on a train, or over dinners at a restaurant, or in my own head, I do not hear anywhere else.

This is not to say that I've become so deluded as to have crowned myself the public voice for anyone. My ambition remains much simpler: to put the most complex, complicated people I can on stage and to let them talk about their country today.

Sweet and Sad

(Written for the Opening on September 11, 2011)

I have begun to wonder or fantasize that after the (imagined) four plays of this series are completed, that there might be something in putting them all together into one very long evening; the hope being that the very specificity of the plays combined with the overriding arc of them covering the same people over several years, might tell a rich and compelling story. So instead of feeling dated or "disposable," the plays, as a whole, might just feel true. We'll see. As I say, it might all be a fantasy.

But what I do know is that writing these plays, which are so incredibly specific in time and place, has been liberating for this writer. I feel I have found a way to address my questions of our society/culture/time/politics that derives not from ideas or (god help us) an ideology, but rather from human beings talking to human beings.

The theater has a unique place in the history of societies. After all, the theater is the only artistic form that *uses the entire live human being as its expression*, and, hence, carries within itself a very specific view of the world; and that view, in a word, is humanistic. The individual is at the center of the play, and the world of the play revolves around the individual—that is simply what a play is. By a play's very nature, the heart of any play is the individual voices of its characters. And in times like our own, when human voices seem more disembodied than ever, where words seem pulled from their meanings and turned into rants and weapons, the theater can, I believe, be a necessary home for human talk; that is, a place where human beings talk about their worries, confusions, fears and loves. And where they also listen.

So in one sense then, I'm hoping that these are plays about the need to talk, the need to listen, and the need for theater.

SORRY
(Written for the Opening on November 6, 2012)

This is now the third play with the same characters on the same set (only Tim is absent here). But what is not immediately apparent reading the play is that this is the third play with the *same* actors playing the same characters on the same set. As I have also directed these plays, I have to say what a unique experience this has been; often on the first day of rehearsal, actors are just getting to know each other, and the long journey of making an ensemble begins. Here, on the first day, they are not just an ensemble, but like a real family. And, this writer has begun to cross a line between writing characters and uncovering people who he sees before him. In other words, I have now begun to use the personalities, the complexities, the confusions of the people who are acting in these plays to help me probe the depth of the characters themselves.

Earlier this year I opened a play called *Farewell to the Theatre* in London; its central character is the playwright, director, actor, theater visionary Harley Granville Barker. In that play I have Barker speak words he wrote in his essay "The Heritage of the Actor":

> One is tempted to imagine a play—to be written in desperate defiance of Aristotle—from which doing would be eliminated altogether, in which nothing but being would be left. The task set the actors would be to interest their audience in what the characters were, quite apart from anything they might do; to set up, that is to say, the relation by which all important human intimacies exist.

I'm learning more and more that this is an ambition of these *Apple Family* plays; to put characters in a room with an audience, who then can watch them *be*. To where the private thoughts of the characters, derived often from the very actors playing them, work to make the relation between actor and audience as intimate as relations in real life. To let the audience not only share the same space, but find themselves inside the characters' minds. In other words, to create "the relation by which all important human intimacies exist."

And so as I wrote in the note to *Sweet and Sad*: "It is my hope that these plays are about the need to talk, the need to listen, the need for theater," *and*, I now add, the need to be in the same room together.

Regular Singing
(Written for the Opening on November 22, 2013)

When I began this series, I wrote about how I felt it was quite likely that these plays would end up "disposable." Perhaps foolishly and with a certain amount of hubris, I have come to think or at least hope that the plays might have a somewhat longer shelf life and, when experienced as a group over two or four days, might even add up to something greater than its parts. We can soon see. Surrounding the opening of *Regular Singing*, the other three plays will be remounted with the same cast.

In notes for the earlier plays, I have yet to mention two very important ways in which these plays have come about. Each of the plays has been commissioned by Oskar Eustis and The Public Theater, and in each case I was given an opening date before a word of the play had been written. Such confidence in a writer is very rare. And I am grateful. I have also yet to mention that most every Saturday night over the past many years a small group of friends has spent a few hours in my living room, talking—about life, themselves, their hopes, their art, their jobs and parents and families, what they have been reading and seeing, and, of course, about their country. *The Apple Family* plays originate from those Saturday nights.

In my note for *Sorry* I wrote that: "It is my hope that these plays are about the need to talk, the need to listen, the need for theater, *and* the need to be in the same room together."

Maybe it's just saying the same thing another way, but after completing *Regular Singing*, I want to add that I hope that these plays are also about the need to know, in small and even some bigger ways, that we are not alone.

Richard Nelson
Rhinebeck, New York

ACKNOWLEDGMENTS

These four plays are all works of fiction and not based upon any living person or persons; any similarities are coincidental.

For *That Hopey Changey Thing*:
I wish to thank my good friend Marian Faux for allowing me permission to give Jane Apple authorship of a book very similar to Marian's own wonderful *Wild Civility*. I have used Marian's research with elasticity, and therefore any misreading or errors are strictly mine and not hers.

For *Sweet and Sad*:
I read numerous books and articles while writing *Sweet and Sad*, and some have influenced the play, in large and small ways. In particular, Matt Taibbi's enjoyable *Griftopia* (Spiegel & Grau, 2011) is the book that Tim has been reading, and that has been depressing him so much. Others: Paul Goldberger's *Up from Zero* (Random House, 2005), Robert B. Reich's *Aftershock* (Vintage Books, 2011), Marian Klamkin's *The Return of*

Lafayette (Scribner, 1975). Tim's story about the rescue of Yiddish books comes from a video I saw at the extraordinary Yiddish Book Center in Amherst, Massachusetts, in which the founder describes the beginnings of the Center.

For *Sorry*:

Numerous books and articles influenced the writing of this play: Oliver Sacks's *The Mind's Eye* (Vintage Books, 2011); *A History of Private Life* (Volumes II, III and IV), Philippe Aries and Georges Duby, series editors (The Belknap Press of Harvard University Press, 1992); Roy Franklin Nichols's *Franklin Pierce: Young Hickory of the Granite Hills* (American Political Biography Press, 1993); Nathaniel Hawthorne's *The Life of Franklin Pierce* (Acheron Press, 2012); *Occupy!: Scenes from Occupied America*, edited by Astra Taylor, Keith Cassen and the editors from *n+1* (Verso, 2011); essays by David Brooks, Charles M. Blow and Michael Winerip ("On Education" column) in the *New York Times*. My daughter, Jocelyn, and her friends: Evan, Mat, Holly, Margaret, Sarah, Adrienne and Hilary, supplied me with invaluable insight into a younger generation's take on Occupy Wall Street, President Obama, and so much more. My friend Oliver Cotton (unwittingly) supplied the anecdote about making the film about Columbus; and the edit and reordering of Oscar Wilde's *De Profundis* was adapted from a version originally edited by Merlin Holland. The book Jane has been referring to and from which she quotes/paraphrases is: Michael J. Sandel's brilliant *What Money Can't Buy* (Farrar, Straus and Giroux, 2012). The song Evan had on her iPod is Regina Spektor's "Us" (from *Soviet Kitsch*, 2004). The story about the urinals and the fish comes from *Tynan*, a play adapted by me with Colin Chambers from *The Diaries of Kenneth Tynan*, edited by John Lahr (Bloomsbury, 2001).

For *Regular Singing*:

I read and consulted many books and articles while writing *Regular Singing*. Here are the most important: Oliver Sacks's

Hallucinations (Vintage Books, 2013) and *An Anthropologist on Mars* (Vintage Books, 1996); James Thomas Flexner's *History of American Painting* (Volumes One, Two and Three; Dover, 1969); David Nasaw's *The Patriarch* (Penguin, 2012); Paul Grondahl's *Mayor Corning* (Washington Park Press, 1997); Robert S. McElvaine's *Mario Cuomo* (Scribner, 1988); William Kennedy's *O Albany!* (Penguin, 1985); John P. Papp's *Albany's Historic Street* (Papp Historical Publications, 1976); Stephen Rodrick's *New York* magazine article "The Reintroduction of Kirsten Gillibrand" (June 7, 2009); William Safire's essay for the *New York Times*, "The New Rainmaker" (August 28, 1986); Sari Brewster Tietjen's *Rhinebeck: Portrait of a Town* (Phanter Press, 1990); Michael J. Sandel's *Justice* (Farrar, Straus and Giroux, 2010); J. L.Austin's *How to Do Things with Words* (Harvard University Press, 1975); Tom Wicker's reporting for the *New York Times* on the assassination of President Kennedy; the newspaper Tim holds up is a copy of an issue of the *Dallas Times Herald*; Thomas Walter's *The Grounds and Rules of Musick Explained* (Gale ECCO, 2010); Lorraine Inserra and H. Wiley Hitchock's monograph *Music of Henry Ainsworth's Psalter* (Institute for Studies in American Music, 1981); the compact disc collection *America Sings: The Gregg Smith Singers* (VoxBox, circa 1976). The story of the actress playing Rosalind is stolen (without her knowledge) from my friend Jemma. The story of Samuel Beckett's slippers is from my friend Gregory. Barbara recites from Euripides' *Alcestis* as translated by Ted Hughes (Farrar, Straus and Giroux, 2000). My daughter Jocelyn and her friends Evan and Margaret were very helpful in describing what such an event of fifty years ago might mean to a younger generation today.

R. N.

CREDIT INFORMATION

Continued from the copyright page

That Hopey Changey Thing
Bundling: Its Origin, Progress and Decline in America, by Henry Reed Stiles; Knickerbocker Publishing Company, Albany, New York, 1871. Lyrics to "Sweetly She Sleeps, My Alice Fair," by Charles G. Eastman, music by Stephen Collins Foster; 1851. *The Cherry Orchard*, by Anton Chekhov; 1903. Lyrics to "All Through the Night," translated and adapted by Harry Boulton; 1884.

Sweet and Sad
Herzog, by Saul Bellow; Viking Press, New York, 1964. "The Wound-Dresser," by Walt Whitman;1881.

Sorry
Three Sisters, by Anton Chekhov, 1900. "Better Farther On," lyrics and music by Doyle Lawson, copyright © 1998 Bug Music (BMI), Southern Melody Publishing Company (BMI)

and Top O'Holston Publishing (BMI), all rights administered by Bug Music, Inc., a BMG Chrysalis company, all rights reserved, used by permission, reprinted by permission of Hal Leonard Corporation. *A History of Private Life*, Volumes II, III and IV, by Philippe Aries and Georges Duby, series editors; © President and Fellows of Harvard, Belknap Press of Harvard University, 1988, 1992. *What Money Can't Buy*, by Michael J. Sandel; Farrar, Straus and Giroux, New York, 2012. Lyrics to "Us," by Regina Spektor; copyright © 2005 EMI Blackwood Music Inc. and Soviet Kitsch Music, all rights on behalf of EMI Blackwood Music Inc. and Soviet Kitsch Music, administered by Sony/ATV Music Publishing LLC, 424 Church Street, Suite 1200, Nashville, Tennessee, 37219, all rights reserved, used by permission. *De Profundis*, by Oscar Wilde; 1905.

Regular Singing

In Search of Lost Time, Volume I: Swann's Way, by Marcel Proust, translated by C. K. Scott Moncrieff and Terence Kilmartin, copyright © 1981; Random House, New York, 1981. Psalm 13, *The Ainsworth Psalter*, by Henry Ainsworth; 1612. Psalms 23, 39, *The Bay Psalm Book*; 1640. "Kennedy Is Killed by Sniper as He Rides in Dallas; Johnson Sworn in on Plane," by Tom Wicker; from the *New York Times*, November 22, 1963, © 1963 the New York Times. All rights reserved. Used by permission and protected by the Copyright Laws of the United States. The printing, copying, redistribution, or retransmission of this content without express written permission is prohibited. *How to Observe Morals and Manners*, by Harriet Martineau; Harper & Brothers, New York, 1838. *Alcestis*, by Euripides, translated and adapted by Ted Hughes, copyright © 1999 by The Estate of Ted Hughes; Farrar, Straus and Giroux, New York, 1999. *The Cherry Orchard*, by Anton Chekhov; 1903.

Author's Notes

"The Heritage of the Actor," by Harley Granville Barker; *Quarterly Review* CCXL, No. 476, July 1923, pp. 53–78 (p. 70).

RICHARD NELSON's plays include *Nikolai and the Others*, *Farewell to the Theatre*, *Conversations in Tusculum*, *How Shakespeare Won the West*, *Frank's Home*, *Rodney's Wife*, *Franny's Way*, *Madame Melville*, *Goodnight Children Everywhere*, *New England*, *The General from America*, *Misha's Party* (with Alexander Gelman), *Two Shakespearean Actors* and *Some Americans Abroad*. He has written the musicals *James Joyce's The Dead* (with Shaun Davey) and *My Life with Albertine* (with Ricky Ian Gordon), and the screenplays for the films *Hyde Park-on-Hudson* and *Ethan Frome*.

He has received numerous awards, including a Tony (Best Book of a Musical for *James Joyce's The Dead*), an Olivier (Best Play for *Goodnight Children Everywhere*) and two New York Drama Critics' Circle Awards (*James Joyce's The Dead* and *The Apple Family*). He is the recipient of the PEN/Laura Pels Master Playwright Award, an Academy Award from the American Academy of Arts and Letters; he is an Honorary Associate Artist of the Royal Shakespeare Company. He lives in Upstate New York.